INDIA'S WAR ON TERROR

INDIA'S WAR ON TERROR

Editors
Gurmeet Kanwal
N Manoharan

KNOWLEDGE WORLD
KW Publishers Pvt Ltd
New Delhi

Centre for Land Warfare Studies
New Delhi

First reprint November 2012

The Centre for Land Warfare Studies (CLAWS), New Delhi, is an autonomous think tank dealing with contemporary issues of national security and conceptual aspects of land warfare, including conventional and sub-conventional conflicts and terrorism. CLAWS conducts research that is futuristic in outlook and policy-oriented in approach.

Centre for Land Warfare Studies
RPSO Complex, Parade Road, Delhi Cantt, New Delhi 110010
Tel: +91.11.25691308 **Fax**: +91.11.25692347
Email: landwarfare@gmail.com **Website**: www.claws.in

The views expressed in various chapters are the personal views of individual authors and do not have any official endorsement. They do not necessarily represent the views of CLAWS.

ISBN 13: 978-93-80502-06-9

Published in India by
Kalpana Shukla
KW Publishers Pvt Ltd
NEW DELHI: 4676/21, First Floor, Ansari Road, Daryaganj, New Delhi 110002
Tel: +91.11.23263498 / 43528107 **Email**: mail@kwpub.in / knowledgeworld@vsnl.net
MUMBAI: 15 Jay Kay Industrial Estate, Linking Road Extn., Santacruz (W), Mumbai 400054
Tel: +91.22.26614110 / 26613505 **Email**: mumbai@kwpub.in **Website**: www.kwpub.in

Printed and Bound in India

CONTENTS

List of Figures

CONTRIBUTORS

Dr **Shah Alam** is a Research Fellow at CLAWS. He is presently working on "Pakistan Military's Role in Governance".

Dr **Monika Chansoria** is a Research Fellow at CLAWS. She is presently working on "Modernisation of China's PLA". She has recently authored *Chinese WMD Proliferation in Asia: US Response* and has also written extensively on American security policy and strategy in Asia.

Brig **Anil Chauhan** is presently commanding an infantry brigade in Manipur. Previously, he was Senior Fellow at CLAWS, where he worked on "Consequence Management in the Aftermath of a Nuclear Strike".

Col **Hardev Faujdar** is presently Deputy Commander of a brigade in the Western sector. Previously, he was Senior Fellow at CLAWS, where he worked on "Modernisation of Infantry in India".

Mr **Samarjit Ghosh** is an Associate Fellow at CLAWS. He is presently working on "Fourth Generation Warfare in the South Asian Region". He has written on the insurgency in the FATA and NWFP, as also on Pakistan and terrorism.

Mr **Avinash Godbole** is a Doctoral Scholar at the School of International Studies, Jawaharlal Nehru University, New Delhi. At present, he works with the Institute for Defence Studies and Analyses, New Delhi.

Brig **Gurmeet Kanwal** (Retd) is the Director of CLAWS. He commanded an infantry brigade on the Line of Control (Operation Parakram, 2001-03) and an artillery regiment in counter-insurgency operations in Kashmir Valley (Operation Rakshak, 1993-94).

Dr **Rajesh Kapoor** is an Associate Fellow at CLAWS. He is presently working on "Indo-Myanmar Relations: A Study of Security Dimensions". He has written on security challenges in East Asia, South Asia and Southeast Asia.

Brig **M L N Sravan Kumar** is presently commanding an artillery missile brigade. Previously, he was Senior Fellow at CLAWS, where he worked on "Future Trajectory of United Nations Peace Support Operations".

Dr **N Manoharan** is Senior Fellow at CLAWS. He is presently working on "Comprehensive Internal Security Strategy in the Indian Context". His areas of interest include Sri Lanka, Maldives, human rights, ethnic conflicts, multi-culturalism, terrorism, and national security.

Dr **Mansi Mehrotra** is an Associate Fellow at CLAWS. She has recently completed a study on Security Challenges to "India-Bangladesh Relations and Conflict Management in Northeast India". She has written on security concerns in Central Asia.

Brig **S C Meston** is presently commanding a brigade in the Eastern sector. Previously, he was Senior Fellow at CLAWS, where he worked on "Challenges to National Leadership in the 21st Century India".

Ms **Swapna Kona Nayudu** is an Associate Fellow at CLAWS. She is presently researching on "Defence Diplomacy as a Tool of Foreign Policy". Her work is centred on the security complexes at work in South and Central Asia (with a particular focus on Afghanistan).

Mr **Rohit Singh** is a Research Assistant at CLAWS. His areas of interest include defence affairs and sub-conventional warfare.

Brig **S M Singh** is presently commanding a brigade in the Eastern sector. Previously, he was senior fellow at CLAWS, where he worked on "Internal Security Management at National Level".

Brig **Harish Thukral** is presently commanding Assam Rifles in Manipur sector. Previously, he was Senior Fellow at CLAWS, where he worked on "India's Defence Economics".

Col **Ravi Tuteja** is presently serving in a corps in the Northern sector. Previously, he was Deputy Director, CLAWS. An Infantry Officer, he has served in various parts of the country. He has also served in Sri Lanka.

INTRODUCTION: INDIA IS IN FOR THE LONG HAUL

Gurmeet Kanwal

And death will be our darling and fear will be our name.
—Richard Fariña, from the lyrics of *Bold Marauder*, 1972

Terrorism is not an enemy. It cannot be defeated. It's a tactic... We're not going to win the war on terrorism.
—General William Odom, US Army, on C-SPAN's *Washington Journal* programme, November 2002

On 26 November 2008, the tsunami of 'new terrorism' hit India's commercial capital. Ten mercenary marauders from Pakistan, armed to the teeth, belonging to the Lashkar-e-Tayyeba (LeT), and trained, equipped and controlled by their Inter-Services Intelligence (ISI) handlers, sneaked in undetected from the sea and unleashed wanton attacks on innocent civilians returning home after a hard day at work at the Chhatrapati Shivaji Terminus at Mumbai. During the course of the evening, they also attacked two upmarket hotels, a Jewish centre, a hospital and a café. By the time they were through with their devilish plans, they had left almost 200 people dead and over 300 injured, including several police officers and personnel. It took India's National Security

Guard (NSG), an elite counter-terrorism commando force, 60 hours to flush them out and end their orgy of violence. One terrorist was captured alive. Though he confessed publicly that he was from Pakistan, his country (initially) disowned him – in keeping with its short-sighted policy of living in denial. Till the time of writing (early-October 2009), Pakistan has not yet taken back the bodies of nine other terrorists who were killed by Indian security forces, despite overwhelming evidence that they were Pakistani citizens.

The age of 'new terrorism' hit India with the Mumbai serial bomb attacks of March 1993, well before the term had become prevalent, and in the same year, when a group of Islamist extremists led by Ramzi Yousef had launched the first attack on the World Trade Centre in New York. In 1995, Aum Shinrikyo attacked the Tokyo underground with Sarin gas. Soon after that, a large truck bomb killed 168 people in Oklahoma City and visions of apocalypse through terrorism began to haunt the world. The London and Madrid train bombings further heightened the pervasive fear psychosis. Walter Laqueur, the well known terrorism historian, wrote in 1999 that the character of terrorism was assuming catastrophic proportions and changing in a revolutionary manner. "Rather than the vicious yet calculated application of violence that everyone had become familiar with, the world was now confronted with terrorists whose aim was 'to liquidate all satanic forces [and destroy] all life on earth'."

The11September 2001 attacks were a catastrophic confirmation of a major shift in the trend lines of transnational terrorism and there is now ready agreement that the age of 'new terrorism' is well and truly upon us. However, 'new terrorism' is in many ways still a catchphrase that heralds change as no clear understanding of its characteristics is as yet forthcoming. Even as the world attempts to enhance its understanding of what exactly has changed, four pointers can be clearly discerned. Firstly, modern terrorist organisations are both diffuse and opaque in nature. They have cellular structures that resemble networks, rather than a clearly demarcated chain of command. Secondly, they are increasingly more transnational in their geographical spread, with shifting centres of gravity and constantly changing recruitment bases. Thirdly, their ideological motivations are driven by religious fundamentalism and they seek to achieve their political objectives through radical extremism, even though no religion justifies violent means. Fourthly, 'new terrorism' is far more violent than 'old terrorism'. In the mid-to-late-20th century, terrorist organisations wanted "a lot of people watching, not a lot of people dead" but this has changed and they now wish to inflict horrendous casualties so that they can impose their will on governments and societies.

India's response to the Mumbai terror attacks was slow and laborious, and poorly coordinated among the Central and state governments and their various agencies. Coastal security was virtually non-existent; the marine police were too few in number to effectively patrol the vast area entrusted to them; they were ill-equipped and inadequately trained; and, there was poor coordination between the coast guard and the marine police. It took far too long to begin flushing out operations and then to eliminate the nine terrorists who were holed up at three separate locations. The army battalion located at Mumbai was only given the responsibility to establish a perimeter cordon when it could have launched flushing out operations at least three hours before the NSG commandos arrived on the scene and before the terrorists had consolidated their positions. The media were telecasting live pictures of ongoing military operations when they should have been at least a couple of kilometres away from the scene. Generally speaking, the country's response left much to be desired.

It is in order to study the changes that are underway in the character of terrorism and the need to fight it cohesively at the national level that the Centre for Land Warfare Studies (CLAWS), New Delhi, has undertaken this in-house project with various chapters being written by individual or joint authors based on research, interviews, round-table discussions and seminars. Dr. N Manoharan has undertaken an analytical review of the concept of 'new terrorism', its amorphousness, its organisational structures and likely future developments. Mr. Samarjit Ghosh has traced the history of this new or 'fourth wave' of terrorism, with particular reference to India. Colonel Anil Chauhan (now Brigadier) and Colonel Hardev Faujdar have examined the motivations, identified the perpetrators and analysed their methods. Colonel Harish Thukral and Colonel M L N Sravan Kumar (both are now Brigadiers) have gone into the support systems, internal and external, and studied finance structures, state sponsorship of terrorism and the impact of narcotics as a tool for financing terrorism. Ms. Swapna Koyna Nayudu has listed the principal targets and the victims of 'new terrorism', usually innocent bystanders, and sought to establish patterns by studying various similar acts of terrorism. Colonel Ravi Tuteja and Dr. Mansi Mehrotra have identified the chinks in India's border management, including coastal security. Colonel S M Singh (now Brigadier) has examined the efficacy of India's force structures, military and civilian, to successfully fight the war on terror and has gone into police reforms and strengthening of India's counter-terrorism laws.

Colonel Sanjay Meston (now Brigadier) has looked holistically at the intelligence gathering and dissemination apparatus, including the technologies that are necessary to cope with the increasing sophistication of the tools of terror being employed by post-modern terrorists. Dr. Monika Chansoria has analysed the status of international cooperation in fighting the new scourge and how India can enhance its counter-terrorism efforts through better international support. Dr. Shah Alam has analysed the role of the media and how it aids as well as hampers counter-terrorism. Mr. Avinash Godbole has studied the role played by the community and suggested how ordinary people can contribute better. Dr. Rajesh Kapoor has undertaken case studies to understand lessons India could learn from the experiences of Israel, Japan and the United States. Mr. Rohit Singh has chronologically listed the terror attacks in India from 1993 to 2009. The chapter authors and the concluding chapter suggest policy measures to enhance capabilities, cooperation and coordination for qualitatively upgrading India's counter-terrorism efforts.

Peter R Neumann has written: "Regardless of whether governments are dealing with 'old' or 'new', the aim must be to prevent terrorist attacks whilst maintaining legitimacy in the eyes of the population. In doing so, governments need to 'harden' potential targets; develop good intelligence in order to disrupt terrorist structures; bring to bear the full force of the law whilst acting within the law; address legitimate grievances where they can be addressed; and, not least, convey a sense of calm and determination when communicating with the public." This prescription cannot be faulted and Indian policy planners would do well to draw up a counter-terrorism policy on these lines as part of a comprehensive national security strategy.

The Mumbai terror attacks have left a deep scar on the national psyche. The mood in the country, particularly in the urban areas that have been the victims of 'new terrorism', is that of anger and grim determination. If there is another attack of similar magnitude – and given the extent of radical extremism and creeping Talibanisation, there will surely be many more such attacks – the Indian people will demand military retribution against the perpetrators and their handlers. And, that could mean war, if a clear linkage can be established with state sponsors of terrorism from across India's western border.

Contrary to General William Odom's rather pessimistic assessment that the war against terrorism cannot be won, there is no option but to successfully defeat the terrorist organisations that are inimical to India's national security interests and are determined to create a communal-sectarian schism with a view to destabilising India on behalf of their handlers in the ISI and the Pakistan Army. They must be prevented from launching major terrorist strikes in the future and, in case some terrorists do manage to sneak through comprehensively organised and coordinated intelligence and police defences, they must be quickly eliminated with minimum collateral damage. Like many other countries, India is in for the long haul in the war on terror.

This book could not have been published without the untiring efforts of Dr. N Manoharan, Senior Fellow, CLAWS, who coordinated the project; Dr. Manpreet Sethi, Senior Fellow, Centre for Air Power Studies, who reviewed each chapter and gave very valuable suggestions; Mr. Samarjit Ghosh, Associate Fellow, CLAWS, who helped with editing and coordination and Mr Jose Mathew of KW Publishers Pvt Ltd, who patiently executed the publication process. Thanks also go out to each of the contributors who worked to tight deadlines while writing their chapters. Finally, if this book contributes to understanding and successfully fighting the scourge of 'new terrorism' that will continue to confront the country for many years to come, the effort would have been worthwhile.

1

CONCEPTUALISING 'NEW TERRORISM'

N Manoharan

Evolution of the 'Old'

In the final decade of the last millennium, the phenomenon of terrorism came to be redefined. Ever since the French Revolution, when the term 'terrorism' first gained prominence, its connotation has repeatedly undergone changes. It is claimed that there are at least 212 different definitions of 'terrorism' in existence throughout the world, with 90 of them being used by various governments and institutions over the past two centuries.[1] Yet, there is no single internationally acceptable definition of 'terrorism,' making it one of the most disputed terms in the social sciences.[2] The aim here is not to add yet another definition of 'terrorism', but to describe the term in the traditional sense so as to place the concept of 'new terrorism' in the proper context.

For the layman, terrorism can be defined as the illegal use of political violence. But, when the term first came to the fore during the French Revolution, it had a positive connotation and was used as "an instrument of governance" to "consolidate the new government's power by intimidating counterrevolutionaries…"[3] However, with the advent of democracy and liberalism in Europe in the 19th century, the term started gaining a revolutionary and anti-state connotation, the exact reverse of the earlier Robespierreian context. In the late 19th and early 20th centuries, terrorism meant "propaganda by deed" to attract public attention to the then existing anarchist terrorist groups and their causes.[4] Except during the inter-War period, when state terrorism dominated, the revolutionary connotation of terrorism continued even after World War II. Significantly, it meant violence used by anti-colonialist and indigenous nationalist groups, especially with the sponsorship of some sovereign states.

During the Cold War, some American scholars went to the extent of describing terrorism "as a calculated means to destabilise the West as part of a vast global conspiracy by the USSR."[5] 'Terrorism' was also associated with "proxy war" employed by the smaller states to take on more powerful ones without risking formal retaliation. The two superpowers also resorted to this tactic during the Cold War. This was when the well-known phrase of "one man's terrorist is another man's freedom fighter" came to the fore, bringing in the problem of moral judgement while defining the term 'terrorism'. This problem continues even today, not as a moral dilemma, but more as a usage for convenience by the states that sponsor terrorist groups to "bleed their enemies". Use of terrorists as "surrogate warriors" by some states to take on their powerful adversaries has become a kind of asymmetric warfare strategy, mainly to escape identification, retaliation, and sanction. In its evolution, the term "terrorism", thus, from a "positive" origin has reached the other end of the spectrum to bear a "pejorative" and subjective connotation.[6]

Birth of the 'New'?

Down the evolutionary ladder, the term further became more pejorative, but less subjective. In the 1990s, the concept of 'new terrorism' started appearing in the terrorism literature as a "gray area phenomenon" mainly to describe catastrophic and religiously motivated terrorism threatening "immense regions or urban areas".[7] Soon, new patterns of terrorist attacks were conspicuous and forced the acceptance, if not formalisation, of the concept of 'new terrorism'. The New York World Trade Centre bombing in

1993 and Sarin gas attack in Tokyo 1995 can be taken as defining timelines between the 'old' and the 'new'. In the Indian context, it was the Mumbai (then Bombay) serial blasts of March 1993. Some called it "postmodern"[8] or "catastrophic"[9] terrorism, while others described it as the "fourth wave" in the evolution of terrorism, a metamorphosis of terrorism from being focussed in the past on the break-up of empires, decolonisation, and anti-Westernism to a new kind of phenomenon.[10] It has now come to be described as a "new evil in our world"[11] that encompasses "both the dark forces that threaten 'civilisation' and the fears they arouse."[12]

Walter Laqueur observes, "There has been a radical transformation, if not a revolution, in the character of terrorism."[13] Although 'new terrorism' is not fundamentally or qualitatively 'new', but grounded in an evolving historical context, there are some distinctions that should be acknowledged. These differences are evident in its amorphous and global nature, the character of its perpetrators, and the organisational structure, motivation, lethality, support systems and technological sophistication.

Characterising the 'New Terrorism'

Global and Amorphous: While the old style terrorism was mainly, though not wholly local, the 'new terrorism' is mostly global. As a result, the traditional distinction between local and international terrorism has blurred. The globalised "flat world"[14] has facilitated not only an easy movement of terrorists, but also transformation of their operations, support systems and methods. With advancements in information and communication technology, the terrorists are now in a position to guide operations thousands of kilometres away. The World Wide Web is also being used as a tool of propaganda and fund-raising by terrorist groups.[15]

The organisational structure of the new terrorist groups is more networked than the traditional-formal-hierarchical of the old. Pyramids have been flattened, with multiple leaders wielding authority. Decision-making and operations are decentralised, allowing for local initiative and autonomy.[16] Although network-based structures existed earlier, what is new is the professional way of networking in the globalised world. Most of the present-day terrorist groups prefer operating as small, dispersed and autonomous entities, linked by advanced communications and "shared principles, interests and goals – at best an overreaching doctrine or ideology – that spans all nodes and to which their members wholeheartedly subscribe."[17] Simon and Benjamin term such an arrangement as a combination of "a 'hub and spoke' structure (where nodes communicate with the centre) with a 'wheel' structure (where nodes in the network communicate with each other without reference to the centre)."[18] Overall, the structure "sometimes appears acephalous (headless), and, at the other times, polycephalous (hydra-headed)."[19] This phenomenon is called by various names: "leaderless resistance", "phantom cell networks", "network of networks", "lone wolves" and "franchise terrorism."[20]

The new form gives terrorists more flexibility and adaptability to the rapidly evolving situations. To be in the form of a network also increases their resilience as even if a few of its constituent entities are destroyed, the others can carry on.[21] As the result of a loose, informal organisational structure, it is difficult to find terrorist groups having a permanent infrastructure in place. For training, they tend to utilise more of the 'how to do' or 'do it yourself' sources that are freely available on the Internet; for physical/weapons training, they take the help of freelance, retired or disbanded military personnel. They are trained not only in the military art, but also the "black arts".[22] Amateur groups prefer taking short-term training courses from established terrorist groups. For instance, cadres of the Indian Mujahideen are trained by the Lashkar-e-Tayyeba in Pakistan. It is due to this amorphous nature that the new terrorists are more difficult to spot and neutralise.[23] The anonymous nature of modern-day terrorists is further reinforced by their comparative disinterest in claiming credit for their attacks. According to statistics, only about 30 percent of all terrorist attacks in 2004 were claimed.[24]

Wide-Ranging Motivation: 'New terrorism' is also characterised by perpetrators who are paranoiac and fanatic elements, especially from the right wing spectrum of ideology. Religion has emerged as a predominant impetus for terrorist attacks, unlike predominantly secular motivations of the 'old'.[25] The political impulse for terrorist acts has drastically fallen from being the priority number one. Consequently, the new terror groups have "radically different value systems, mechanisms of legitimisation and justification, concepts of morality and Manichean world views."[26] Their sense of alienation makes them all the more deadly because for "the religious terrorist, violence is first and foremost a sacramental act or divine duty executed in direct response to some theological demand or imperative."[27] The struggle is seen as "good against evil" and, therefore, large scale violence is morally justified as necessary for the advancement of their religious cause. They hold themselves accountable to none other than to "their own God" or their representatives.[28] The inevitability of their victory is taken for granted for "God too plans" for them and "would grant victory".[29]

The rapid motivation of present-day terrorists also lies in "inhuman hatred, all-consuming ill-will and raging fanaticism"[30] in addition to personal vengeance. Suicide attacks are mostly "motivated by the desire for revenge and retaliation" rather than out of deprivation or love for a political cause. Significantly, most of the Islamist terrorists have a deep-rooted hatred towards the West in general, and the United States in particular. A *fatwa* issued by the World Islamic Front: Jihad Against Jews and Crusaders on 23 February 1998 pointed out, "The ruling to kill the Americans and their allies—civilians and military—is an individual duty of every Muslim who can do it in any country in which it is possible to do it ..."[31] Osama bin Laden made "holy war" between Islam and the Western world his sole mission and went on to invoke religion to spur terrorist attacks.

Larger Numbers and Innocent Victims: Present-day terror attacks have become bloodier. Accordingly, the choice of victims by the new terrorists is indiscriminate. The aim is no longer just to conduct "propaganda by deed" but to effect maximum destruction.[32] Thus, the 'new terrorism' is not only deadlier, but also more indiscriminate and unpredictable, which is evident in attacks like the Oklahoma City bombing, Tokyo subway attacks by the Aum Shinrikyo cult, Kobar Towers in Saudi Arabia, 9/11, London train bombings, and, more recently, the Mumbai attacks.

For 'new terrorism', destruction is an end in itself, while the 'old terrorism' used violence that was "targeted and proportionate in scope and intensity to the practical political objectives being pursued."[33] In other words, it is "a terrorism that seeks the total collapse of its opponents."[34] As some experts aptly put it, "They [the new terrorists] believe that their violence is divinely justified and that great goals require dramatic means, and the dramatic means is mass bloodshed."[35] This is evident in the increase in the number of casualties per attack. They are "freed from ordinary constraints of morality. ... There is less inhibition to kill in quantity and a greater willingness to die in the process."[36] Although use of suicide/suicidal tactics existed before, its use is more predominant now because martyrdom is seen as a way of reaching heaven. The "suicide terrorist production line"[37] has become easier than ever before. This is one of the main characteristics of the 'new terrorism'.[38]

Unlike in the past, the incidents of terrorist attacks as well as the casualties per attack have both increased. For instance, 0.17 percent of international terrorist attacks in 1995-99 caused 67 percent of the casualties.[39] In this regard, the urban terrain, the new playground of terrorism, holds significant advantages for terrorists. It is in urban areas that targets are most varied and abundant: laymen, officials, foreign nationals, corporate heavyweights, government buildings with symbolic/strategic value, crowded bus stands, railway stations, airports, markets, foreign embassies, strategic communication centres, etc. By attacking high profile symbolic targets, the terrorists can make a point that if a government is unable to protect high value targets, its inability to protect ordinary people and places is obviously in doubt. The spread of such a perception seriously undermines the credibility of the government of the day.

Since the quality and quantity of the "defined enemy" of the terrorists is high in cities, the impact of a destructive act is more widespread and likely to spread more terror. Urban operations for terrorists also often demand less in the way of brute physical strength and endurance than do operations in mountainous or rural terrain.[40] Neither do they need sophisticated, long-range weapons to inflict the desired damage. As is characteristic of urban areas, the population is not only high, but also dense. Inhabitants in cities and towns are more heterogeneous, which allows more space for anonymity, enabling the terrorists to easily merge with the background; the urban setting provides them an excellent place for camouflage. For terrorists, logistic support like arms, medicines, food, and lodging are readily available in an average urban area.[41] Manoeuvrability of terrorists is guaranteed by the presence of public and private transportation facilities that are both dependable and unobtrusive. In urban areas, terrorist groups may also find it easier to recruit prospective members for their cause from the large pool of alienated and marginalised sections of society. Indeed, cities are the nerve centres of a country.[42]

Since terrorism is "propaganda by deed", the attention seeking goal of the terrorist is well served in the urban environment, where the immediate audience is large and where representatives of the print and electronic media are readily available and ever eager to "break news". Such coverage also magnifies the fear-generating capabilities of terrorists. If the general population begins to live in fear and terror, the objective of the terrorist group would have been achieved. Overall, an urban landscape facilitates terrorists in realising their goals: of surprise, of causing maximum damage with minimum risk, of garnering media attention and of quick disappearance through merging with the anonymous crowds.[43]

More Lethal Attacks: New terrorism is described as "far more lethal than anything that has come before it."[44] Accordingly, the choice of weaponry, techniques, and tactics is devised to meet the objective of causing mass casualties in a more lethal manner.

The new terrorists are more "high tech". Their arsenal is not only deadlier, but also more miniaturised and sophisticated, and therefore, easier to hide and more effective in capability. Through the general diffusion of scientific skills and dual-use technologies, there is also a danger of weapons of mass destruction (WMDs) falling into the hands of terrorists, who wish to use them for mass destruction.[45] For instance, Al Qaeda considers it a "religious duty" to acquire WMDs.[46] WMDs are highly destructive, but also difficult to defend against. They are also likely to produce an enormous psychological impact. The new terrorists have no taboo, nor morality, nor reason to limit extreme violence. Their "purpose is not to intimidate or persuade but rather simply to destroy."[47] They believe that they have to do something spectacular to receive grand attention. To them, according to Bruce Hoffman, "both the public and media have become increasingly inured or desensitized to the continuing spiral of terrorist violence. Accordingly, these terrorists feel themselves pushed to undertake ever more dramatic or destructively lethal deeds today in order to achieve the same effect that a less ambitious or bloody action may have had in the past. Indiscriminate lethal attacks against civilians are also motivated to demonstrate that the state is incapable of protecting its citizens."[48] They feel driven by the urge to surpass previous "body counts" and the scale of destruction. Thus, there is an unrelenting upward spiral of violence.

Diverse Support Systems: State sponsorship has also become more subtle and diverse in the new form of terrorism. Today, one can see resources from many countries for terrorist groups routed through a single organisation or state. Diverse state sponsorship has, in fact, acted as a "force multiplier" by enhancing planning, intelligence, logistic capabilities, training, finances, and sophistication of the new terror groups, making them akin to elite commando units. In addition, support from non-state "amorphous constituencies" has also swollen[49] even as a new dimension of private sponsorship has come to the fore. Now, individuals like Osama bin Laden run organisations like Al Qaeda to support terrorist projects they consider worthwhile. The declining costs for conducting terrorist attacks have increased the confidence of terrorist groups to become less dependent on state sponsors. The modern-day terrorist groups also increasingly rely on their own income generation through illegal sources such as drug-trafficking, human smuggling, video piracy and credit card fraud, as well as legal business investments, donations from wealthy individuals, charities and the diaspora.[50] Due to advanced communication and information technology, appealing to their supporters and sympathisers, near and far, has become very easy.

Countering the 'New Terrorism'

'New terrorism' is seen as "a threat to all states and to all peoples, which can strike any time, anywhere."[51] Yet, the world has not fully grappled with the enormity of the challenge, nor been able to arrive at a consensus on ways to deal with this new form of threat. The amorphous nature of the present-day organisational structure of terrorist groups is deliberate, to not only thwart easy identification, but also to facilitate the escape of the terrorists. The 'new terrorism' is more lethal, claiming more casualties than ever before. Religion and revenge factors constitute the major ingredients of motivation to the new cohort of terrorists. They are high-tech, professional and leave fewer footprints.[52] The present-day terror groups are difficult to penetrate. The funding for them has become diverse and, at the same time, opaque. Therefore, it is difficult to identify and fully block the funding sources. Since the target of the new form of terrorism has become more urban oriented, it gives an added advantage to terrorists to prevent any kind of indiscriminate counter-terrorist operation by the state, given the fear of high collateral damage. For the same reason, use of aerial bombardment against terrorists becomes difficult.

Countering this complex nature of terrorism effectively requires a 'new' set of counter-terrorism policies. The entire counter-terrorism mechanism demands a thorough overhauling based on a clear understanding of the threat potential of 'new terrorism'. A comprehensive approach based on thinking beyond conventional methods is urgently required.

The basic premise for any counter-terrorism policy, at the least, should be "zero tolerance": Terrorism, as a means of redressing grievances, should be deemed unacceptable under any circumstances. Addressing the "root causes" of grievances is also vital. Some of the important "root causes" that require immediate attention are deprivation, inequity, religious intolerance, discrimination, etc. By neutralising the causes, most, if not all, militants can be dissuaded from resorting to violence as a means of achieving their ends. Appropriate methods should be used to prevent as well as to deter terrorists. The appropriateness should be such that "one does not use a tank to catch field mice—a cat will do the job better."[53]

A multi-pronged and multilateral approach and solidarity within the international community is imperative. The strategies should involve the prevention and elimination of sources of terrorism wherever they are rooted, effective imposition of sanctions, and transnational cooperation amongst all law enforcement authorities. Despite 12 international treaties related to terrorism, a comprehensive convention covering all aspects of counter-terrorism is still missing. Such a convention should be powerful enough to deter states from supporting terrorist groups. The multilateral instruments, however, should not prevent states from having bilateral arrangements aimed at enhancing intelligence between the security agencies of their countries, mutual sharing of database and experiences on counter-terrorism, and joint training/exercises of their forces.

At the same time, the counter-terrorism strategies must be compatible with fundamental freedoms and human rights. The argument is that if we compromise on "core values"[54] in our responses, we would be handing a victory to the terrorists. In other words, any disregard for human rights by a counter-terrorism strategy would keep alive the underlying tension, hatred and mistrust of the government among precisely those sections of the population where terrorists are most likely to find recruits. A vicious cycle should not start all over again.

Notes

1. Jeffrey D Simon, *The Terrorist Trap* (Bloomington: Indiana University Press, 1994), p. 29. Also see David Rapoport, "Terrorism," in Mary Hawkesworth and Maurice Kogan (eds.), *Routledge Encyclopedia of Government and Politics* (London: Routledge, 1992), p. 1061.
2. Alexander Spencer, "Questioning the Concept of 'New Terrorism'," *Peace, Conflict & Development*, Issue 8, January 2006, p. 2.
3. Bruce Hoffman, *Inside Terrorism* (New York: Columbia University Press, 2006), p. 3.
4. See James Joll, *The Anarchists* (Boston: Little Brown, 1964).
5. See, for instance, Claire Sterling, *The Terror Network* (New York: Henry Holt & Co., 1981), which claimed that the Soviet Union was the source of all international terrorism in the world.
6. Paul Wilkinson, "Terrorism," in Michael Foley (ed.), *Ideas That Shape Politics* (Manchester: Manchester University Press, 1994), p. 189.
7. The main works that highlighted this emerging phenomenon were Max G Manwaring (ed.), *Gray Area Phenomena: Confronting the New World Disorder* (Boulder: Westview, 1993); Xavier Raufer, "Gray Areas: A New Security Threat," *Political Warfare*, No. 19, Spring 1992.
8. Walter Laqueur, "Postmodern Terrorism," *Foreign Affairs*, Vol. 75, No. 5, 1996, pp. 24-36.
9. Ashton B Carter, John Deutch & Philip Zelikow, "Catastrophic Terrorism," *Foreign Affairs*, Vol. 77, No. 6, 1999, pp. 80-94.
10. David C Rapoport, "The Fourth Wave: September 11 and the History of Terrorism," *Current History*, December 2001, pp. 419-24. According to Rapoport, the "four waves" were the Anarchist Wave, Anti-Colonial Wave, New Left Wave and Religious Wave.
11. George Jones, "We Will Help Hunt Down Evil Culprits," *London Daily Telegraph*, 12 September 2001.
12. Geoffrey Nunberg, "The War of Words: 'Terror' and 'Terrorism'," *International Herald Tribune*, 22 July 2004.
13. See Walter Laqueur, *The New Terrorism: Fanaticism and the Arms of Mass Destruction* (London: Oxford University Press, 1999).
14. For a detailed exposition on the "flat world", see Thomas L Friedman, *The World*

is Flat: The Globalized World in the Twenty-First Century (London: Penguin Books, 2006).

15. Paul R Pillar, "Terrorism Goes Global: Extremist Groups Extend Their Reach Worldwide," Brookings Institution, 23 February 2009.
16. Ian Lesser et al, *Countering the New Terrorism* (Santa Monica, CA: Rand, 1999), p. 51.
17. Ibid.
18. Steven Simon and Daniel Benjamin, "America and the New Terrorism," *Survival*, Vol. 42, No. 1, 2000, p. 70.
19. John Arquilla, David Ronfeldt & Michele Zanini, "Networks, Netwar, and Information-Age Terrorism," in Lesser et al., n. 16, p. 51.
20. Raymond Whitaker, "Bin Laden Hunt Stepped up," *Canberra Times*, 22 March 2004.
21. David Tucker, "What's New About the New Terrorism and How Dangerous Is It?" *Terrorism and Political Violence*, Vol. 13, Autumn, 2001, p. 1.
22. Col Russ Howard, "The New Terrorism," MIT Security Studies Programme Seminar, 09 March 2005.
23. Tucker, n. 21, p. 2.
24. Craig Whitlock, "Terror Probes Find 'the Hands, but Not the Brains'," *Washington Post*, 12 July 2005. Also see Bruce Hoffman, "Why Terrorists Don't Claim Credit," *Terrorism and Political Violence*, Vol. 9, No. 1, Spring 1997, pp. 1-6.
25. Kumar Ramakrishna & Andrew Tan, "The New Terrorism: Diagnosis and Prescriptions" in Andrew Tan & Kumar Ramakrishna (eds.), *The New Terrorism – Anatomy, Trends and Counter-Strategies* (Singapore: Eastern Universities Press, 2002), p. 6. According to Nadine Gurr and Benjamin Cole, only two out of 64 international terrorist organisations in 1980 could be classified as religious. This figure had risen sharply to 25 out of 58 by 1995. By 2009, religious-based terrorist groups were predominant. See Nadine Gurr & Benjamin Cole, *The New Face of Terrorism: Threats from Weapons of Mass Destruction* (London: I.B. Tauris, 2000), pp. 28-29.
26. Bruce Hoffman, *Inside Terrorism* (New York: Columbia University Press, 2006), p. 88.
27. Ibid., pp. 88-89.
28. Bruce Hoffman, "'Holy Terror': The Implications of Terrorism Motivated by a Religious Imperative," *Studies in Conflict and Terrorism*, Vol. 18, No. 4, 1995, p. 273.
29. Gamat al-Islamiya (Islamic Group), "Statement on US Sentencing of Sheikh Rahman," 19 January 1996.

30. B S Raghavan, "Fight the War on New Terrorism to the Finish," http://www.rediff.com//news/2008/may/14guest1.htm, accessed on 30 January 2009.
31. Quoted in Yonah Alexander and Michael S Swetnam, *Usama bin Laden's al Qaida: Profile of a Terrorist Network* (Ardsley: Transnational, 2001), Appendix 1 B.
32. Walter Lauquer, *No End to War* (New York: Continuum, 2003), p. 9.
33. Simon and Benjamin, n. 18, p. 65.
34. Dore Gold, *The American Spectator*, March/April 2003.
35. Karen DeYoung and Michael Dobbs, "The New Terrorism: Global in Scope, it's Based not on Politics but Fervor," *The Washington Post*, 18 September 2001.
36. Ibid.
37. The elements of this "production line" include the establishment of a social contract, the identification of the "living martyr" (which accrues great prestige within the community), and – in the culminating phase – the production of the final video. See Jerold M Post, "Addressing the Causes of Terrorism Psychology," paper presented at the International Summit on Democracy, Terrorism and Security, 8-11 March 2005, Madrid.
38. Except the LTTE and PKK, all other terrorist groups that employ(ed) suicide attacks are religiously motivated.
39. The US State Department's *Patterns of Global Terrorism* (2002), http://www.state.gov/s/ct/rls/crt/2002/pdf/index.htm, accessed on 01 February 2009.
40. Edward L Glaeser and Jesse M Shapiro, "Cities and Warfare: The Impact of Terrorism on Urban Form," Harvard Institute of Economic Research, Discussion Paper No. 1942, December 2001.
41. "Why is Terrorism an Urban Phenomenon?" *Financial Express*, 15 February 2009.
42. Joshua Woods et al, "Terrorism Risk Perceptions and Proximity to Primary Terrorist Targets: How Close is too Close?" *Human Ecology Review*, Vol. 15, No. 1, 2008, p. 64.
43. Jo Beall, "Cities, Terrorism and Urban Wars in the 21st Century," Crisis States Research Centre, Working Paper No. 9, February 2009.
44. Gold, n. 34.
45. For a more detailed look at terrorism and WMDs, see Richard A Falkenrath, Robert D Newman, and Bradley A Thayer, *America's Achilles' Heel: Nuclear, Biological, and Chemical Terrorism and Covert Attack* (Cambridge: MIT, 1998); Jessica Stern, "Getting and Using the Weapons" in Russell D Howard & Reid L Slayer (eds.), *Terrorism and Counterterrorism – Understanding the New Security Environment* (Guildford: McGraw-Hill, 2003).

46. Osama bin Laden's interview to Rahimullah Yusufzai dated 23 December 1998. cited in Ben Venzke and Aimee Ibrahim, *The al Qaeda Threat: An Analytical Guide to al Qaeda's Tactics and Targets* (Alexandria: Tempest Publishers, 2003), p. 53.
47. Tucker, n. 21, p. 3.
48. Bruce Hoffman, "Terrorism: Trends and Prospects," in Lesser et al, n. 16, p. 13.
49. Mathew J Morgan, "Origins of New Terrorism," *Parameters*, Spring 2004, p. 37. Also see Jessica Stern, *The Ultimate Terrorists* (Cambridge, Mass.: Harvard University Press, 1999).
50. Nimrod Raphaeli, "Financing of Terrorism: Sources, Methods, and Channels," *Terrorism and Political Violence*, Vol. 15, No. 4, 2003, pp. 59-82.
51. Kofi Annan, "A Global Strategy for Fighting Terrorism," Keynote Address to the Closing Plenary of the International Summit on Democracy, Terrorism and Security, 10 March 2005.
52. Raymond Whitaker and Paul Lashmar, "Franchise Terrorism: 'Trying to Hit al-Qa'ida is like Trying to hit Jelly'," *The Independent*, 10 July 2005.
53. Charles Foley (ed.), *The Memoirs of General Grivas* (London: Longmans, 1964), p. 71.
54. The United Nations identifies these "core values" as the rule of law; the protection of civilians; mutual respect between people of different faiths and cultures; and peaceful resolution of conflict.

2

TRACKING 'NEW TERRORISM' IN THE INDIAN CONTEXT

Samarjit Ghosh

Things fall apart, the centre cannot hold; Mere anarchy is loosed upon the world.

— W B Yeats

South Asia, which is home to more than a quarter of the world's population, is terminally beset with problems ranging from rebellions and insurgencies to militant movements, thus, giving repeated occasion to terrorist incidents.[1] The spread of militancy and terrorism in the region is closely linked to the Afghan War of the 1980s, and the joint United States-Saudi Arabia funnelling of arms to the Mujahideen through Pakistan's Inter-Services Intelligence (ISI) Directorate. It is these veterans of the Afghan War, who have come to haunt the security of the United States and several Muslim states in general, and India's in particular. Substantial portions of the billions of dollars given to the rebels in Afghanistan were siphoned off by the ISI and utilised to ignite the separatist movement in the state of Punjab, and, following its failure, the insurgency in Kashmir.[2]

Thus, while India was no stranger to terror activities, it had never witnessed the likes of the attack which struck the city of Bombay in 1993, when, on 12 March, a series of colossal explosions rocked the city. The blasts, which killed more than 200 people and injured about 1,200 others, occurred in several localities simultaneously, with the police going on record to say that the detonations, and coordination and extent of the attacks, were of a variant never before experienced in either the city or the country. Additionally, the explosives used (primarily SEMTEX and RDX), though commonly available to military personnel and mercenaries alike, had never been used in India, especially on such an extensive scale.[3]

S B Chavan, the erstwhile Minister of Home Affairs, also went on record to say that the attacks were part of an international conspiracy,[4] an opinion which was in concert with observers from the United States, who believed that the Bombay attacks not only bore similarities to the Islamic fundamentalist terrorism rampant in the Middle East, but also the February 1993 bombing of the World Trade Centre in New York City.

While it was later posited that the bomb blasts in Mumbai were in retaliation to the riots in late 1992, which, in turn, had been ignited by the demolition of the Babri Masjid by Hindu fanatics,[5] setting into motion a chain of events which continues to wreak havoc today, it did mark a watershed in terror attacks in the country, considering both its extent, and what it portended for the nation at large. While the recent 26/11 attacks in Mumbai were calamitous, in the sense of the terrorists holding entire sections of the city hostage, particularly localities that had remained sheltered from previous incidents, these attacks were only a technological and sociological upgrade of the attacks which the city had previously experienced since 1993.

Krieger and Meierrieks[6] have drawn certain conclusions, with regard to the reasons for the occurrence and flourishing of terrorism, which may be equally applied to the Indian example:

- The factors leading to terrorism may be magnified by political and institutional instability, as also socio-cultural divides on ethnic and religious fronts.
- Large and populous countries, suffering perhaps from institutional handicaps as also social fault lines and a general lack of opportunity for the populace, are more often targeted by terrorism.

- Target countries in a regional neighbourhood do seem to be chosen because of their economic success.
- While democratic states are not especially vulnerable to terrorism, the presence of the democratic institution does not serve as a detractor to a potential terrorist.

The Neighbourhood

The geographical location of the country is not an inconsequential factor in the development of terrorism in the country. Historically, South Asia has been viewed as a region of protracted animosity for a variety of reasons ranging from political, ethno-cultural and religious conflicts of various nature, sporadic terrorist activities with cross-border repercussions, illegal trafficking of small arms, etc. The region, thus, remains politically volatile, with the dubious honour of being able to threaten the peace and stability in areas both within and beyond. Needless to say, repetitive ethno-religious problems in India, particularly in Jammu and Kashmir (J&K), the Maoist insurgency in Nepal, the situation with the Tamil Tigers in Sri Lanka, the bomb attacks and mutinies in Bangladesh, and a pervasive crisis in Pakistan, each with a different prioritisation of security implications for the region, have drawn the attention of academics and terrorists alike.

Thus, on the terrorist front, India is living in an unenviable neighbourhood. Islamic terrorism herein is inherently of an imported nature, whether it is manpower, financing, weaponry, motivation or operational planning and barring Kashmir, where some youth may venture into Pakistan for training in subversive tactics, only a microscopic proportion of Indian Muslims join the ranks of the terrorists.[7] However, the escalating effects of propaganda and extremism have made its presence felt in the country.

In Pakistan, India has a neighbour founded on the basis of religion, and whose government, along with those of Iran and Saudi Arabia, has been a principal exporter of militant Islamic fervour. Bangladesh, too, is host to quite a panoply of *jehadi* groups. As in Pakistan, no meaningful effort to control those who use the country as a launching pad for orchestrating mayhem in India has been successful.[8]

In the case of India, the lack of a firm response to terrorism has only served to embolden terrorists and their sponsors over the years. Pakistan, thus, has not hesitated in employing veterans of the Soviet-Afghan War,[9] and its own cadres of home-grown terrorists, to inflict on India the self-proclaimed policy of bleeding India through the "war of a thousand cuts".[10]

Terrorist incidents in India constitute almost 75 percent of the total such incidents worldwide, as far as 'free' countries are concerned,[11] and while it might be reasonable to assume that groups based in Pakistan are responsible for a fair number of them, especially those occurring in Kashmir, they cannot be blamed for all of them. Geographic and international factors can only amplify the conditions which may foster terrorism. Therefore, the threat of terrorism in India does not come exclusively from the neighbourhood, for, apart from being a country where the divide between the rich and the poor grows wider everyday, people also continue to clash on the basis of religion, caste and language. These internal divisions are as effective a training ground for terror as *jehadi* camps across the border, for the form of *jehad* practised by terrorists is not restricted by religion. Thus, apart from external factors (and actors), India also has homegrown terrorists.[12]

At a broader level, India has actually become a laboratory of sorts, so far as acts of terror are concerned, with the perpetrators believing in the logic that if the world's largest democracy can be rattled, so can other democracies. For instance, the bombing of Pan Am 103 over Scotland in 1988 bore shades of the mid-air bombing over the Atlantic Ocean of an Air India flight from Canada in 1985. Similarities have also been posited between the 1999 hijacking of flight IC 814 to Kandahar, and the 9/11 hijackings, including, but not limited to, the use of box cutters and the terrorists' knowledge of aviation systems.[13]

The Trajectory

Many different interest groups in India use terror as a tool to get their aims across to the government at different levels, including but not limited to, separatist movements in the Northeastern states, Naxalites in the central and eastern states, and extremists of both the Muslim minority and the Hindu majority.[14] However, to be accurate about the appropriate usage of the term, the Indian government takes care to distinguish what it believes to be extremism from terrorism. Thus far, going by governmental fulminations, the term terrorism is applied, quite possibly unintentionally, to the violent activities perpetrated by either Muslim actors or groups, while Naxalites are said to carry out extremism.[15]

Following the 1993 Mumbai attacks, which delineated the beginning of 'new terrorism' in India, several terror incidents have occurred in the country, some with a frequency and lethality that has shocked even the regrettably jaded Indian psyche towards such acts. Of them, certain particular attacks bear mention, as the evolution, and indeed, exacerbation of incidents of 'new terrorism' may be traced through their occurrence:

2001 Attack on Parliament: On 13 December 2001, five men infiltrated the Parliament complex in New Delhi, in cars bearing ministerial labels, and opened fire. They were subsequently killed by the security staff present there.[16] Even by standards of new terrorism, this was an extraordinary attack. By targeting the legislature of the world's largest democracy, the terrorists (shown to have linkages to the Lashkar-e-Tayyeba in Pakistan)[17] were purposefully seeking to provoke India to strike back at the terrorists' sponsors.[18] This attack also bore similarity with an attack which had occurred earlier in the year on the Legislative Assembly of the state of Jammu and Kashmir, when a car had blown up inside the Assembly complex with approximately 80 kg of plastic explosive inside it; 38 people had died in the blast and the subsequent exchange of fire, making it, at that time, the worst individual attack in the state. Had it occurred a mere 30 minutes earlier, the entire political machinery of the state would have been eliminated.[19] New Delhi, considering the audacious December attack the last straw, responded by mobilising the Indian Army to the frontiers with Pakistan, resulting in a prolonged military stand-off between the neighbours. However, the objective of the same, which was the cessation of cross-border terrorism, was not completely achieved.[20]

2005 Delhi Blasts: The bombings occurred on 29 October, 2005, in New Delhi, resulting in the death of 62 people and injuring at least 210 others in three successive explosions.[21]

2006 Mumbai Blasts: The train bombings on 11 July were a series of seven bomb blasts that took place over 11 minutes on the western line of the suburban railway network. The bombs were set off in pressure cookers.[22] Some 209 people lost their lives and over 700 were injured. Investigations revealed that the groups responsible for the blasts were the Lashkar-e-Tayyeba and Students Islamic Movement of India (SIMI).[23] Although the Mumbai rail network had been hit by terrorists in 2003,[24] the impact and extent of the damage in 2006 was more severe.

The switch of targets from aircraft to railways seems to make sense for the terrorists, not because they no longer want to seize aircraft and use them as flying bases or guided missiles, but because the Kandahar and 9/11 experiences had unveiled the advantages and limitations of commandeering an aircraft. Also, airline security has been significantly hardened in recent times, making air operations more difficult. Trains are a much more difficult target to secure. Mumbai alone has six million rail passengers a day, more than three times the total daily number of airline passengers in the entire United States. And the inconvenience caused by placing security checkpoints forces both the government and the people to rethink the enterprise in the long run.[25]

2007 Hyderabad Blasts: On 18 May 2007, a blast occurred inside the Mecca Masjid. It was caused by a cell phone-triggered pipe bomb. Fourteen people were reported dead in the immediate aftermath, of whom four were killed in the police firing after the incident.[26] The blast occurred near the open air section of the Masjid. At the time of the blast, thousands of people were inside the mosque premises for Friday prayers.[27]

Just three months later, two bombs again exploded almost simultaneously on 25 August in Hyderabad. The first bomb exploded in an amusement park and the second, only five minutes later, in a restaurant about five kms away. At least 44 people were reported to have died in the two bombings.[28] A day after the blasts, police discovered 19 unexploded bombs across the city.[29]

Incidents in 2008: On 13 May 2008, Jaipur was hit by a series of nine synchronised bomb blasts, within a span of fifteen minutes at various locations. A tenth bomb was eventually found and defused. Official reports confirmed 63 dead with more than 216 injured.[30] This was the first time terrorists had targeted Jaipur.[31] Two days after the blasts, a previously unknown Islamic militant group known as the Indian Mujahideen, sent an e-mail to the Indian media in which they claimed responsibility for the attacks.[32]

On 25 July 2008, blasts in Bangalore occurred when a series of nine bombs exploded in which two people were killed and about 10 others injured. According to the police, the blasts were caused by low-intensity crude bombs triggered by timers.[33] It was reported that either the Students Islamic Movement of India or Lashkar-e-Tayyeba was behind these blasts.[34]

On 26 July 2008, a series of 16 bomb blasts hit Ahmedabad within a period of 70 minutes; 45 people were killed and over 200 were injured.[35] The blasts were considered to be of low intensity, and were similar to the Bangalore blasts which had occurred the day before.[36]

A series of five synchronised bomb blasts took place within a few minutes on 13 September 2008 at various locations in New Delhi, India. The first bomb exploded at 6:10 pm and four other blasts followed in quick succession, ending with at least 30 people killed and over 90 injured.[37]

Eighteen bombs went off on 30 October 2008, in markets in Guwahati city and the surrounding area of western Assam, causing at least 84 deaths and 470 injuries.[38]

Even for a country like India, which loses more people to terrorism in a year than most countries do in a decade, the 26

November terror attacks in Mumbai signified a turning point. By no means was it the first significant terrorist attack in India. Rather, the July 2006 train bombings had led to more casualties. Yet, certain aspects of this attack were significant, such as its scope, the operational complexity of the attack, its boldness of execution, and the sophistication of the weapons used. Also, for the very first time, foreign nationals – including, but not limited to, Americans, Japanese and Israelis – were among the nearly 200 dead and over 295 wounded. The magnitude of these attacks, which were carried out in many places simultaneously, by a group of 10 men, made the 2001 assault on the Parliament appear almost inconsequential in comparison.[39]

Post the attack, there was much criticism about the way the Indian security forces handled the situation, or rather, their inability to do so. Commentators, both in India and elsewhere, did not shy away from indicating the various fronts where the security and intelligence agencies might have checked the terrorists.[40] But the point that must not overlooked is that the tactical skill and cohesion required to confront the perpetrators of such an attack would perhaps not be within the capabilities of even the most developed nations.[41]

The Trends

The terror incidents recounted above, which form the trajectory of 'new terrorism' in India, are not entirely distinct from those that are deemed to occur on different ideological (and otherwise) grounds. For instance, certain techniques witnessed in incidents of 'new terrorism' appear to be of the same vintage as those in terror attacks occurring in the state of Jammu and Kashmir for many years. In fact, given that terrorism in that state appears to be reaching a saturation point, the incidence of terror attacks in the rest of the country seems to have increased as a counter-balance.

Similarities may also be found in expressions of left wing extremism, especially when it is a question of the tactics and weapons employed, though these extremists have shied from making much use of improvised explosive devices (IEDs) as compared to their urban counterparts. However, while the left wing extremists have restricted themselves primarily to the rural sector, 'new terrorism' is now far more prevalent in the urban sector. Certain modifications in techniques, thus take place, since unlike their rural counterparts, urban terrorists are not interested in territorial control, barring what they deem fit for their limited objectives (if any). And while the former attempt to make their presence felt by targeting specific individuals and establishments for what they represent (specifically in terms of the government), the latter simply look for the most visible and "media-friendly" target.[42]

Indeed, one of the most disturbing trends of 'new terrorism' is that those who indulge in the same, become eventually subsumed with the act itself and tend to forget the ideas which were germane to their initial motivation for the act.[43] Or perhaps we come to know so little of what it is that motivates the terrorists, because they simply do not feel the need to justify any cause to fight for.[44] Accordingly, these individuals indulge in terrorism simply because they can and allow their victims and the like to fabricate their *raison d'être*.

In terms of terrorism in the Northeastern part of the country, the conflicts therein range from insurgency for secession to insurgency for autonomy, and from sponsored terrorism to ethnic clashes, to conflicts generated as a result of a continuous inflow of migrants from across the borders, as well as from other states of the country. Terrorism in this region can, at best, be understood as a strategy to achieve political and personal ends, through the use of both extreme violence and intimidation, even with the tacit complicity of the state.[45]

Yet another defining trend, which may be observed in the evolution of 'new terrorism', is that urban centres are becoming more and more susceptible to terrorist violence, primarily because of the probability of greater visibility afforded by cities.[46] It is, therefore, no coincidence that all major terrorist attacks in India have taken place in cities.[47] Cities of the developing world are specifically vulnerable because poverty, urbanisation and the rapid and unplanned expansion of the same may well exacerbate the impact of terrorism.

The physical environment of an urban setting, as compared to a rural scenario, is very conducive to acts of terrorism, not only because it provides several potential targets, both individual (in the sense of government officials, businessmen, and the like) and infrastructural (offices, transport stations and the like), but also allows the terrorist the convenience of both logistics and anonymity. In India, this perspective, along with the previous one, becomes very crucial, because: (a) the people of the country share common sociological and anthropological attributes with the other countries in the subcontinent, allowing people (if they so choose) to blend seamlessly with the particular location they find themselves in; (b) rapid, and at times, unplanned urbanisation has left even the most prominent cities with a citizenry consisting of both the highly privileged and the completely marginalised sections. Also, a number of satellite towns have begun congealing with the city at large, leaving people to confront realities, both forgotten and unseen, which may not be entirely appreciated. This leads to a situation which often does not encourage mutual coexistence and provides a conducive breeding ground for terrorism amongst the alienated population.

However, when terrorists target a city, it is not just the built environment of the city that attracts them, but also the idea that the city portends, at both a local/domestic and an international level. At the local level, it is a fault line which the terrorist exposes, in the sense that if the government cannot secure a major city, it could hardly be in a position to safeguard the rest of the country. At a broader level, it is an attack on the very idea of urbanism itself, on the city as a social institution, with an impact that transcends national borders and ricochets across the globe.

In the Indian scenario, the attacks on various cities can be marked through their particular attributes. Mumbai, for instance, is not only one of the international faces of India, it is also the financial capital of the nation. Bangalore, in turn, is a technological hub, often referred to as "India's Silicon Valley", and Delhi, of course, is the capital of the nation, and, therefore, the most representative of the same. However, it is with the attacks on cities such as Jaipur, Ahmedabad, Hyderabad and so on, that another trend has come to be defined. The fact that now terrorists are able to strike at even smaller towns and cities, locations which would have been deemed safe before indicates that they are able to muster local support and aid from dissatisfied and malicious sections of society, which remain hidden from the security lens of the state.[48] A further trend is the incidence of simultaneous strikes on multiple targets, which not only fulfils the agenda of maximum damage, but with the bonus of leaving the government's intelligence and security agencies with egg on their faces.

However, with the November attacks in Mumbai, 'new terrorism' could no longer be confined to incidents involving hit-and-run tactics, for on 26/11, Mumbai witnessed urban warfare.

The Response

The model of 'new terrorism' is not free from error. It encourages a top-down approach to the processing of information. It leads policy-makers to depend on a defined set of assumptions about terror acts and their perpetrators. As a result, they believe they can remain unconcerned with understanding what is, in truth, a contradictory and confusing set of circumstances. In such a scenario, policy-makers are liable to rely on metaphors and analogies that make plain sense of what might otherwise be difficult to comprehend.[49]

Therefore, although terrorism has been a national security problem right since the 1980s, and has only worsened since the turn of the century, successive governments at the Centre have done little to combat it, insofar as crafting a concrete counter-terrorism strategy and/or doctrine is concerned. Terrorism has been, for the most part, treated as a law and order problem. Therefore, every time a major attack takes place, the Centre promises to send more security forces to the region, not realising, or ignoring, the fact that they are playing right into the hands of the perpetrators by thinning out and exhausting their forces.[50] At this juncture, it merits mention that the government of the day has gone on record in admitting its understanding of certain new characteristics of terrorism, insofar as its global, and more often than not, non-state character is concerned, and that India is a part of the trajectory of attacks occurring internationally.[51] However, the security authorities have, either by action or inaction, not entirely come to terms with the phenomenon of 'new terrorism', and, hence, the action that they have taken thus far has been found lacking.

On the face of it, terrorists are simply common criminals, guilty of acts of murder, grievous bodily harm, arson, criminal damage and so forth. However, states seldom treat them as such,[52] and India is no exception to this fact.

The primary difficulty with regard to terrorism legislation in India is that law and order is legislated at the state government level, and state governments, traditionally, bridle against central government directives. At the level of the central government, terrorist threat intelligence is assessed and disseminated by a Joint Intelligence Committee that lacks the time, resources and adequate expertise to process and prioritise such material. The domestic intelligence service of the Centre, the Intelligence Bureau, is constitutionally and legally handicapped, and there is a gross lacuna in coordination between the Intelligence Bureau and the Research and Analysis Wing (which is the external arm of intelligence). Both guard their respective turf zealously, and prefer to deal unilaterally with the political leadership, rather than with each other, or, for that matter, with the Joint Intelligence Committee – an unfortunate circumstance since, had it not been for these ego and administrative clashes, many terrorist attacks could have been avoided.[53]

Initially, terrorism did not even figure as an offence in the Indian Penal Code of 1860, nor in its amended versions. In India, the first law that was enacted to deal specifically with terrorism was the Terrorist and Disruptive Activities (Prevention) Act (TADA), in 1987. It was legislated for a limited period of two years in the backdrop of the escalation of terrorist activities in the country. However, after several extensions, and an equivalent number of complaints against it, it was allowed to lapse in 1995.

With the hijacking of flight IC 814 in 1999 and the assault on the Parliament in 2001, a need was felt for a legislative mechanism to deal with terrorism. Hence, the Prevention of Terrorism Act (POTA) was promulgated in 2002. Again, following gross misuse and ineffectiveness, in equal parts, it was repealed in 2004. The Unlawful Activities (Prevention) Act of 1967 (UAPA) was amended in 2004 to include the scope of terrorist activities.[54]

On 17 December 2008, following 26/11, the Indian Parliament passed two major legislations: the National Investigative Agency (NIA) Act and the Unlawful Activities (Prevention) Amendement Act.

The NIA, set up as an outcome of the eponymous Act, has an overarching jurisdiction over law and order matters all over the country. It is a police force created and administered by the central government, which would endow all personnel above the rank of sub-inspector with powers throughout the territory of India. And though law and order is technically a state subject, all information pertinent to the jurisdiction of the NIA would be forwarded to it, and if and when the NIA decides to take control, the authority of the state government would be superceded, including in matters of records and evidences. While the Terrorist and Disruptive Activities (Prevention) Act of 1987 and the Prevention of Terrorism Act of 2002 endowed both the state and the Centre the power to establish courts to try the pertinent cases, the NIA revokes the state's powers in this matter, leaving the Centre in charge.[55]

The UAPA is meant to facilitate investigations and trials of the accused in terrorism cases. It differs from its precursors in only so far as doubling the time allowed to the police to keep a suspect in detention to 180 days. Measures to control terrorist financing have also been included. However, as had been the case with the previous Acts, this one has raised the hackles of human rights advocates as well, with Amnesty International issuing a warning that the UAPA is in violation of accepted international human rights treaties, and, hence, should be rejected.[56]

Laxity in the administration is another reason for the rise of terrorism. Let us take the recent Mumbai attacks as an example. In 2001, a Ministry of Defence report,[57] aimed at the reformation of the national security system, warned that India's long coastline and prime coastal cities, have to a great extent, been left unprotected and unsecured. Given the ubiquitous disputes between the state governments and the Coast Guard, so far as coastal security is concerned, there was need for greater clarity on the subject, especially since the coast's vulnerability to smuggling and infiltration has increased. Hence, an updated security system in concert with rising threats had been long overdue. And while this report was approved by the Cabinet Committee on Security, even several years down the line, the measures therein have not been implemented.

Another major factor that has affected the growth of terrorism in India is the selective nature of justice when it comes to prosecution for the same. While the government continues to push for the extradition of Dawood Ibrahim for his involvement in the 1993 attacks, many who perpetrated and instigated the 2002 Gujarat riots, were never brought to book. [58] Such contradictions, whether deliberate or not, serve as powerful motivators.

Also, in the public spectacle surrounding the Mumbai attack, an important aspect which might be missed out is that this was an attack which would have required a great deal of logistic and operational planning, probably enabled by the involvement of at least ten times the number of people actually carrying out the attack, and yet, the government suspected nothing.[59] Much after the effect, Hasan Gafoor, the Mumbai police commissioner admitted that some Indian nationals were also suspected of being involved in the Mumbai terror attacks, especially in providing reconnaissance, financial and logistics support.[60] However, no sooner had he made these allegations that denials and procrastinating statements couched in the ambit of "due process" were issued *ad nauseam* from the Centre, prompting the commissioner to retract his remarks and profess a gap in communication. Till date, this disturbing aspect of the attack remains unexplored.

The Indian strategic rejoinder to terrorism, then, may be seen as a combination of the country's soft and hard power, which has, at times, invited more than its fair share of criticism. However, it must not be assumed that the particular issues unique to India, given its historical experience, its regional position, and its international aspirations, and their overarching effect on its counter-terrorism policy would be necessarily obvious to other South Asian or Western analysts.[61]

Having said that, the most effective manner of dealing with the problem of terrorism is to:

- gain a firm understanding of the fundamental issues which lead people to commit such acts in the first place; and
- the ramifications of the act, not only on the affected target, but on society and the people at large.

Unfortunately, most government efforts focus on just the immediate incident, and fails to address the systemic challenges and problems behind the same. It is this myopic tendency that ensures that terrorism will continue and grow. Policy-makers need to think systematically about the future, and plan out scenarios for the same – an aspect of governance lacking in current administrations.

Therefore, one must not be too eager to indulge in criticism when it comes to this aspect of governance. While the series of attacks which the country has experienced in the past few years may be testament to the government's inability to take care of internal security, the frequency and complexity of the same would have taxed the abilities and resources of even the most well-prepared nation.[62] Perhaps, terror attacks of the complexity that is visible today may be relatively better detected and defused by the developed nations since they might have greater resources and efficiency to deal with them. Yet, we must not overlook the fact that these nations have themselves not remained impervious to the effects of terrorism either and that it is only through bitter experience that they have come to a position where they can combat it effectively. However, in the case of a nation like India, although it is an ancient civilisation, it is a young democracy consisting of a montage of ethnicities, languages, cultures and religions, unlike any other nation.[63] People in India live concurrently in the past, present and future, and there are many viable targets for terrorists to strike, and precious few frontiers which are completely defensible.

A defining characteristic of this 'new terrorism' is that its practitioners have been able to combine their cobbled interpretation of religious fundamentals with the conveniences and innovations, technological and otherwise, of the modern world.[64] And when attempting to reason what the future of terrorism might be, it is these developments, particularly in connection with weaponry, telecommunications and transport, which must be kept in mind. Terrorist violence is also increasingly becoming decentralised, and though efforts to combat the same must also be decentralised, it has not happened yet.[65]

The world we live in is fraught with old rivalries, festering inequalities and divergent value systems. Until very recently, the scholarly literature on terrorism, both in India and abroad, was dominated by psychologists and sociologists, searching for deep-seated reasons to explain the behaviour of terrorists, and the outward manifestation of the same, which seemed, at first glance, to be absurdly irrational. These aberrations included not only the ease with which terrorists could take innocent lives, but also how easily they could give up their own, for a cause others might not be able to fully appreciate.[66] Thus, we must accept that while acts of terrorism may seem mindless to us, there is a logic and reasoning to them, which is perceptible to those indulging in them.[67] And it is in this context, in particular, that the future looks bleak, insofar as terrorism is concerned. It was theorised by the proponents of globalisation that it would lead to people coming closer together all across the world – what they neglected to mention was that perhaps not everyone would be ready for it. The issues which led to the conception and escalation of terrorism, have not been addressed yet, and may perhaps only be amplified in the future. Experience shows that the terrorist is not a finite entity and manages to rise up against all odds. However, time and time again, so does the nation.

Notes

1. The Failed States Index, brought out by *Foreign Policy*, ranked 146 nations according to their viability, as per 12 criteria, including human flight and economic decline. Pakistan and Bangladesh have been placed 9th and 19th respectively. Nepal, Sri Lanka, and India have been placed 20th, 25th, and 93rd respectively. Even giving latitude to the credibility of the compilation, the region shows a generic tendency towards weakening of the state. Pakistan and Afghanistan sank in their viability over 2005 in the current year.
2. According to one account, barely 30 percent of the military aid reached the Afghan guerrillas. See Anthony H Cordesman and Abraham R Wagner, *The Lessons of Modern War* (Boulder, Colo.: Westview, 1991), Vol. 3, p. 20.
3. Clark Staten, "Indian Bombings Caused by 'Foreign Extremists,' According to Police," *Emergency News*, March 1993.
4. "On This Day – 12 March 1993," *BBC News*, 12 March 1993.
5. Ibid.
6. Tim Krieger and Daniel Meierrieks, "What Causes Terrorism?" Centre for International Economics, Working Paper No. 5, June 2008.
7. Ajit Doval, "Islamic Terrorism in South Asia and India's Strategic Response," *Policing*, Vol.1, No.1, 2007.
8. Sadanand Dhume, "India's Antiterror Errors," *The Wall Street Journal*, 28 November 2008.
9. Richard Ehrlick, "Outsiders Join *Jihad* in Kashmir," *Washington Times*, 02 November 1992.
10. Celia W Dugger and Barry Bearak, "Falling Out: You've Got the Bomb. So Do I. Now I Dare You to Fight," *The New York Times*, 16 January 2000.
11. F Gregory Gause, "Can Democracy Stop Terrorism?" *Foreign Affairs*, September/October 2005, http://www.foreignaffairs.com/articles/61021/f-gregory-gause-iii/can-democracy-stop-terrorism, accessed on 1 February 2009. In fact, since 2004, India has lost more lives to terrorist incidents than all of North America, South America, Central America, Europe and Eurasia put together. All of these sectors lost a total of 3,280 lives in terror incidents between

January 2004 and March 2007, while India alone lost 3,674 lives during the same period. See Shankar Raghuraman, "India Loses Maximum Lives to Terror," *The Economic Times*, 28 August 2007.

12. Anand Patwardhan, "Terror:The Aftermath," *The Hindustan Times*, 09 December 2008.
13. Brahma Chellaney, "Fighting Terrorism in Southern Asia: The Lessons of History," *International Security*, Vol. 26, No. 3, Winter 2001/02, p. 98.
14. Bruce Riedel, "Terrorism in India and the Global Jihad," *Qatar Tribune*, 03 December 2008.
15. Government of India, Second Administrative Reforms Comission, "Combating Terrorism: Protecting by Righteousness," Eighth Report, June 2008.
16. Kanchana Suggu, "The Militants had the Home Ministry and Special Parliament Label," http://www.rediff.com/news/2001/dec/13parl14.htm, accessed on 01 February 2009.
17. Ramananda Sengupta, "The Attack on Parliament, Two Years Later," 13 December 2003, http://www.rediff.com/news/2003/dec/13spec.htm, accessed on 01 February 2009.
18. Bruce Riedel, "How 9/11 is Connected to December 13," *The Hindustan Times*, 11 September 2008.
19. Sessions for the day had closed 30 minutes prior to the attack. Praveen Swami, "An Audacious Strike," *Frontline*, Vol. 18, No. 21, 13-26 October 2001.
20. Srinath Raghavan, "Terror, Force and Diplomacy," *Economic & Political Weekly*, 06 December 2008, p. 10.
21. AFP, "Delhi Blasts Death Toll at 62," http://www.news24.com/News24/World/News/0,,2-10-1462_1826434,00.html, accessed on 01 February 2009.
22. "Scores Dead in Mumbai Train Bombs," *BBC News*, http://news.bbc.co.uk/2/hi/south_asia/5169332.stm, accessed on 01 February 2009.
23. "India Police: Pakistan Spy Agency Behind Mumbai Bombings," *CNN*, http://www.cnn.com/2006/WORLD/asiapcf/09/30/india.bombs/index.html?section=cnn_world#, accessed on 01 February 2009.
24. Vijay Singh, "Blast in Mumbai Train, 10 killed," http://www.rediff.com/news/2003/mar/13mum.htm, accessed on 01 February 2009.
25. James S Robbins, "The Mumbai Blasts: A Repeat Victim," *National Review*, 12 July 2006.
26. "Mob Violence after Hyd Blast, 4 Killed," *IBN Live*, http://ibnlive.in.com/news/india/05_2007/4-killed-as-cops-fire-on-frenzied-mob-40874.html, accessed on 01 February 2009.
27. "Bomb Hits Historic India Mosque," *BBC News*, http://news.bbc.co.uk/2/

hi/south_asia/6668695.stm, accessed on 01 February 2009.

28. "Death Toll in Hyderabad Serial Blasts Rises to 44," *IBN Live*, http://ibnlive.in.com/news/death-toll-in-hyderabad-serial-blasts-rises-to-41/47450-3.html, accessed on 01 February 2009.
29. "Day After Blasts, 19 Timer Bombs Found in H'bad," *The Indian Express*, 26 August 2007.
30. "Defused Bomb in Jaipur had only RDX Traces," http://www.thaindian.com/newsportal/world-news/defused-bomb-in-jaipur-had-only-rdx-traces_10050850.html, accessed on 01 February 2009.
31. Bappa Majumdar, "Unknown Terror Group Claims Responsibility: Report," *Hindustan Times*, 15 May 2008.
32. "For the First Time in 280 Years," *Times News Network*, 14 May 2008.
33. Nirmala Ravindran and Swagata Sen, "Terror Strikes Bangalore; Two Killed, 12 Injured in Nine Blasts," *India Today Group Online*, http://www.itgo.in/index.php?option=com_content&task=view&issueid=&id=7025&sectionid=5&secid=28&Itemid=1, accessed on 01 February 2009.
34. "SIMI, LeT may be behind Bangalore Blasts: IB," *Times News Network*, http://timesofindia.indiatimes.com/SIMI_LeT_may_be_behind_Bangalore_blasts_IB__/articleshow/3279993.cms, accessed on 01 February 2009.
35. "Ahmedabad Blasts: Toll Rises," *NDTV*, http://www.ndtv.com/convergence/ndtv/mumbaiterrorstrike/Story.aspx?ID=NEWEN20080058856&type=News, accessed on 01 February 2009.
36. "Ahmedabad, Bangalore Blasts Share Similarities," *NDTV*, http://www.ndtv.com/convergence/ndtv/mumbaiterrorstrike/Story.aspx?ID=NEWEN20080058893&type=News, accessed on 01 February 2009.
37. Rahul Tripathi, "Serial Blasts Rock Delhi; 30 Dead, 90 Injured," *The Times of India*, 14 September 2008.
38. "At Least 61 Killed and Over 470 Injured in 18 Blasts in Assam," *Associated Press of Pakistan*, http://www.app.com.pk/en_/index.php?option=com_content&task=view&id=57515&Itemid= 2, accessed on 01 February 2009.
39. Sadanand Dhume, "Terror in Mumbai: Two Faces of Globalization," *YaleGlobal*, 01 December 2008.
40. Edward Luttwak, "Ten Men Willing to Die, and a Pathetic Security System," *The Globe and Mail*, 03 December 2008.
41 Greg Grant, "Urban Warfare Mumbai Style," http://www.defensetech.org/archives/004579.html, accessed on 31 January 2009.
42. B Raman, "From Green Revolution to Red Revolution," *International Terrorism Monitor*, Paper No. 239, 03 January 2008

43. V R Raghavan, "Response to Pakistan's Terrorism," *The Hindu*, 25 December 2001.
44. Paul Cornish, "The Age of Celebrity Terrorism," *BBC News*, 30 November 2008.
45. Archana Upadhaya, "Terrorism in the North-East: Linkages and Implications," *Economic & Political Weekly*, 02 December 2006.
46. Jo Beall, *Cities, Terrorism and Urban Wars of the 21st Century*, Crisis States Research Centre, Working Paper No. 9, February 2007, p. 4.
47. N Manoharan, "Targeting Urban Terrain," *The Hindu*, 11 January 2009.
48. Abhay Vaidya, "Pattern of Terrorism Changing in India," *The Times of India*, 03 June 2006. Also see Wilson John, "Terrorist Tentacles in India," *Indian Defence Review*, Vol. 21, No. 2, January 2008.
49. Martha Crenshaw, "The Debate over "New" vs. "Old" Terrorism," Draft paper presented at the Annual Meeting of the American Political Science Association, Chicago, 30 August - 02 September 2007.
50. Chellaney, n. 13, p. 99.
51. Government of India, n. 15.
52. Paul Gilbert, *Terrorism, Security and Nationality: An Introductory Study in Applied Political Philosophy* (London: Routledge, 1994), p. 47.
53. "Terror in Mumbai," *IISS Strategic Comm*ents, Vol. 14, No. 10, December 2008
54. Government of India, n. 15.
55. "Laws Without Accountability," *Economic & Political Weekly*, 20 December 2008, Vol. 23, No. 51, p. 5.
56. "India Seeks to Sooth Public with New Terror Law," *Reuters*, 18 December 2008; Amnesty International, "India – New Anti-Terror Laws Would Violate International Human Right Standards,"18 December 2008.
57. Ministry of Defence, "Group of Ministers' Report on Reforming the National Security System," http://mod.nic.in/newadditions/chapter-v.pdf, accessed on 15 January 2009.
58. Ryan Clarke, "The Indigenisation of Terrorism in India," *RSIS Commentaries*, 137/2008, 26 December 2008.
59. Mobasher Javed Akbar, "India's Agony," *Daily Times*, 30 November 2008.
60. "Mumbai Police Admit Local Support for Mumbai Attack," *Press Trust of India*, 12 February 2009.
61. Doval, n. 7.
62. Grant, n. 41.
63. K Alan Kronstadt, "Terrorist Attacks in Mumbai, India, and Implications for

US Interests," *Congressional Research Service Report R 40087 – 7-5700*, 19 December 2008.

64. Karen DeYoung and Michael Dobbs, "The New Terrorism: Global in Scope, It's Based Not on Politics but Fervor," *The Washington Post*, 18 September 2001.
65. Jean-Jacques Rosa, "The Future of Terrorism," *The Wall Street Journal*, 30 January 2003.
66. William F Shughart II, "An Analytical History of Terrorism, 1945 – 2000," *Public Choice*, Vol. 128, No. 1, pp. 7-39.
67. John L Petersen, "The Future of Terrorism," archive.arlingtoninstitute.org/library/The % 20 Future % 20 of % 20 Terrorism.doc, accessed on 15 January 2009.

3

Motivation, Perpetrators and Methods

Hardev Faujdar and Anil Chauhan

Those youths are different from your soldiers. Your problem will be how to convince your troops to fight, while our problem will be how to restrain our youths to wait for their turn in fighting and in operations

— Osama bin Laden, 26 August 1996

Motivation

Psychologists define motivation as "the needs, wants, interests, and desires that propel people in certain directions." Indeed, it is not going too far to assert that terrorists are psychologically "normal" in the sense of not being clinically psychotic. They are neither emotionally disturbed, nor crazed fanatics. Indeed, terrorist groups and organisations screen out emotionally unsound individuals since they represent a security risk to their own organisation and cadres. There is a multiplicity of individual motivations. For some, it is to give a sense of power to the powerless; for others, revenge is a primary motivation; for still others, to gain a sense of significance. Within each group, there will be motivational differences among the members, each being motivated to different degrees by group interest versus self-serving actions as well as those inspired by ideology.

Terrorist Life Cycle

The process of becoming a terrorist involves a collective, incrementally sustained and focussed commitment to the group. It is useful to unpack the life course of terrorists to consider the psychological process they undergo at different phases of their lives. The feeling of attraction for, and entrance into, the terrorist path is a gradual process, which for some groups begins in early childhood. In particular, what initially attracts a potential terrorist to a terrorist group will differ from what he or she experiences within the group in terms of radicalisation and consolidation of group and collective identity. This, in turn, will differ from what leads the terrorist to carry out acts of violence, and finally, from what leads a terrorist to become disillusioned and leave the group. The power of group dynamics, especially for the closed group, is intense, and once an individual is in the group, it is very difficult to penetrate his psychology and extricate him. Hence, early intervention is required to extricate a person before he is firmed into the group. To do that, it is important to understand what leads the youth to the path of terrorism and also what leads terrorists to leave it. Each of these phases will differ from group to group, and from terrorist to terrorist.

Motivational Categories

Motivation categories describe terrorist groups in terms of their goals or objectives. Some of the common motivational categories are separatist, ethnocentric, nationalistic, and revolutionary.

Separatist: Separatist groups have a goal of separation from existing entities through independence, political autonomy, or religious freedom or domination. The ideologies that separatists promote include social justice or equity, anti-imperialism, as well as the resistance to conquest or occupation by a foreign power.

Ethnocentric: Ethnocentric groups see ethnicity as the defining characteristic of a society and a basis of cohesion. Group members promote the attitude that a particular group is superior because of its ethnic characteristics.

Nationalistic: The motivating factor behind these groups is the loyalty and devotion to a nation and the national consciousness that places one nation's culture and interests above those of other nations or groups. This can aim to create a new nation or to split away part of an existing state in order to join with another nation that shares the perceived national identity.

Revolutionary: These groups are dedicated to the overthrow of an established order and replacing governance with a new political or social structure. They are often associated with communist political ideologies.

Motivational Factors

Individuals who become terrorists are often unemployed, socially alienated individuals who have dropped out of society. Those with little education, such as youths in the Algerian ghettos, Gaza Strip, Pakistan, India or Sri Lanka may try to join a terrorist group out of boredom and a desire to have an action-packed adventure in pursuit of a cause they regard as just. Some individuals may be motivated mainly by a desire to use their special skills, such as bomb-making. The educated youth, on the other hand, may be motivated more by genuine social, political or religious convictions.

Religious: The terrorist activities by the Al Qaeda as a group are motivated by religious convictions. This group believes it is justified because of religious commands found in the Koran, and they use these beliefs to recruit more followers. The Al Qaeda sees Americans as being self-righteous, and power hungry. They loathe what they see as a Hollywood-centric, immoral, and perverted society. Their hope is not so much to convert the US to Islam, but more to destroy the offending parts of US society in order to please Allah.

Abdallah Azzam, a renowned writer, defines *jehad* as fighting the infidels with the sword, and considers death for the sake of God as the ultimate goal of the fight. Azzam says that those who honestly pray to God to be martyrs shall attain a home in paradise even if they die in their beds. Azzam argues that women should contribute in the *jehad* through giving their money and the money of their children in case the enemy attempts to inflict damage. Azzam states that those who die in the battlefield cannot be judged as martyrs going to heaven, since entering heaven is linked to the intention not the act, and intentions are known only by God, as the Sunni doctrine does not judge anyone to heaven or hell.[1]

Socio-cultural: Some are motivated to do better in life simply because they want to move up the social ladder. Others may be motivated to do something so that they can remain in their peer group. Another aspect of social motivation is the widespread unemployment and corruption in Arab societies. Even the loss of Islam's position as a dominant culture centuries ago may have added to that anger which has driven some Arabs to terrorism. Radwan Masmoudi of the Centre for the Study of Islam says that appropriate means should be evolved to find peaceful solutions to serious problems.

Psychological/Achievement Oriented: Everyone has an inherent desire to achieve something in life, and what we feel we need to achieve is relative to who we are as a person. What may be easy for one to achieve might be difficult for another. However, when you have this desire to achieve, and when you recognise it as a driving force, nothing is impossible once you put your mind to it. Even terrorists may be getting motivated by the desire to achieve something as taught to them.

Psychological motivation for a terrorist arises from the individual terrorist's personal dissatisfaction with his own life, government, or accomplishments. A terrorist who is psychologically motivated will always project his own anti-social behaviour and values (motivations) onto anyone he can influence, creating a polarised "Us vs Them" situation. His predictable rationalisation is: everyone outside his own group is evil. This type of terrorist always needs a group to belong to, similar to the gang psychology. The terrorist defines his social status or ego by the psychology behind group acceptance.

Political: Traditionally, terrorism has been used by the people in society who believe their voice is not being heard. Terrorism then becomes a means to disrupt an oppressive government. The leaders of the given idea or movement come together in the form of a militia or rebel group, and aim to bring about political change in order to rid society of an undesired ruling power. In some cases, they can take over as the political power themselves. If this rebellious terrorist group is able to gain the support of the general public, then it is more likely to take control.

Nationalism: Probably the most contested cause of terrorism is an aggrieved group resorting to violence for nationalist or separatist reasons; depending on one's point of view, this can be considered as resistance against an (external) oppressor. Thus far, only Indians have managed to liberate themselves from foreign occupation by peaceful means, whereas in most other colonised states nationalism movements commonly turned to terrorism. The fear of loss of identity of a nation could also drive its people to adopt terrorism. Muslims feel that the Western countries are trying to suppress them socially, politically and economically, which has united them to fight for a cause, individually and collectively.

Revenge/Attention: Another motivation for terrorism is revenge. There have been many instances where terrorism has been used as a means to avenge what is considered an unjust or offensive act. As mentioned earlier, Al Qaeda seems to have a personal vendetta against America. Terrorism has been used as an effective means of gaining the attention of the public by using fear. Most terrorism occurs without warning and at random. This reduces perceived control and increases the sense of helplessness, vulnerability, and disequilibrium. The more random a terrorist act seems, the more attention it will receive as more individuals perceive it as a possible threat. The attention of the world is drawn to the magnitude/intensity of the attack and thereafter the crucial role played by the media. Another important issue is the manner in which the attack is carried out.

Symbolism: Every terrorist act is designed to convey a specific message. The attacks of 11 September or 26/11 had very specific symbolic messages. The attack on the World Trade

Centre was designed to weaken confidence in the American economy. The attack on Washington DC (whether it was intended to hit the Pentagon or the Capitol Hill) was intended to degrade confidence in government security. The attack on Mumbai on 26/11 was carried out to weaken the economic centre of India. Even seemingly random terrorist acts convey the specific message: "We can get you anywhere, at any time. There is no one to protect you." In recent months, terrorism has come to the forefront of our everyday lives and is something we are struggling to understand. Even though we may not see it personally on a day-to-day basis, we are all affected by its far-reaching consequences.

Fear Factor: Fear of punishment may also be a motivating factor for terrorists. This could be looked upon as the opposite of incentive as a motivation, and often both, incentive and punishment, go hand-in-hand. While a terrorist could be rewarded for doing the right thing, he could well be penalised if he did not do it or did it wrongly. For the top hierarchy of a terrorist organisation, this may be an efficient way of keeping terrorists sharp and focussed.[2]

Perpetrators

The inability of the global community to arrive at a universally acceptable definition of terrorism has been a major problem in identifying and labelling (as terrorists) the perpetrators of senseless violence against innocents. In fact, the UN is still struggling to arrive at a consensus among its member states on the definition of terrorism. The attempt has not met with success because of two major reasons. Firstly, on whether the definition of terrorism should include acts of violence perpetuated by the state or not. Secondly, the failure to distinguish between a 'terrorist' and a 'freedom fighter,' when viewed from different perspectives.

In case one considers terrorism in its broadest term as any violent act that terrorises innocent people resulting in intimidation of the society at large or the coercion of their government, then the "shock and awe" bombing of the Iraqi people during the second Gulf War and the asymmetrical use of military force against Palestinians in Gaza in January 2009 by the Israeli Defence Forces can also be termed as terrorist acts. Going by the same yardstick, violence that is generally perpetuated by dictatorial and radical regimes against their own people such as by Saddam Hussein's regime against the Kurds, can also be considered as an act of terrorism. However, there exist several international and regional mechanisms to look after the problems of violence generated by a state, such as the UN and its Security Council, human rights groups and other non-governmental organisations (NGOs). The problem of state terrorism gets accentuated when a state sponsors terror in the garb of providing 'moral' or 'diplomatic' support to an insurgent movement fostered by itself, especially in a disputed area. At the extreme end of such a policy continuum actually lies a strategy to use terror as a tool to achieve politico-military aims that otherwise would not be possible through diplomatic means or even through a conventional war. Nations like Iran, Libya and North Korea had been labelled as the "axis if evil" by the Bush Administration in the recent past, but there is still no legal yardstick to judge nations sponsoring terror, as part of their state policy, for being castigated as "terrorist states". After the 26/11 Mumbai terror attacks, India has proposed the establishment of an International Committee to deal with countries that harbour and aid terrorists. However, the success of such initiatives will primarily depend upon the ability of the international community to first distinguish "one man's terrorist from another man's freedom fighter."

Unlike the haziness surrounding state sponsored terrorism, there is a difference, howsoever thin, between freedom fighters or insurgents and terrorists. The former enjoy popular public support, whereas the latter not only lack such support but, due to their desperate acts of violence, are further deprived of public sympathy. It may be pertinent to note that insurgents also use terror but do so selectively. Generally, their targets are government agencies and institutions or the security forces and their supporters or informers among the common public. The insurgents generally avoid mass killing, an act which is easily used by terrorists in pursuit of their absolute, yet abstract goals. An insurgent can also be distinguished from a terrorist because the former has an ideology with a pragmatic and achievable goal, which makes him a rationalist even while perpetuating violence. Since he is a rationalist, he is also willing to negotiate. A terrorist, on the other hand, is either bereft of ideology or the goals of his ideology are so utopian that they are unachievable in a real world.[3] He is never willing to compromise and even if a threatened government, society or international community is inclined to negotiate with these groups, the terrorist's own ideology often precludes compromise. Unlike guerrillas and insurgents who operate in distinguishable uniforms, terrorists often masquerade as civilians while perpetuating the crime, which makes their act even more heinous. Hence, any organisation that uses terror selectively in support of a larger political strategy that includes a range of tactics (like subversion, guerrilla warfare, etc) to gain control of a government, region or country, deserves to be called "insurgent". An organisation that lacks the capacity to do anything but carry out terrorist attacks could be labelled as "terrorist".[4]

The perpetrators of terror, hence, can range from nation-states to organisations and, in some cases, individuals also. A nation-state may terrorise its own people within the confines of its national boundary or defenceless people of other states who are considered inimical to the former's interest. Nation states may also sponsor both insurgencies and terror in other states for their selfish political ends. There may also be examples of home grown, indigenous and self-supporting insurgencies and terrorist movements, but such cases are scarce. Finally, terrorism is also perpetuated by organisations like the International Islamic Front (IFF) and Al Qaeda, which have a global footprint. Wherever such organisations do not have a physical presence, their ideology inspires terrorist groups and even individuals to undertake terror operations independent of

Fig 3.1: Perpetrators of Terror

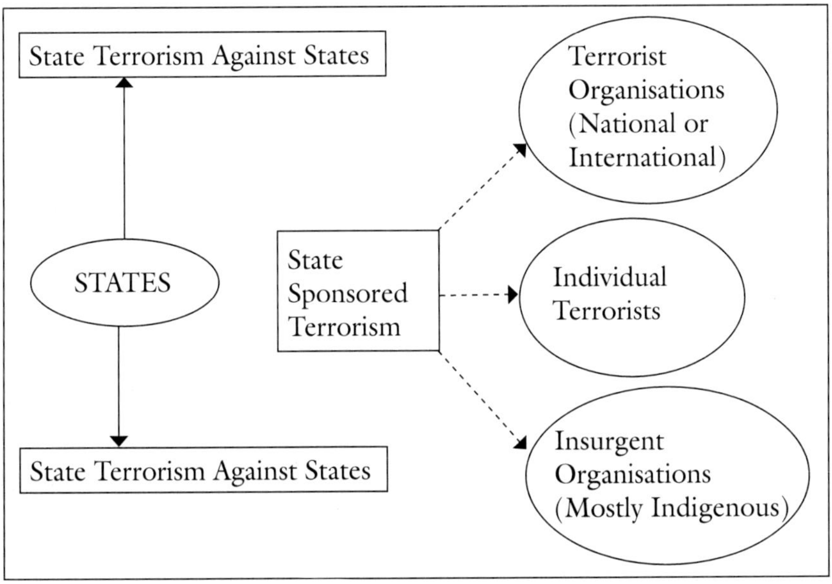

the original organisation. Terrorism unleashed by such groups is what is generally referred to as 'new terrorism' — terrorism that is irrational, uncompromising in ideology, and ruthlessly lethal in approach and execution. Such terrorism is spreading like a virus and is a major threat that not only haunts the Western world but also Asia, including India, which has been at the receiving end of such a movement during the past few decades. There is, hence, an overarching need to focus on such organisations.

The emergence of myriad and yet mutually exclusive ideologies and motivations has given root to various types of insurgent movements and resultantly terrorist activities in India. The waxing and waning of the ideological mooring of the movement itself or the motivation of its leadership has seen the mushrooming or decline in the foot soldiers, who remain the physical perpetrators of violence. While ideologies, which remain mutually exclusive, are the driving force behind most acts of terrorism, the terrorist groups that are motivated by these ideologies do not necessarily operate in mutually exclusive groups. Hence, one often finds instances of cross-group support like, say, the Maoists cooperating with the United Liberation Front of Asom (ULFA) for training or sourcing their supply of weapons and explosives from the Harkat-ul-Jihad-al Islami (HuJI) located in Bangladesh. As far as India is concerned, organisations that are perpetuating 'new terrorism' can be broadly categorised as follows:

Religious Fundamentalist Organisations: In this category fall Islamic organisations that seek to turn India from a *Dar-ul-Harb* to *Dar-ul-Islam*. Such organisations have a pan-India footprint and its foot soldiers are mostly Indian Muslims. These organisations look for, and more often than not, find, ideological and logistic support from outside the nation due to similar ideologies that are at work in the immediate and extended neighbourhood of India. In the second category are Islamic organisations seeking the secession of Jammu and Kashmir from the Union of India and ultimately its assimilation with Pakistan. Most of these terrorist organisations have their bases in Pakistan Occupied Kashmir (POK) and Pakistan, and draw support from practically all sections of the Pakistani government, including the army and Inter-Services Intelligence (ISI). They operate primarily in Jammu and Kashmir, but of late, have carried out major strikes in the heartland with the help of indigenous militant organisations. In the third category, are Hindu militants seeking to undermine the liberal and secular values, including the constitutional provisions of India, to promote a hardline and Hindutva ideology, and, finally, such a nation state on that basis. Considered by some as ultra-nationalists who are responding in kind to *jehadi* terrorism, the fact remains that such organisations are targeting Muslims who happen to be Indian citizens. Finally, there are Sikh fundamentalists seeking to carve out an independent state of Khalistan from the Indian Union. Currently, the movement has been considerably contained and most of the terrorist organisations which mushroomed in the mid-1980s, drawing inspiration from such an ideology, are today dysfunctional or in a state of disarray. These organisations do not pose any worthwhile threat to India.

Tribal and Ethnicity-Based Terrorist Organisations: Terrorist organisations of all hues and types that draw their inspiration from ethnicity are generally based in the Northeastern states of India. Most of these would actually fall under the category of insurgent movements that have either failed to win popular public support, or have reached a strategic stalemate while combating the security forces, without reaching their enunciated or perceived goals. Some of these organisations, especially from Assam, have turned to violence, bordering on terrorism, either in sheer frustration or to prove that they still remain a force to reckon with. Others have negotiated complete peace with the Indian government like the Mizo National Front (MNF) in Mizoram, and some are on an extended period of truce and ceasefire like the National Socialist Council of Nagaland (NSCN) in Nagaland, so as to negotiate a final settlement with the Government of India.

Terrorist Organisations Seeking Social Restructuring: Some terrorist organisations have a socio-political agenda which they seek to achieve through violence. These are generally labelled in the category of Naxalites or Maoists. There is a large number of such groups operating in various states of India. The stated aim of the Naxalite movement in India is to establish an egalitarian society and the rule of the proletariat by armed revolution, overthrowing the present order and elimination of all class enemies. The movement has taken the threat of terrorism to India's heartland and portends to become a major problem in the years to come.

International Terrorist Organisations: Some terrorist organisations that have a global footprint also have some of their support base in India either directly or through their affiliates. The International Islamic Front (IIF), an umbrella organisation formed by Osama bin Laden in 1998, includes groups like the Taliban, Al Qaeda, terrorist groups from Pakistan, Bangladesh, Egypt, Central Asian Republics, China and Philippines. Terror groups like the Lashkar-e-Tayyeba (LeT) and HuJI-Bangladesh are members of IIF and along with some indigenous groups, draw their motivation from the latter's ideological goal which is the reestablishment of an Islamic Caliphate, ruled by the Shariat, by removal of artificial boundaries separating Muslim nations and reuniting them as one country that stretches from the Atlantic to the Pacific.

Major Terrorist Groups Operating in India

All terrorist groups do not pose similar threats and challenges to the unity and integrity of India. The degree of the threat is related to the assistance they receive from neighbouring countries in terms of diplomatic, financial, material, personnel and moral or ideological support. The threat is also directly proportional to the mass support these organisations may enjoy. Some of the major terrorist organisations, along with their stated objectives and ideologies, are listed below:

Students Islamic Movement of India (SIMI): SIMI is an Islamist fundamentalist organisation which advocates the liberation of India by converting it into an Islamic land, either through forced conversions or through violence. It does not believe in the concept of secularism, a nation-state or the Indian Constitution. It was founded as the student's wing of the Jamaat-e-Islami Hind (JIH), but parted ways with the parent organisation in 1981, when serious differences developed between them over the visit to India of Yasser Arafat, who SIMI considered a Western stooge. SIMI continued to function as an independent organisation under Dr Shahid Bader Fateh as its president and Safder Nagori as its general secretary till it was banned in 2001.

Indian Mujahideen: The Indian Mujahideen is a new terrorist organisation which came into prominence after it claimed responsibility for the terror attacks in Ahmadabad, Jaipur and New Delhi in 2008. It was first noticed in November 2007, when it claimed to have carried out the bombings in Uttar Pradesh, by sending e-mails to the media just before some of the bombs planted by it actually exploded. It is believed that the Indian Mujahideen may be composed of lower-tier SIMI members who have taken on a new identity because the top leadership of SIMI had been detained. The name reflects a desire of this nascent organisation to seek the support of Indian Muslims rather than be seen as a foreign terrorist entity. The organisation is said to be founded by Riyaz Bhatkal and Mohamed Sadiq Sheikh, both of whom are now absconding.

Abhinav Bharat: Abhinav Bharat was originally floated by Vinayak Damodar Savarkar as a revolutionary outfit to fight the British imperialism but was wound up in 1952 after India gained independence. The present Abhinav Bharat was floated in 2006 in Maharashtra. A similar outfit was also started in Madhya Pradesh in 2008 by some right wing members after their expulsion from the Rashtriya Swayamsevak Sangh (RSS). Presently, Lt Col Prasad Srikant Purohit, Swami Dayanand Pandey, Sadhvi Pragya, Maj Ramesh Upadhyay (Retd) and Sameer Kulkarni, are all part of Abhinav Bharat or associated with it. They are under investigation for their role in right wing extremist activities.

Lashker-e-Tayyeba (LeT): Founded by Hafiz Muhammad Saeed and Zafar Iqbal, the main headquarters (HQ) of the organisation is currently located in Muridke near Lahore. While the immediate objective of LeT is to liberate Muslims residing in Indian administered Kashmir, its long-term aim is the restoration of Islamic rule over all parts of South Asia. This Islamic rule is later to be be extended to include Russia and even China. The LeT draws ideological support from its political arm, the Jamaat-ud-Dawa, alongwith which it is now internationally banned. The LeT has been responsible for most of the *fidayeen* and suicide attacks in India.

Jaish-e-Mohammed (JeM): JeM was formed in 1994 and is a major Islamic terrorist organisation based in Pakistan. The group's primary motive is to separate Kashmir from India and it was formed after the supporters of Maulana Masood Azhar split from another Islamic militant organisation, the Harkat-ul-Mujahideen. The group gets considerable funding from Pakistani expatriates in the United Kingdom and other parts of the world.

Harkat-ul-Jihad-al-Islami, Bangladesh (HuJI-B): The organisation was established in 1992, reportedly with assistance from Osama bin Laden's International Islamic Front (IIF). The HuJI-B continues to maintain active links with the Al Qaeda network and remnants of the Taliban militia. Its aim is to establish an Islamic republic in Bangladesh. HuJI-B has strong links with Pakistan based terrorist groups and the ISI.

Leftwing Extremist (LWE) Groups: Presently, there are about 40 LWE groups in India. However, only 19 of them are operationally active. These could be divided under three broad categories. In the first category are groups that participate in parliamentary politics like the CPI-ML (Liberation). The groups in the second category have raised armed underground cadres but still participate in parliamentary democracy, like the CPI-ML (New Democracy), and in the third category are groups that consider parliamentary democracy a sham and have declared their unflinching support to the idea of carrying on with an armed struggle. The third category contains groups like the CPI (Maoists) and CPI-ML (Naxalbari), of which the former is the largest and most violent. Most of the Naxal related violence during the past few years can be attributed to the military wing of the CPI (Maoists) called the People's Liberation Guerrilla Army. The front organisations of the Maoists movement include trade unions, intellectual forums, human right activists and NGOs that are actively engaged in furthering the cause of the movement.

United Liberation Front of Asom (ULFA): ULFA was formed in April 1979 at the Rang Ghar in Sibsagar to establish a "sovereign socialist Assam" through an armed struggle. The organisation has been banned by the Government of India since 1990.

Methods

The world in general, and India in particular, has been the victim of a number of spectacular and high profile terrorist attacks in the past few years. The success of these horrendous acts of terror can be attributed to the relative freedom enjoyed by terrorists in selecting their targets, including the time and mode of attack besides the use of innovative and ingenious methods. On the other hand, the security forces that are required to prevent such acts of terror and combat the perpetrators, not only lack credible and timely intelligence but also remain relatively ill-trained and ill-equipped to handle 'new terrorism' and its perpetrators.

In any nation, the security forces are the visible symbols of its state power and the only entities legitimately licensed and equipped to use force. Accordingly, the world over, the security forces have been the main targets of insurgents and terrorists. However, in the past, the general population was considered by insurgents as neutral and was sought to be cultivated for espousing the cause of their movement. In fact, the insurgents thrived on popular public support and survived, as Mao put it "like a fish in the sea of humanity". The ultimate objective of all insurgent movements is to overthrow the existing regime by turning its own people against it.

In the age of 'new terrorism', such a paradigm is no longer true. 'New terrorism' considers that the general public can be coerced through violence. A sense of uncertainty and insecurity among the general population and conditions of anarchy can lead to the loss of credibility of the government, which would finally lead to changes in the established order. Hence, "terrorism for the sake of terrorising alone" seems to be the philosophy behind 'new terrorism' where focus is not mass disruption, but mass destruction. The bigger the horror or the carnage, the bigger sound bytes it will attract in the media and the bigger will be the impact on the public. When the focus of terrorism shifts from the security forces to the common man, not only do the numbers of targets that can be easily attacked get multiplied manifold, but the success rate of the terrorists' action against such targets is also high as most of them are generally unprepared to undertake evasive action or counter-measures. The relative ease with which success is achieved is sometimes taken by terrorists, especially those driven by religious motivation, as divine approval of their act and, hence, the righteousness of their cause – "they died because they deserved to die" type of perverse reasoning.

Terrorist methods have undergone radical changes in their tactics and *modus operandi*, both of which are always evolving. An insurgent or terrorist of yesteryears generally adopted "hit and run tactics" so that he could "live to fight another day". These generally resulted in the terrorists undertaking operations like ambushing of security forces, hijacking of airplanes or hostage situations, followed by negotiations for ransom, demands for freeing of captured terrorists or to espouse the terrorist cause. This style has been sidelined in favour of newer methods like suicide bombing and *fidayeen* attacks, where a certain loss of terrorist life is juxtaposed against the number of innocent lives such an act will be able to take.

In this context, suicide terrorism driven by religious fundamentalism, especially by Islamic terror groups, needs special mention because suicide *per se* is banned in Islam. Although popularised by the Liberation Tigers of Tamil Eelam (LTTE), suicide terrorism, initially caught the fancy of Shia terrorist groups operating in Lebanon, like the Hezbollah, who used the *shahadat* or martyrdom of Hussain in Karbala to draw inspiration from such an act. The success of this "poor man's cruise missile" which could achieve devastating effects with pin-point accuracy, further motivated Sunni terrorist groups like Hamas, Islamic Jihad and Al Aqsa Martyrs Brigade that operated in Israel or territories occupied by it. Suicide terrorism is now used by most Islamist terrorist groups, especially those operating against US forces and their allies in Iraq and Afghanistan. A *fidayeen* attack, though equally if not more deadly than a suicide attack, is slightly different from the latter. A *fidayeen* does not take his life himself although he knows that he is sure to die in the operation he is about to undertake.

The changes being ushered by 'new terrorism' are not restricted to change in tactics and *modus operandi* alone. The changes in methods include recruitment, motivation and training of cadres, organisational restructuring, use of the media and the exploitation of technology.

Recruitment, Motivation and Training: While the unemployed youths of the society form the mainstay of most terrorist groups, if the videos released by the Taliban and Al Qaeda to the media are to be believed, they are also recruiting and training very young children to undertake terrorist acts. There have been cases of women, including suicide bombers, in the ranks of terror groups like the LTTE, and Palestinian terror groups like the Hamas, Islamic Jihad and Al Aqsa Martyrs Brigade but these have not found favour among Afghan-based terror groups like the Taliban. Similarly, it would be unwise to assume that the uneducated and unemployed fill the ranks of all terror groups because most of the high profile terrorist attacks in Europe and the US have been carried out by educated middle class youth or well-to-do professionals. Some of these terrorists were even married, with families, including children. Most of the foot soldiers of terror groups are the products of religious seminaries preaching the superiority of their ideology and, hence, motivation is not a major problem. The recruits are further brainwashed by religious discourses, including accounts of injustices and atrocities being perpetuated on their co-religionists, during their basic and advanced training. Basic training of terrorists includes a wide variety of subjects so that they can operate effectively and achieve their objectives. Since most terrorist incidents involve bombs, training in handling of explosives is of paramount importance, followed by handling of firearms, communication equipment and physical fitness. These instructions are often combined with small unit tactics like fire and move, maintaining fire discipline and techniques of guerrilla warfare like mounting of covert surveillance. Depending on the mission, advanced training is imparted which could include navigation on land or high seas, underwater demolitions, deep sea diving or even piloting of small boats, patrol craft, ships, even gliders or aircraft.

Organisational Structures: Insurgent organisations of yesteryears had an hierarchical set-up even though the structures and their linkages were not so well defined. Most of these organisations had political and military wings under a command

and control element which was headed by the top leadership. Even Al Qaeda, during its formative years, had four committees, each headed by an *emir*, who reported to the *shura majlis*, which functioned as a kind of a higher committee. Each of these committees dealt with military affairs, finance and business, *fatwas* and Islamic laws and media and publicity. However, the present day Al Qaeda, most analysts believe, is no longer a hierarchical organisation but has transformed itself, first, into a network through the formation of the IIF and, finally, has morphed into an ideology. It is the appeal of this ideology that is inspiring terrorist groups in different countries to perpetuate violence without any direct linkage or communication with the parent organisation. However, a terrorist group working within the limited confines of an area is generally organised in small modules or cells to avoid detection, akin to those devised by the Bolshevik revolutionaries in Russia. A typical clandestine cell may comprise four to five members, with only one member knowing only one person of the higher or lateral module.

Use of the Media: The mass media occupies a central position in the formation of public opinion and any coverage of terrorist acts enjoys high viewership ratings, not only in India but the world over. Most terrorist groups believe that media coverage of their violent act assists their long-term objectives of discrediting the government, its security forces and the judicial system of the land, besides creating a sense of helplessness among the common public. Terrorist organisations like the Al Qaeda and Indian Mujahideen have also used the media to covey their ideas and messages to their cadres and warnings to the government and public. On the other hand, during the coverage of terrorist acts, often, although unwittingly, the media becomes a convenient tool in the hands of terrorists, providing their services free of charge. Live coverage of such events sometimes may also assist the actual perpetrators either though direct access or through their proxies located outside as was witnessed in the 26/11 attacks on Mumbai.

Exploitation of Technology: The developments in technology can enable a single terrorist to be extremely destructive, as was evident during the 9/11 attacks where passenger aircraft were used as guided missiles to target the World Trade Centre (WTC) and the Pentagon. Terrorists sponsored and equipped by states can also use anti-aircraft missiles on passenger aircraft with devastating results. When the aim of terror becomes "mass destruction and large-scale killing", the possibility of use of weapons of mass destruction (WMD) also becomes a grim reality. Biological, chemical and radiological weapons can kill thousands of people relatively easily and are, thus, considered by many to be the most serious terrorism threat. It is also possible for some of these weapons to be produced by individuals or to be fabricated in rudimentary workshops, which increases the scope of the potential threat. Use of technology is not restricted to the mode of attack or the weapon system only but can also be exploited by terrorists to communicate and navigate as was evident during the 26/11 Mumbai attacks.

Shifting Focus of Terror: While Figs 2 and 3 identify various terrorist groups based on the acts committed by them in their area of preeminence, Fig 4 presents countries or regions that have been the victims of terrorism during the period 2001-2008. The representation is based on actual locations where terror acts have been committed. However, in some Muslim, especially Arab countries, the victims have been mostly foreigners and people of other faiths. Hence, to that extent, the picture being presented in Fig 4 from a 'victim of terror' point of view will be slightly skewed. However, the figure confirms that the centre of global terrorism is shifting from the Middle East to South Asia. Terrorist action in Israel and Russia has shown a marked decline, whereas there has been a general increase everywhere else. However, the increase has been sharpest in India and Pakistan, especially the latter. Hence, Pakistan is not only emerging as the epicentre of global terror but also as its victim.

Fig: 3.2: Terror Groups: Worldwide

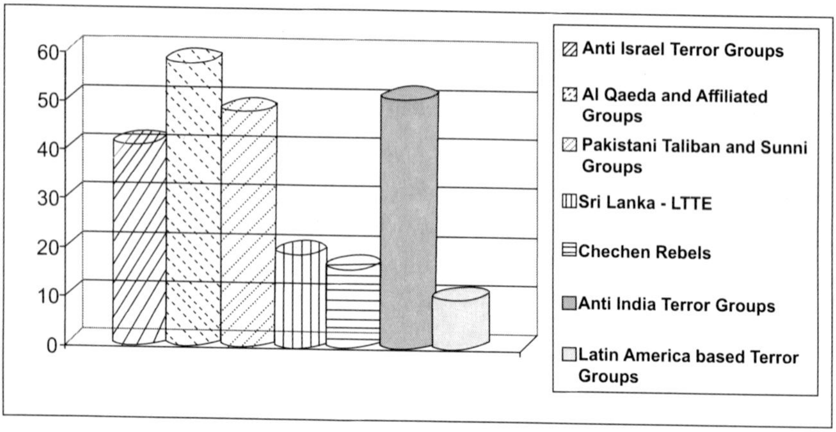

Fig 3.3: Anti-India Terror Groups

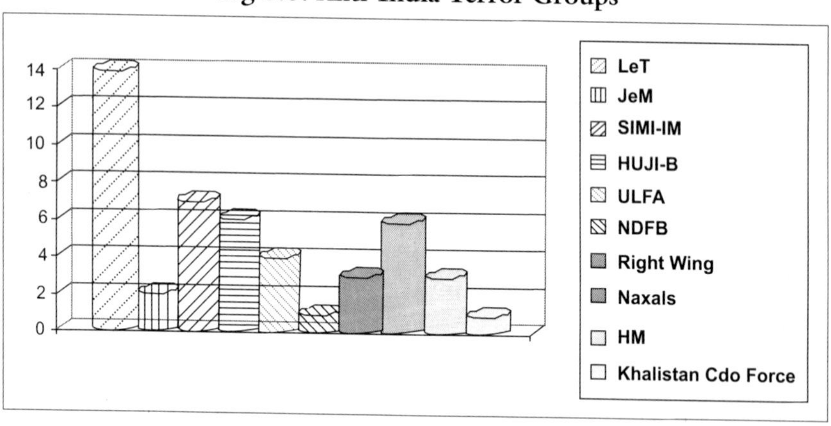

Fig 3.4: Shifting Focus of Global Terror

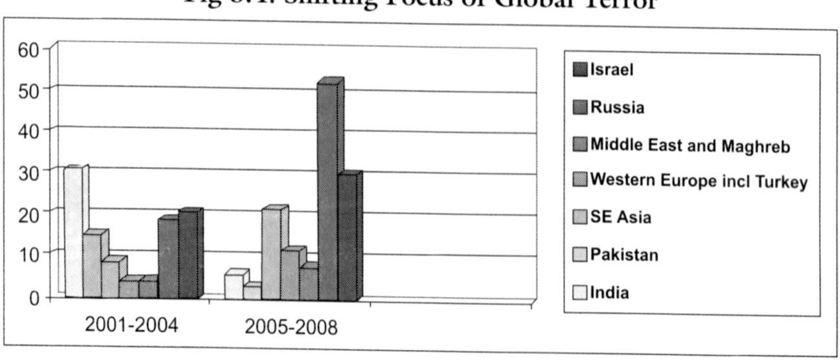

Modes of Attack: The *modus operandi* adopted by terrorists to perpetuate violence worldwide and in India, during the period 2001-2008 is summarised in Fig 5. When viewed against a global perspective, suicide attacks (human or car bombs) along with pre-placed bombs/improvised explosive devices (IEDs) or landmines appear to be the most preferred forms of attack. On the other hand, in India, the *modus operandi* of terrorists has been to detonate IEDs, landmines or carry out serial bomb explosions.

Fig 3.5: Modes of Attack

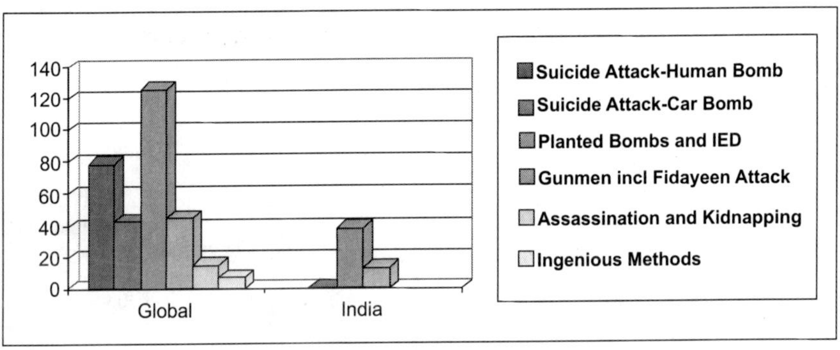

Suicide Attacks: Suicide attack is emerging as a major tool in the hands of terrorists. Figs 6 and 7 establish a correlation between frequency of such attacks and the countries targeted either by human or vehicle based suicide bombers. Israel, which was once a victim of human suicide bombers during 2002 to 2005, has shown an absence of such terror attacks during the period 2006 to 2008. It may also be noticed that even when suicide bombing was the most preferred mode of attack, there were hardly any instances of car bomb attacks in Israel. The weight of suicide attacks now has shifted to Pakistan where terror groups of all hues prefer this mode of attack.

Fig 3.6: Suicide Attacks by Human Bombs

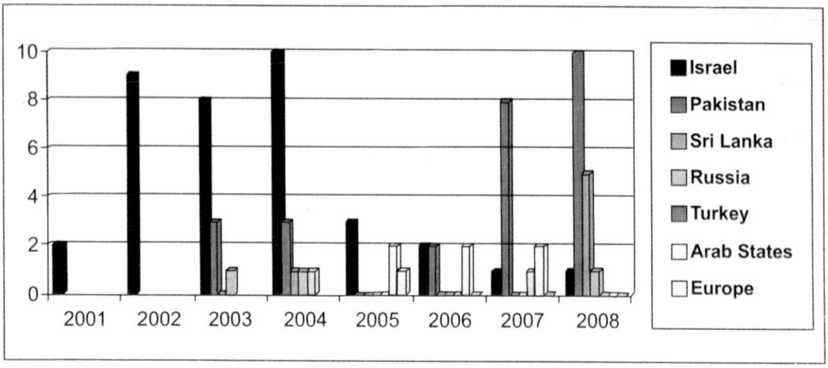

Fig 3.7: Suicide Attacks by Car and Truck Bombs

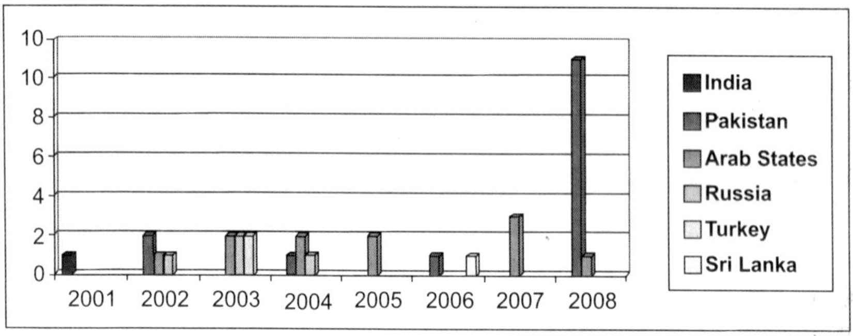

Gun, Grenade and Fidayeen Attacks: All attacks by terrorists using guns and grenades cannot be categorised as *fidayeen attacks.* In most cases, the perpetrators plan for, and make good, their escape after committing the crime. *Fidayeen* attacks generally involve forced entry into heavily barricaded places, the taking of hostages and a fight to a bitter end. Examples of large scale *fidayeeen* attacks include the seizure of a cultural theatre in Moscow, the local school in Beslan and the 26/11 attacks in Mumbai. Fig 8 presents attacks involving armed gunmen which may or may not be *fidayeen* attacks, as a correlation to time period and target countries. As may be seen, such attacks have been mostly carried out in the Arab states, Russia and India.

Fig 3.8: Attacks Involving Guns and Grenades

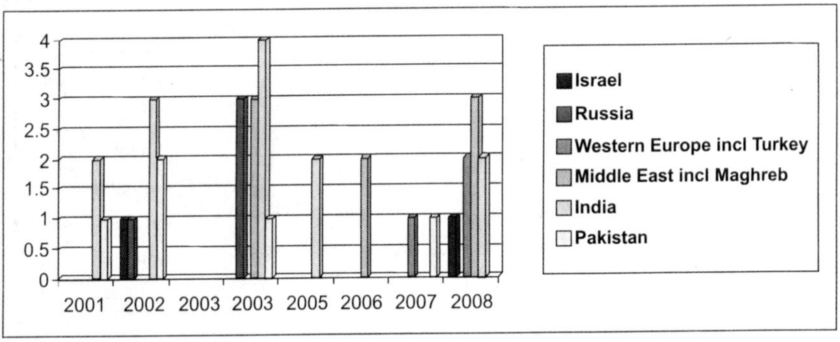

Severity of Attack: Has the focus of 'new terrorism' shifted from mass disruption to mass destruction? Which are the organisations responsible for the largest number of deadly attacks? While there is no yardstick to classify the severity of a terrorist attack, for the purposes of this analysis, any terrorist incident in which more than 20 people have been killed has been taken as a major terrorist strike. Figs 9 and 10 establish the correlation between location of severe terror strikes and the organisations responsible for them respectively.

Conclusion

While there has been a general rise in terrorist activities worldwide, the focus of terrorist activity has shifted from the Middle East to South Asia, with Pakistan emerging as the epicentre of global terror. An analysis of terrorist incidents for the period 2001-2008 indicates that suicide terrorism is becoming the preferred mode of attack for perpetuating violence as there is no defensive mechanism to guard against it. Increased instances of suicide terrorism in our neighbourhood, especially in Pakistan, have serious portends of such techniques being imported to India. There is, hence, an overarching need to sensitise our security forces, intelligence agencies and also the general public about such threats so that counter-measures can be developed. Hence, close cooperation with foreign nations that have been a victim of such terror in the past and have been able to successfully counter it, is imperative.

Fig 3.9: Location of Severe Terror Attacks

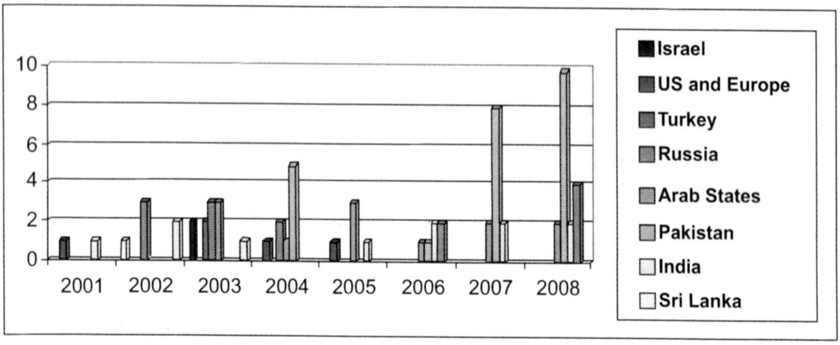

Fig 3.10: Groups Responsible for Severe Terror Attacks

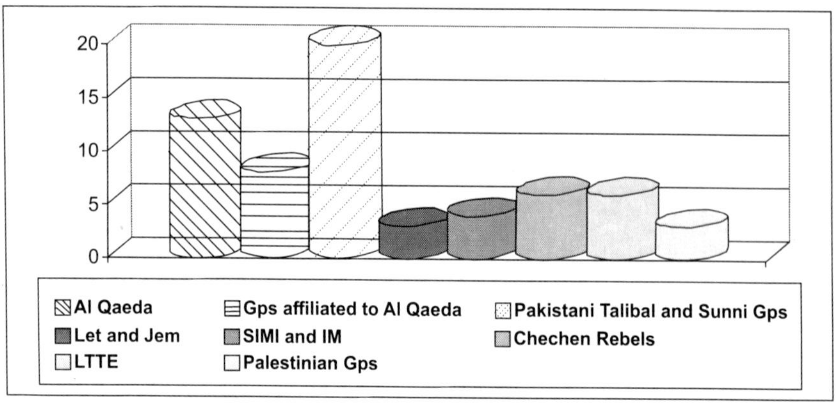

India's fight against terrorism cannot remain restrictive in scope. The focus cannot just be on combating the perpetrators or arresting the modes and methods of attack. To eradicate terror, there is a need to address the root causes of terror itself. The roots of such terror are mired in the fundamentalist ideology which motivates misguided youth towards terrorist organisations. The battle against terrorism can only be won if we are able to wean away the youth from the fundamentalist ideology that inspires them. This will require a multi-dimensional approach and cooperation from all sections of the society.

Notes

1. F Keane, "The Mind of a Terrorist," in J Baxter and M Downing (eds.), *The Day that Shook the World: Understanding Sept 11* (London: BBC Worldwide, 2001), pp. 54-67.
2. See R Falk, "The Terrorist Mindset: The Moral Universe of Revolutionaries and Functionaries," in R Falk (ed.), *Revoultionaries and Functionaries: The Dual Face of Terrorism* (New York: E P Dutton, 1988).
3. Thomas R Mockaitis, *The New Terrorism: Myths and Reality* (Connecticut: Praeger Security International, 2008), p. 8.
4. Ibid., p. 9.

4

FEEDING THE FIENDS: TERROR SUPPORT SYSTEMS

Harish Thukral and MLN Sravan Kumar

Introduction

The motivations and methods for the germination and spread of terrorism are truly myriad, as has been discussed in the previous chapter. While the underlying motivation gives life to this monster, it is the public attention and publicity that provide the monster with the oxygen for survival. However, for continued sustenance and growth, the agencies of terrorism require enormous financial backing and elaborate support systems. In the context of "terror without borders", it is axiomatic that the flow of terror funds, its support mechanisms and collusive elements extend beyond political and physical boundaries of states and regions. Any meaningful measures to tackle terrorism, therefore, necessitate international cooperation and transnational endeavour.

Terror Financing: Facts and Challenges

Continuance of terrorism has made it clear that no amount of talk, persuasion or diplomacy will lead to terrorists giving up violence and terror. Terrorism will continue to grow unless a determined offensive is launched both against terrorist organisations and the factors that help terrorism thrive globally. Among many factors, financial assistance to terrorist groups is, perhaps, the most crucial for their survival. Terrorist activities in most cases require substantial financial support. Such activities generally involve the propagation of an ideology advocating militant action to achieve their goals, increasing the number of cadres willing to carry out violent action, acquisition of, and training in the use of arms and explosives, planning and execution of violence, etc. All these activities require significant funding. Apart from the proceeds of illegal operations, such funding may be sourced even from the proceeds of lawful activities such as contributions to non-profit or charitable institutions set up as fronts for terrorist organisations or by working in concert with cartels involved in drug-trafficking, smuggling, etc. – without having to resort to money-laundering *per se*. Funding may also involve counterfeiting of currency. In all the activities mentioned above, the end result is that money reaches the persons involved in carrying out terrorist acts. This brings into focus the crucial issue of transfer of funds – both within and beyond national boundaries. International organised crime makes use of a wide range of methods and networking routes to transfer funds with a view to launder the proceeds of crime. Apart from using the facilities provided by international trade, such organisations also take recourse to bulk cash smuggling and use of informal channels of transfer of money (like *hawala*). This is the reason that internationally there has been a tendency to merge the anti-money laundering and counter-terrorist finance (AML/CTF) regimes. However, the following two features distinguish the activities related to money laundering operations from those related to financing of terrorist activities:[1]

- In money laundering, the activity begins with the generation of proceeds from unlawful activities/crimes and ends with their conversion into legal assets (movable or immovable). On the other hand, financing of terrorist activities could be from legal or illegal funds and it culminates when it reaches the perpetrators of a terrorist act, sometimes involving money laundering activity en route. This widens the scope of investigation in cases involving terrorist finance.

- In the case of money laundering, even if the proceeds of unlawful activities get 'laundered', enforcement authorities can undo the effect on the basis of *post facto* investigation. Whereas in the case of terrorist finance, once the finance chain is completed and an act of terrorism has taken place, *post facto* investigation is limited to generating evidence leading to conviction of the perpetrators; loss of life, damage to property and erosion of public confidence would have already taken place.

It follows from the above that the law enforcement and investigation regime has to be wider in scope while dealing with terrorist financing as compared to money laundering operations. Further, in dealing with financing of terrorist activities, the emphasis has to be more on obstructing such activities while in progress. Thus, a comprehensive understanding of the entire gamut of terror financing is essential to evolve an effective strategy to combat terrorism and disrupt the financing of terrorist groups and their activities.

This section seeks to put forth a comprehensive overview of the vital facets concerning terror financing to enable the formulation of an effective strategy to counter the flow of funds to the terrorists.

End Use of Funds by Terrorists

The first step in identifying and forestalling the flow of funds to terrorists is to understand the funding requirements of modern terrorist groups. While the funding requirements of terrorist organisations vary too widely to be described by any single typology, recent literature does suggest some common activities and tasks on which terrorists actually use funds.[2] The demand-side of terrorist finance includes:

Direct Costs of Terrorist Attacks and Conflict: The materials necessary to stage specific attacks are highly diverse and include, for example, explosives, arms and ammunition, improvised bomb-making components, vehicles, maps, surveillance material, etc. These direct costs of terrorist attacks are often very low, relative to the damage they can yield. For instance, the 9/11 attacks are estimated to have cost between 400,000-500,000 dollars.[3]

Training: Aspects such as setting up training camps and other infrastructure, buying arms for training, payment to trainers, acquisition of indoctrination and motivation material, etc, require substantial financial outlays.

Salaries/Subsistence and Communications: Individual operatives need to cover their day-to-day expenses and perhaps also those of their dependents. This is a more significant commitment if there is no other source of income for the operatives (such as employment or welfare payments). A cell also needs to communicate with its members and perhaps the parent network, incurring expenses on communication.

Travel and Logistics: The financial facilitation of travel, for training as well as for operations, which can include the procurement of false documentation, represents an important cost for many terrorist networks.

Shared Funding: Where a cell is part of a network or shares a common goal or ideological or religious background with another cell or network, it may be called upon, or feel compelled, to provide financial support to fellow terrorists.

Broad Organisational Requirements: Beyond the funds needed to finance terrorist attacks and provide direct operational support, terrorist organisations require funding to develop a supporting infrastructure, recruit members and promote their ideology. In addition, this infrastructure spending may go to support charitable organisations and media owned or controlled by the terrorist organisation in question. Terrorist groups such as Al Qaeda have been especially adept at manipulating the media through the release of videos. In addition, virtually every terrorist organisation has a website dedicated to recruitment and spreading the message of their "mission".

Mode of Raising Funds

Terrorist organisations may raise funds through legitimate sources, including through abuse of charitable entities or legitimate businesses and self-financing, criminal activity, state sponsors and activities in failed states and other safe havens.

Raising Funds from Legitimate Sources: Terrorist organisations receive considerable support and funding through legitimate sources, including charities, businesses, and through self-funding by terrorists and their associates from employment, savings, and social welfare payments. This includes the phenomenon known as "black-washing" where legal funds, for example, money stemming from collection by charities or governmental subsidies and social benefits, is diverted for purposes of radicalisation, recruitment or acts of terrorism. In developing the key financial standards to combat terrorism, the Financial Action Task Force (FATF) has found that "the misuse of non-profit organisations for the financing of terrorism is coming to be recognised as a crucial weak point in the global struggle to stop such funding at its source."[4]

Raising Funds from Criminal Proceeds: Some terrorist groups derive much of their funding and support from state sponsors of terrorism. With increased international pressure, many of these funding sources have become less reliable and, in some instances, have disappeared altogether. In addition, newer, decentralised, independent cells often do not have the same level of access to foreign funding as traditional terrorist groups. As a result, terrorist groups have turned to alternative sources of financing through criminal activities such as arms trafficking, kidnap-for-ransom, extortion, racketeering, and drug trafficking as well as credit card fraud.

Role of Safe Havens, Failed States and State Sponsors: Whether through the absence of effective jurisdictional control, tolerance of terrorist organisations and their activities, or by collusion, safe havens, failed states and state sponsors not only create enabling environments but also provide active support to terrorist organisations. They continue to represent crucial sources of support for terrorist organisations today, including those based in Somalia, and the Pakistan-Afghanistan border.

Moving Terrorist Funds

There are three main methods by which terrorists move money. The first is through the use of the financial system; the second involves the physical movement of money (for example, through the use of cash couriers); and the third is through the international trade system.

Formal Financial Sector: Financial institutions and other regulated financial service providers represent the formal financial sector and serve as the principal gateway through which retail and commercial transactions flow. The speed and ease with which funds can be moved within the international financial system allow terrorists to move funds efficiently and often without detection between and within jurisdictions.

Cash Couriers: Physical movement of cash is another way terrorists move funds without being encumbered by the AML/CFT safeguards established in financial institutions. It has been suggested[5] that some groups now convert cash into high-value and hard-to-trace commodities such as gold or precious stones in order to move assets outside of the financial system. As legitimate financial institutions tighten their due diligence practices, it has become an attractive method of transferring funds without leaving an audit trail.

Trade Sector: The international trade system is subject to a wide range of risks and vulnerabilities which provide terrorist organisations the opportunity to transfer value and goods through seemingly legitimate trade flows. The specific methods and techniques used to launder money through the trade system were described in the 2006 FATF Typology Report on trade-based money laundering[6] although terrorist financing was not a focus of that work. Further examination of the specific methods and techniques used to exploit the trade system for terrorist financing purposes could assist in the development of measures to identify and combat such activity.

Response to Terrorist Financing

Disrupting and dismantling terrorist financing networks is essential to combat terrorism. Choking funding flows to terrorist-linked activities is an effective means of checking them. Interdicting cash flows can degrade the capability of terrorist groups over time, limiting their ability to launch attacks, increasing their operational costs and injecting risk and uncertainty into their operations, which can have tactical benefits, such as damaging morale, leadership and legitimacy within a network and/or forcing terrorist groups to shift activity into areas where they are more vulnerable, including areas that they would otherwise avoid.[7] The main planks of a strategy to deal with the financial aspects of terrorist activities should involve the following:[8]

- Asset recovery and obstruction powers.
- Legal penalties against persons/organisations involved in financing terrorism.
- Insistence on adoption of diligent customer identification programmes and standard record keeping procedures by financial institutions/agencies.
- Reporting of suspicious financial activity by individuals and institutions.
- Anti-money laundering measures.
- Capacity building and coordination mechanisms between agencies involved.
- International cooperation.

Role of the United Nations: The International Convention on Suppression of the Financing of Terrorism (ICSFT) came into force in 2002. It requires each country to criminalise the funding of terrorist activities under its domestic law, seize terrorists' funds, and lays down a framework for financial institutions to cooperate with other countries in investigation and follow up on crimes related to such activities. UN Security Council Resolution 1373 mandated an establishment of a permanent counter-terrorism legal and executive infrastructure under Chapter VII. It also called on all members to join the ICSFT.

Pioneering Work by FATF: FATF is an inter-governmental body whose purpose is the development and promotion of policies at national and international levels, to combat money laundering and terrorist financing. FATF's 40 Recommendations and nine Special Recommendations provide some of the most powerful investigative and intelligence tools to gather financial information. As money moves through the financial system, it leaves a verifiable trail that can in many cases indicate illicit activity, identify those responsible, and locate the proceeds of criminality that can then be recovered. The value of financial information in counter-terrorist investigations has increased dramatically in recent years. Financial information is now used as part of the evidential case to hold criminals and terrorists to account. It also has a key intelligence role for example, by allowing law enforcement agencies to:[9]

- Look backwards, by piecing together how a criminal or terrorist conspiracy was developed and the timelines involved.
- Look sideways, by identifying or confirming associations between individuals and activities linked to conspiracies, even if overseas, often opening up new avenues for enquiry.
- Look forward, by identifying the warning signs of criminal or terrorist activity in preparation.

To highlight the issues involved in dealing with financing of terrorism, the response measures are discussed under two separate heads as under:

- Anti-money laundering measures and due diligence in the financial system.
- Measures to block the flow of funds for financing of terrorist activities.

Anti-Money Laundering Measures and due Diligence in the Financial System

United States of America and United Kingdom: Post-9/11, the USA introduced 'The Uniting and Strengthening America by Providing Appropriate Tools Required to Intercept and Obstruct Terrorism (USA PATRIOT) Act of 2001.' The Act establishes money laundering as a federal crime; criminalises the financing of terrorism and requires financial institutions to adopt due diligence procedures. The United Kingdom has also put in place a sound anti-money laundering system by implementing the 'Proceeds of Crime Act 2002' (POCA) which provides for a single set of money laundering offences applicable throughout the UK to proceeds of all crimes. Thus, in one stroke, POCA "opens up new legal avenues to prosecute those associated with criminal finance and to deprive them of any benefit they might enjoy from criminal assets."[10] It has been claimed that POCA "delivers one of the world's most powerful legal tools against money laundering."[11] Application of financial safeguards involves procedural mechanisms and monitoring measures to be adopted by players in the financial system, including due diligence measures to be undertaken in the case of customer identification; record-keeping, procedures and training; supervision and registration of high value dealers, money service businesses and trusts or company service providers, etc. The information is to be provided to the UK Financial Investigation Unit (FIU), which in turn analyses the information and makes it available to law enforcement agencies. The FIU also has a specialised Terrorist Finance Team.[12]

India: The provisions related to money laundering are contained in the 'Prevention of Money Laundering Act, 2002' (PMLA) as amended by the 'Prevention of Money Laundering (Amendment) Act', 2005. Based on the recommendations of the Second Administrative Reforms Commission, the PMLA (Amendment) Bill, 2008 has been introduced in the Parliament and is in the final stages of consideration. Based on the recommendations of the Parliamentary Standing Committee on Finance, India has applied to be a member of FATF. However, there is a large number of recommendations of FATF that have not been incorporated by India either in the Act or the Bill. The issues on which India faces criticism are:[13]

- India has not criminalised money laundering as per the UN Convention against Transnational Organised Crime, 2000 (not ratified by India).
- India has not undertaken a comprehensive risk assessment of money laundering or the financing of terrorism.
- There is no unified set of customer due diligence standards for the financial sector. In addition, many provisions related to the "Designated Non-Financial Business" (DNFB) category have not been complied with.
- There are no explicit legal gateways allowing for regulatory cooperation with foreign counterparts in any of the Acts governing the operations of the Reserve Bank of India, the Securities Exchange Board of India or the Insurance Regulatory and Development Authority. All employees of these agencies are covered by the Official Secrets Act as public servants.
- Money laundering is not a stand-alone offence, and, therefore, a conviction for a scheduled offence is required before a conviction for money laundering. If a third party has laundered the proceeds of crime, unless that third party is charged with criminal activity relating to a scheduled offence, he cannot be charged with the offence of money laundering. This requirement causes difficulties in securing convictions for money laundering.

Measures to Block the Flow of Funds for Financing of Terrorist Activities

While an effective money laundering regime is an essential element of the fight against terrorist finance, certain additional measures are required to prevent financing of terrorist activities. Steps taken in this connection in the United States of America, United Kingdom and India are detailed below in brief:

United States of America and United Kingdom: Terrorist finance is an offence under the laws of both countries which also allow for direct freezing of assets and funds on the grounds of suspected involvement with terrorism.

India: Anti-terrorist legislations in India have always contained provisions pertaining to financing of terrorist activities and proceeds of terrorist acts. Both the Terrorism and Disruptive Activities (Prevention) Act (TADA) as well as the Unlawful Activities (Prevention) Amendment Act, 2004 provide for punishment for knowingly holding a property derived or obtained from the commission of a terrorist act or acquired through terrorist funds. Owing to the fact that any terrorist act would necessarily involve financial backing, the strategy to counter financing of terrorism should not only contain measures for post-incident investigation and prosecution, but also measures providing legal and institutional basis to gather intelligence/information and undertaking prophylactic action for blocking of funds and essential material support. In other words, apart from making the raising of funds for terrorism an offence, focus also has to be on the prevention of terrorist acts. Towards this end, the recent strengthening of the FIU-IND (financial reporting regime) would prove very useful wherein it is mandatory to report any transaction which "gives rise to a ground of suspicion that it may involve financing of the activities relating to terrorism."[14]

Recommendations with Respect to India: Terrorist financing is a global problem and accordingly India's strategy to counter it has to be in harmony with international as well as regional measures. This is not to suggest the availability of a universally applicable template to fight terrorist financing. Each country needs to evolve its own model based on regional and domestic conditions. PMLA 2008 is an essential step to strengthen the country's legal framework for preventing money laundering and financing of terrorism. Additional recommendations of the Parliamentary Standing Committee on the issue are also relevant and must be actively considered, especially with regard to initiating necessary steps to become a full-fledged member of FATF. A few supplementary recommendations to further reinforce the existing legal and institutional framework for combating terrorist financing are enumerated below:

- The new legal framework on terrorism financing may incorporate provisions regarding freezing of assets, funds, bank accounts, deposits, cash, and so on when there is reasonable suspicion of their intended use in terrorist activities. Such actions may be undertaken by the investigating officer with the prior approval of a designated authority, subject to adequate safeguards.
- A specialised cell may be created in the proposed National Counter-Terrorism Centre on the lines of Terrorism Financing Operations Section (TFOS) of the Federal Bureau of Investigation (FBI) which "works not only to identify and track financial transactions and links after a terrorist act has occurred; it exploits financial information to identify previously unknown terrorist cells, to recognize potential terrorist activity or planning, and to predict and prevent potential terrorist acts,"[15] drawing upon expertise from the Ministries of Finance and Home Affairs and the Cabinet Secretariat for taking concerted action on the financial leads obtained from various sources. Further, different investigative agencies dealing with financial transactions may set up anti-terrorist finance cells within their organisations to augment the efforts of intelligence agencies involved in counter-terrorism activities.
- For speedy investigation into the financial aspects of specific cases/group of cases related to terrorist activities, dedicated teams may be formed within the agencies charged with the responsibility of investigating offences related to terrorism. This may be accomplished by inducting officers having specialisation in different aspects of financial investigation for short periods, say three to six months. A protocol for achieving this may be arrived at between the concerned union and state ministries/departments to facilitate capacity building

and strengthening the effectiveness of the counter-terrorist measures.

Narco-Terrorism: Perils of the Terror Weed

The relationship between drugs and terror,[16] typified as "narco-terrorism", had more modest, albeit equally macabre, beginnings than its current diabolic manifestation. Former President Fernando Belaúnde Terry of Peru introduced the term in 1983 to describe the terror unleashed by drug smugglers against the police and the attempts of narcotics traffickers to influence the policies of a government and to hinder the enforcement of the law through violence and intimidation. Druglord Pablo Escobar's use of violence against Colombian government officials is arguably one of the best known examples of narco-terrorism.[17] Terror, then, was only a means to sustain the narcotics trade. However, towards the later part of the 20th century, the drug trade came under the control of terrorists wherein its proceeds began to sustain terrorism. Some of the prominent militant organisations known to have benefited from drug trade are the Taliban and the Northern Alliance in Afghanistan; the FARC (Revolutionary Armed Forces of Colombia), the AUC (United Self-Defence Forces), the ELN (National Liberation Army), and the M-19 (19th of April Movement) in Colombia, the Shining Path and the MRTA (Tupac Amaru Revolutionary Movement) in Peru, the IRA (Irish Republican Army) in Great Britain, the KLA (Kosovo Liberation Army) in Yugoslavia, the Hezbollah in Lebanon, the PKK (Kurdistan's Workers Party) in Turkey, and the ETA (Basque Fatherland and Liberty) in Spain.[18] While Al Qaeda maintains a low profile about its involvement in the drug trade, it has actively supported the Taliban's drug-related activities.[19] The Liberation Tigers of Tamil Eelam (LTTE) in Sri Lanka is widely believed to have obtained substantial finances from the drug trade. In India, the infamous D Company of the underworld don Dawood Ibrahim is actively engaged in the trafficking of narcotics.

Fig 4.1 : World Drug Trafficking Routes

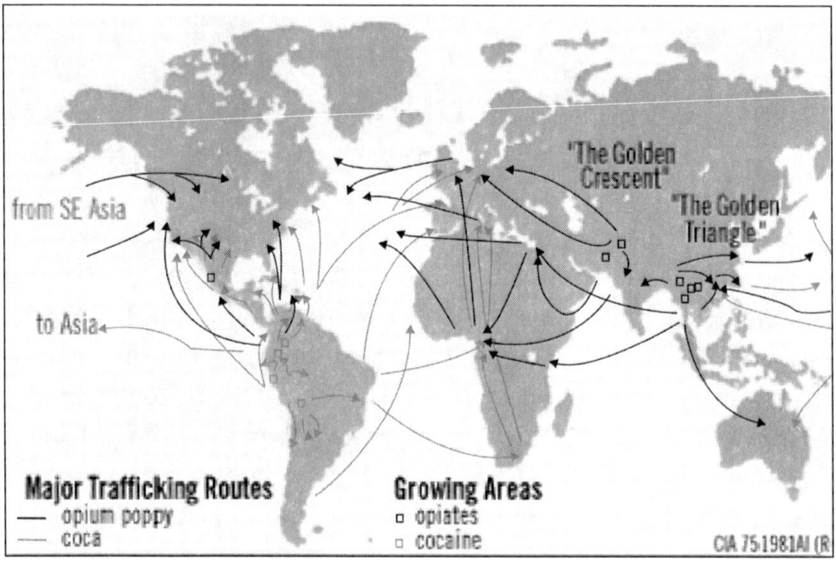

Source : http://www.princeton.edu/~ina/drugs/sources.html

The Gilded Pincers

In geo-strategic terms, India is wedged between the 'Golden Crescent' (Afghanistan, Iran and Pakistan) and the 'Golden Triangle' (Myanmar, Laos and Thailand), making it extremely vulnerable to narco-terrorism. These two regions remain the world's key areas for the production of illicit opiates. While traditionally, Myanmar was the world leader in the production of narcotics, Afghanistan overtook it in the 1990s and has thereafter dominated the scene. In war-ravaged Afghanistan as well as strife-torn Myanmar, opium production is one of the means of sustenance for a large number of impoverished farmers. Some of the significant aspects relating to the region flagged by the United Nations Office on Crime and Drugs (UNOCD) in its World Drug Report 2008[20] are as under:

- In 2007, Afghanistan alone accounted for 92 percent of global narcotics production, producing 8,200 metric tonnes (mt) of opium out of a total global output of 8870 mt.
- The total farm gate value of opium production in Afghanistan rose by 32 percent to US$ 1 billion in 2007 while the total

export value of opiates from Afghanistan to neighbouring countries is estimated to be around US$ 4 billion.

- Opium poppy cultivation in Myanmar increased by 29 percent in 2007 while the total potential production value of opium production in Myanmar increased 67 percent to US$ 120 million.

In Afghanistan, after initially banning poppy cultivation, the Taliban came around to the view that eradication was both financially unsound and politically unsustainable.[21] Progressively, it changed its attitude to tolerating poppy cultivation, then to levying a 10 to 20 percent tax on cultivation and processing, and finally to actively encouraging poppy cultivation, teaching farmers how to achieve greater yields and advancing credit under a system known as *salaam*. In Myanmar, opium production has been estimated at 410 mt in 2008, down from over 1,300 mt in the past. This reduction had been largely the result of international pressure on two of the largest opium producers in the 'Golden Triangle', the Kokang and the Wa,[22] both ethnic rebel groups, with large guerrilla forces. But in the past two years, both poppy cultivation and opium production have begun to grow again, owing to the downturn in the economy.

The Vicious Trail

Much of the heroin that originates in Afghanistan is transported to Peshawar via the tribal areas bordering the two countries. The contraband then moves to Karachi from where air and sea routes are used to transport it to markets in Europe and North America. The Indo-Pak border is also used extensively for transporting narcotics, first to India and then to other countries. Significant drug shipments also move through the Central Asian Republics by rail. A large number of mobile labs have been set up in Pakistan's border areas, particularly in the Khyber region adjacent to Afghanistan, to convert opium to morphine and morphine to heroin. Interestingly, Pakistan's biggest drugs bazaar is located close to Peshawar, where the US Drug Enforcement Administration (DEA) and Pakistan's Anti-Narcotics Board have their offices. Dawood Ibrahim is reportedly involved in large scale shipment of narcotics to the UK and Western Europe, sharing smuggling networks in South Asia, Middle East and Africa with Al Qaida and other terrorist outfits.

Fig 4.2: Drug Trafficking Through India

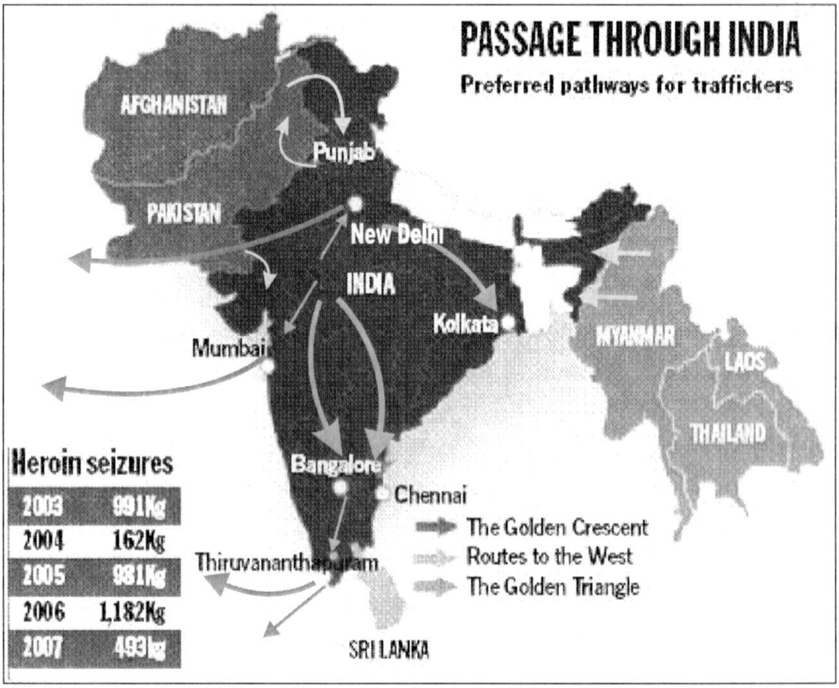

Source: *India Today*, 13 June 2008.

Afghan opiates from Pakistan are sent over the border into Rajasthan, Punjab, Gujarat and Jammu and Kashmir (J&K) and through Indian ports on the western seaboard for onward despatch to international markets. Within India, border districts like Bikaner, Barmer, Sri Ganganagar and cities like Jodhpur and Jaipur are used as transit points.[23] Opiates from Myanmar are mostly confined to the Northeastern states although there have been some reports that these drugs have begun moving deeper into India for domestic consumption or for being carried forward beyond India.

Owing to India's propinquity to the 'Golden Crescent' and the 'Golden Triangle', there has now emerged a lethal relationship among insurgent groups, arms dealers and narco-terrorists, with the sea routes of the Arabian Sea and the Bay of Bengal providing ideal waterways for the supply of both arms and narcotics.[24] Although not all the insurgent groups actively engage in the production or trafficking of drugs, all of them have regularly taxed and extorted money from the traffickers and in return, provided them protection. A large portion of this money goes towards the purchase of sophisticated weaponry from arms dealers. For example, several insurgent groups in Nagaland, including the Isaac-Muivah and Khaplang factions of the National Socialist Council of Nagaland (NSCN), tax and extort money from traffickers in return for protection. The People's Revolutionary Party of Kangleipak of Manipur, and the All Tripura Tribal/Tiger Force in Tripura are other groups that profit from extortion, and they may facilitate cross-border drug-trafficking.

Pakistan is known to have actively supported drug smuggling to finance its nefarious agenda in Afghanistan and India. *India Today* quotes the deputy director of the Narcotics Control Bureau (NCB) as stating that "more than 55 percent of the heroin trafficked into India originates from Afghanistan. There is definitely the hand of the ISI in trafficking. We have statements from arrested traffickers which confirm this information."[25]

Domestic Production and Markets

India is the world's largest producer of licit opium. It is the only country authorised by the United Nations Single Convention on Narcotic Drugs (1961) to produce gum opium for the world's pharmaceutical industry. Opium poppy cultivation is permitted under government control in Madhya Pradesh, Rajasthan, and Uttar Pradesh. In 2006-07, India produced 353 mt of opium gum from 5,913 hectares of opium poppy harvested.[26] However, a portion of the licit opium poppy crop, estimated to be approximately 10 to 30 percent, is believed to be diverted to the illicit market. Further, illicit opium cultivation also occurs in India. In 2008, Indian government agencies destroyed 595 hectares of illicit poppy cultivation. India is also the world's largest producer of illicit methaqualone, usually marketed under the brand name Mandrax. Most of the Mandrax originates in Gujarat and Maharashtra and is shipped in containerised cargo to overseas locations such as South Africa.

In the past decade, a new phenomenon of trafficking nuclear material along established drug and smuggling networks has emerged. In 1998, West Bengal police apprehended members of a smuggling gang transporting uranium stolen from the Jaduguda mines in Bihar across the border to Nepal, for onward movement to Pakistan. Earlier, police in Pakistan arrested an international drug and arms trafficker with 2 kg of heroin, a pistol, and some uranium samples.[27] Although raw uranium by itself is not a fissile material that could cause much harm and India has been conscientious in securing its fissile material sources, trafficking in any radioactive material could lead to dangerous consequences. There is, therefore, a need to reexamine the links between the trafficking patterns of illicit drugs, conventional arms, and nuclear and radioactive material in South Asia. Pirates in the Bay of Bengal and the South China Sea, Afghan warlords, tribal smuggling rings in Pakistan's northern border areas, and drug and arms dealers in both South and Southeast Asia would have no trouble, and little hesitation in exploiting their trafficking proficiency to transport nuclear equipment and material.[28] India is also emerging as a major 'source market' for online drug-trafficking, with international syndicates operating through call centres and software firms to smuggle psychotropic drugs overseas.[29] The scale of this trafficking is truly staggering. For instance, it has been reported that in the United States, 34 illegal Internet pharmacies had dispensed more than 98 million doses of hydrocodone, a powerful narcotic drug, in 2007.[30] These are new threats which require unique and incisive counter-measures.

Acing the Menace

The dimensions of narco-terrorism transcend regional and national barriers. Consequently, the manifestations of the problem are simultaneously immediate and proximate as well as far-reaching and long-term. To be successful, a campaign against the drug trade fuelling terrorism, needs to be transnational in formulation and execution, addressing three principal dimensions, as under:

1. Measures against weed cultivation and drug production:
   - Destruction of standing crops and processing facilities.
   - Incentives for switching to alternative crops such as easy availability of institutional farm credit and procurement guarantees.
   - Enforcement of anti-drug laws.
   - State protection from drug lords and terrorist outfits.
2. Measures against movement and distribution:
   - Interception of drug convoys.
   - Coordination of border protocols.
   - Monitoring of ports and export zones.
   - Generation of street-level intelligence.
   - Collection of cyber intelligence.
3. Measures against laundering of drug money:
   - The previous section has dealt extensively with the issue of money laundering. The International Monetary Fund (IMF) estimated global money laundering to be between $590 billion and $1.5 trillion a year, representing 2-5 percent of global Gross Domestic Product (GDP). A large share of global money laundering as estimated by the IMF is linked to the trade in narcotics. Drug-trafficking constitutes "the third biggest global commodity in cash terms after oil and the arms trade."[31] It is a matter of concern that, despite the menacing proportions of money-laundering, not all countries in the South Asian region have put the necessary legislative counter-measures in place.

Legal Framework and Apparatus in India

NDPS Act, 1985: Control over cultivation of opium and all matters relating to narcotic drugs and psychotropic substances is regulated by the 'Narcotic Drugs and Psychotropic Substances Act and Rules' (NDPS Act & Rules). The NDPS Act, 1985, was enacted by the government to combat the illicit trafficking of narcotic drugs, psychotropic substances and controlled chemicals. Under the NDPS Act, no person can cultivate coca plants, opium poppy and cannabis plants or extract opium, charas and ganja from such plants. The production of opium derivatives such as morphine, heroin and other intoxicating psychotropic substances, except for medical or scientific purposes, is a crime. Possession of these drugs and trafficking for commercial gains is also a crime, punishable with imprisonment ranging from ten to thirty years and fine from Rs one lakh to three lakh. Under the Prevention of Illicit Traffic in Narcotic Drugs and Psychotropic Substances Act, 1988, drug traffickers can be placed under preventive detention for a period of one to two years. The Act also provides for the forfeiture of the properties from earnings related to drug crimes and the award of the death sentence in certain categories of drug offences. Powers have been given to the officers of the Departments of Police, Customs, Central Excise, Border Security Force, Revenue Intelligence, Narcotics Control Bureau, etc. to investigate and inquire into the drug offences and enforce the provisions of the NDPS Act.

The Central Bureau of Narcotics (CBN): The CBN, functioning under the aegis of the Department of Revenue, Ministry of Finance, is responsible for all facets of the licit opium industry. The responsibilities of CBN include:

- Supervision of licit cultivation of opium poppy in India.
- Preventive and enforcement functions, especially in the three poppy growing states.
- Investigation of cases under the NDPS Act, 1985.
- Action for tracing and freezing of illegally acquired property as per the provisions of Chapter V-A of the NDPS Act, 1985.
- Issue of licences for manufacture of synthetic narcotic drugs.

- Issuance of authorisations/certificates for export/import of narcotic drugs and psychotropic substances, precursor chemicals and poppy seeds from permitted countries.
- Monitoring the implementation of the United Nations drug control conventions.[32]

The Narcotics Control Bureau (NCB): While the CBN deals with the licit opium trade in the country, the NCB was set up in 1986 by the Ministry of Finance to attend to the unlawful activities relating to drug trade. The NCB is responsible for:

- Coordination of actions by various offices, state governments and other authorities with regard to the enforcement provisions of the NDPS Act, 1985.
- Implementation of counter-measures against illicit traffic under the various international conventions and protocols that are in force at present or which may be ratified or acceded to by India in the future.
- Assistance to the concerned authorities in foreign countries and concerned international organisations to facilitate coordination and universal action for prevention and suppression of illicit traffic in these drugs and substances.
- Coordination of actions taken by other concerned ministries, departments and organisations in respect of matters relating to drug abuse.
- Collection and analysis of data related to seizures of narcotic drugs and psychotropic substances, study of the trends and modus operandi, collection and dissemination of intelligence, and working in close cooperation with the customs, state police and other law enforcement agencies.[33]

The NCB focusses on the following aspects of counter-narcotics in the country:

- Surveillance and enforcement at import points and land borders.
- Preventive and interdiction efforts along known drug routes.

- Control measures at export points such as air-passenger terminals, cargo terminals and foreign post offices.
- Improved coordination between various drug law enforcement agencies.
- Identification and eradication of illicit cultivation and the wild growth of cannabis and the opium poppy.
- Strengthening of the intelligence apparatus to improve the collection, collation, analysis and dissemination of operational intelligence.
- Increased international cooperation, in both operational and long-term intelligence, as well as in investigations and mutual legal assistance.

Inter-Governmental Measures

India has bilateral agreements on drug-trafficking with 13 countries, including Pakistan, Myanmar and the United States. In order to thwart the maritime trade in arms and drugs, India has been conducting joint military exercises across the Indian Ocean with countries such as Japan, Vietnam and South Korea. Cooperative action with UN and other international bodies is also an issue of serious engagement for the Government of India.

The International Narcotics Control Board (INCB): The INCB was established in 1968 as an independent and quasi-judicial monitoring body for the implementation of the UN international drug control conventions. Its mandate is to:

- Ensure that adequate supplies of drugs are available for medical and scientific uses and that the diversion of drugs from licit sources to illicit channels does not occur.
- Monitor governments' control over chemicals that can be used in the illicit manufacture of drugs and assist in preventing the diversion of such chemicals into the illicit traffic.
- Identify weaknesses in national and international control systems.
- Ensure that the provisions of the international drug control treaties are adequately carried out by governments, and

recommend remedial measures.

- Maintain permanent dialogue with governments to assist them in complying with their obligations and recommend technical or financial assistance where necessary.
- Conduct training programmes for drug control administrators, particularly from developing counties.

Weaknesses and the Way Ahead

The two major weaknesses in the current framework for fighting narco-terrorism in India are the multiplicity of agencies involved in policy implementation and the lack of enforcement capabilities with the monitoring agencies such as the CBN and NCB. As brought out earlier, the implementation of the NDPS Act, 1985, requires integration of the actions of a plethora of agencies such as the police, customs, Central Excise, Border Security Force (BSF), Revenue Intelligence, NCB, etc. India does not have an encouraging record of objective cooperation between various governmental agencies in any field and narco-terrorism is too serious a threat to make-do with the slipshod treatment that such absence of cooperation invariably results in. Therefore, there is a strong case for a federal body that has both monitoring and enforcement capabilities. The DEA model of the United States may be instructive in this regard and should be comprehensively examined for application and adaptation in the Indian context. The DEA was created in July 1973 in order to establish a single unified command to combat "an all-out global war on the drug menace." As of date, it has 5,235 special agents, a budget of more than $2.3 billion and 87 foreign offices in 63 countries.[34] It has comprehensive investigative powers and potent enforcement capabilities to effectively implement its mandate. Considering the implications of narco-terrorism on the internal security of the nation, it may be prudent to place the NCB under the jurisdiction of the Ministry of Home Affairs, which also has the necessary wherewithal for intelligence gathering and enforcement action. Whether in monitoring, enforcement or prosecution, there is much ground to be covered in the nation's fight against narco-terrorism.

State-Sponsored Terrorism

The most defining aspect of terrorism is the absolute randomness in the application of violence, in that it is not circumscribed in either direction or magnitude. It could be directed towards anybody and any number of people. States, on the other hand, have a responsibility to protect. Although mandated to apply extreme violence, states are bound by definite and discrete norms with respect to targets against whom violence can be applied. Such targets are put through a detailed process of identification, validation and legitimisation before being subjected to state-mandated violence. Such is the case equally whether a nation prosecutes war criminals or convicts. When a state loses sight of such distinctions and indulges in violence which is not legitimised, either directly or through proxy, it may be said to be a sponsor of terror. Most often, terrorism is equated with "non-state actors", or groups that are not responsible to a sovereign government. But there are occasions when national governments become involved in terrorism, or utilise terror to accomplish the objectives of governments or individual rulers. This may be undertaken in the following ways:

- Government or state terror.
- State involvement in terror.
- State sponsorship of terrorism.

Government or State Terror: This is popularly known as "terror from above", where a government makes conscious use of its power and instrumentalities to terrorise its own population to control or repress them. It is based on a deliberate policy of the government, and enabled through the use of official institutions such as the judiciary, police, military, and other government agencies. The country's laws may even be changed to permit or encourage torture, killing, or property destruction in pursuit of government policy. The official Nazi policy of extermination of Jews as "state enemies", Stalin's "purges" of "counterrevolutionaries", Saddam Hussein's use of chemical weapons on the Kurdish population are some examples of the use of state machinery to terrorise one's own population.

State Involvement in Terror: These are activities where government personnel carry out operations using terror tactics. These activities may be directed against other nations' interests, the native population, or private groups or individuals viewed as dangerous to the state. In many cases, these activities are terrorism under official sanction, although such authorisation is rarely acknowledged openly. Historical examples include the assassination of dissidents who "defected" during the Cold War era.

Another type is the infamous "encounter", wherein unofficial and illegitimate actions are taken by the functionaries of a regime (such as police, military or intelligence operatives) against their own population to repress or intimidate. While these officials will not openly admit to such activities, it is often made evident that they are acting for the state. Keeping such activities "unofficial" permits the authorities to plausibly deny their role and, thus, avoid the necessity of changing legal and judicial processes to justify oppression.

State Sponsorship of Terrorism: A state is said to be a sponsor of terrorism when the government provides supplies, training, and other forms of support to non-state terrorist organisations. Some types of support extended by governments to terrorist organisations include the provision of safe havens or physical bases, false documentation for personal identification, facilitation of financial transactions and weapons purchases, access to training facilities and expertise, diplomatic protection and services such as immunity from extradition, diplomatic passports, use of embassies and other protected grounds, and diplomatic pouches to transport weapons or explosives.

State-sponsored terrorism reached its zenith during the Cold War era, with neither of the superpowers willing to risk escalation to a full scale war and possible nuclear exchange. The Soviet Union resorted to supporting various dissident and terrorist groups in Europe, directly or indirectly, through Warsaw Pact states and friendly Arab powers such as Libya and Syria. Similar exercises in "plausible deniability" were also carried out by the US, the most notable among them being the Iran-Contra affair,[35] where the US was found to have clandestinely traded arms for hostages with Iran and also divert the funds received from the arms sales to the Contras in Nicaragua. India continues to face the deadly challenge of state-sponsored terrorism owing to the blatant support provided by the Government of Pakistan to terrorist organisations such as the Jaish-e-Mohammed (JeM) and the Lashkar-e-Tayyeba (LeT), whose avowed objective is the disintegration of secular India.

Local Players and Global Burdens

The high costs of modern warfare, concern over escalation of conflict to the nuclear level, the danger of defeat and the unwillingness to appear as the aggressor are factors that have made terrorism an efficient, convenient, and generally discrete weapon for groups seeking to upset the balance of power. Some believe that state-sponsored terrorism can achieve strategic ends where the use of conventional armed forces is not practical or effective. Having suffered defeat repeatedly on the battlefield, Pakistan has adopted precisely this stratagem to humble India. The US military campaigns in Afghanistan (or 'AfPak,' the new US State Department nomenclature for the ungoverned areas on the Afghanistan-Pakistan border) and Iraq highlight the potential cost for any state that has links with international terrorism. However, it would be naïve to expect governments and terrorist organisations not to collude in the future, out of ideological, strategic or existential compulsions.

State sponsors of terrorism also form a vital link in the proliferation of weapons of mass destruction (WMDs). The role of Pakistan, China, North Korea and Iran has been significant in this regard. The problem is further compounded by non-state facilitators, acting in cahoots with the government or operating independently, who provide terrorists with conduits to materials and expertise. In 2007, 74 percent of 117 non-governmental terrorism experts polled by *Foreign Policy* magazine named Pakistan as the country most likely to transfer nuclear technology to terrorists in the next three to five years.[36] Ironically, the very trends driving globalisation, communications and transportation, enable the emergence of proliferation networks that facilitate the terrorist acquisition of WMDs. Globalisation requires that partner nations work together closely to prevent, detect, and disrupt linkages that may develop between terrorists and facilitators.

Dealing with Sponsor States

While much noise is made in India about getting the world to brand Pakistan as a state-sponsor of terrorism, especially in the light of the 26/11attacks in Mumbai, there exist no laws on the statute book of the country to initiate the action. On the other hand, US law requires the Secretary of State to provide to Congress, by 30 April of each year, a full and complete report on terrorism, called 'Country Reports on Terrorism',[37] with regard to such countries as are deemed to be sponsoring terrorism as per the criteria spelt out in the legislation.[38] Also, while the UN has no accepted definition of state-sponsored terrorism, the United States has defined it within its ideological ambit as repeated support for acts of international terrorism by a state and conceptualised a set of sanctions against states that sponsor terrorism as follows:[39]

- A ban on arms-related exports and sales.
- Controls over exports of dual-use items.
- Prohibitions on economic assistance.
- Imposition of miscellaneous financial and other restrictions, including:
    - Requiring the US to oppose loans by the World Bank and other international financial institutions.
    - Lifting diplomatic immunity to allow families of terrorist victims to file civil lawsuits in US courts.
    - Denying companies and individuals tax credits for income earned in terrorist-listed countries.
    - Denial of duty-free treatment of goods exported to the United States.

- Authority to prohibit any US citizen from engaging in a financial transaction with a terrorist-list government without a Treasury Department licence.
- Prohibition of Defence Department contracts above $100,000 with companies controlled by terrorist-list states.

While the US has named Syria, Cuba, Iran and Sudan as states sponsoring terrorism and imposed sanctions against them, India continues to maintain the full range of diplomatic, economic, political and cultural ties with Pakistan, a country alleged to be sponsoring terrorism against India. In fact, Pakistan continues to enjoy most favoured nation (MFN) status for trade with India, a gesture which has not been reciprocated by Pakistan till date. Nor has India been able to mobilise effective regional world opinion against the machinations of Pakistan.

In the case of the 26/11 Mumbai attacks, the diabolic plot may well have been hatched in an Inter-Services Intelligence (ISI) safe-house in Karachi, but it is undeniable that the perpetrators received significant local support in Mumbai. As such, while the Government of India is justified in demanding concrete action from Pakistan and seeking the strident support of the world community, it also needs to address the local conditions which have facilitated the terrorist strike. The strategy would, therefore, need to be three-pronged as under:

- At the international and regional level, to coalesce world opinion against the offending state.
- At the national level, to be prepared to take all measures necessary, including military action, with alacrity and resoluteness.
- At the domestic and local level, to deal with both the underlying as well as manifest causes that provide sustenance to the terrorists.

The approach to dealing with states sponsoring terrorism such as Pakistan has to be markedly different from the approach to deal with terrorist organisations. Poverty, unemployment, absence of civic institutions and social services, widespread low-level corruption, repressive governments, inadequate or unjust law enforcement and legal systems and rabid communalisation are conditions that make the ground fertile for terrorists to recruit their cadres, and garner ideological and logistic support to execute terror strikes. Actions taken at community and local levels are as necessary as those taken at national and international levels in order to effectively deal with such terrorists and terrorist organisations. However, in the case of states sponsoring terrorism, no local or community initiatives are likely to bear significant fruit. It becomes imperative for the international community to close ranks and initiate punitive measures against a renegade state. As the War on Terror has brought home so unmistakably, no country can deal with this challenge single-handedly. In addition to the United Nations, regional partnerships are also necessary to enable states to collectively and resolutely address issues of state-sponsored terrorism.

Conclusion

Creating an understanding of terrorist financing that is distinct from money laundering is critical. Participation of the whole counter-terrorist community could greatly contribute to the development of a better understanding of terrorist financing. It would ensure a common understanding of the financing needs and methods of terrorists and provide insight into the value of financial information when combined with counter-terrorist intelligence. Financial information alone is not sufficient to effectively combat terrorism. However, when combined with counter-terrorist intelligence, financial information can greatly enhance a country's ability to identify and intercept terrorist activity. Because of its predictive value, gathering and sharing financial intelligence is a high priority. Countries could be encouraged to make financial investigation an automatic component of all counter-terrorist investigations. Some of the other important recommendations are:

- Setting up a new legal framework on terrorism, incorporating provisions regarding freezing of assets, funds, bank accounts, deposits, cash, and so on, when there is reasonable suspicion of their intended use in terrorist activities.

- Creation of a specialised cell in the proposed National Counter-Terrorism Centre for taking concerted action on the financial leads obtained from various sources.
- Insistence on adoption of diligent customer identification programmes and standard record keeping procedures by financial institutions/agencies.
- Capacity building and coordination mechanisms between the agencies involved, including international cooperation.
- Induction of specialist officers to investigate different aspects of money laundering and terror financing.

It is also important that the linkages between narcotics trade and terrorism are correctly identified and resolutely dealt with, since these twin evils possess significant potential for unbridled symbiotic growth.

Absence of immediate reciprocal action, whether in diplomatic, economic or military form and awaiting the intervention of other nations and international organisations such as the United Nations, would only embolden states that sponsor or support terrorism. It is, therefore, necessary to strengthen the legal and diplomatic framework of the country so that substantive federal action can be initiated against countries abetting terrorism, directly or indirectly, without always having to invoke third party intervention.

Terror groups all over the world also maintain reciprocal arrangements with other terror and criminal organisations, both within and outside the country.

Notes

1. Government of India, Second Administrative Reforms Commission, "Combating Terrorism: Protecting by Righteousness," Eighth Report, June 2008.
2. Financial Action Task Force (FATF) Report on Terrorist Financing, 29 February 2008, http://www.fatf-gafi.org/dataoecd/11/58/43384540.pdf, accessed on 22 February 2009.

3. National Commission on Terrorist Attacks Upon the United States, "Executive Summary," http://www.9-11commission.gov/report/911Report_Exec.htm, accessed on 23 March 2009.
4. FATF International Best Practices Paper on Special Recommendation VIII, 11 October 2003, http://www.fatf-gafi.org/dataoecd/39/19/34033761.pdf, accessed on 22 January 2009.
5. Ibid.
6. Ibid.
7. HM Treasury, Home Office/Foreign & Commonwealth Office, United Kingdom, "The Financial Challenge to Crime and Terrorism," February 2007, http://www.hm-treasury.gov.uk/d/financialchallenge_crime_280207.pdf, accessed on 22 February 2009.
8. Government of India, n. 1, p. 77.
9. Financial Action Task Force Report on Terrorist Financing, n. 2.
10. HM Treeasury, n. 7.
11. Ibid.
12. Ibid.
13. Asia/Pacific Group on Money Laundering, "Mutual Evaluation Report – India 2005," http://www.apgml.org/documents/docs/8/India%20ME1%20-%20 Final.pdf, accessed on 22 January 2009.
14. Financial Intelligence Unit – India, Ministry of Finance, Government of India, Notification No. 4/2007 – Amendment to Rules, 24 May 2007, http://fiuindia.gov.in/notifications-no4amendments.htm, accessed on 22 January 2009.
15. Statement of John S Pistole, Executive Assistant Director, Counterterrorism/ Counterintelligence, FBI. Before the National Commission on Terrorist Attacks upon the United States, 14 April 2004, http://www.fbi.gov/congress/congress04/pistole041404.htm, accessed on 22 January 2009.
16. In oriental medicine, opium had traditionally been used to treat diarrhoea. Indian households also knew its use as a soporific to quieten restive infants since time immemorial. In fact, cannabis was commonly known all over the world as Indian hemp. In the 17th and 18th centuries, the number of opium addicts in China swelled up alarmingly and crippled the economy, forcing the Manchu rulers to impose punitive tariffs on opium, which mostly came from Turkey and colonial India. This led to the famous Opium Wars between Britain and China. Thus, by the 19th century, opium moved from being a therapeutic remedy to a recreational addiction to a political tool. But, it took another century for it to emerge as manna for terrorists of various denominations.
17. "Terrorism and the Rule of Law: Dangerous Compromise in Colombia,"

Canadian Security Intelligence Service Commentary, No.13, 1991, p. 1.

18. Vanda Felbab-Brown, "Globalization and Narcoterrorism," Paper presented at the annual meeting of the American Political Science Association, Marriott, Loews Philadelphia, and the Pennsylvania Convention Center, Philadelphia, PA, 31 August 2006, http://www.allacademic.com/meta/p151662_index.html, accessed on 22 February 2009.
19. James Emery, "Narcotics in Islam," *Middle East Times*, 21 May 2008.
20. United Nations Office on Drugs and Crime, "World Drug Report 2008," www.unodc.org/documents/wdr/WDR_2008/WDR_2008_eng_web.pdf, accessed on 02 February 2009.
21. Afghan farmers believe that the original ban's only purpose was to allow the Taliban or Arabs who had stockpiled opium and poppy fields to cash in. For a detailed report on the harsh realties of opium cultivation in Afghanistan, see Amy Waldman, "A Nation Challenged: The Opium Trail – A Village at Source of Heroin Trade Fears the Eradication of Its Poppies," *The New York Times*, 12 March 2002.
22. Tom Kramer, "Burmese Daze," *The Irrawaddy*, Vol. 16, No. 11, 15 November 2008.
23. Alok Kumar Gupta, "Western Rajasthan Becoming A Transit Route For Narcotics," Institute of Peace and Conflict Studies, 08 January 2009, available at http://www.ipcs.org/article_details.php?articleNo=2774, accessed on 20 February 2009.
24. Aparajita Biswas, "Small Arms and Drug Trafficking In the Indian Ocean Region," Centre for African Studies, University of Mumbai, Working Paper No. 4, 2007.
25. Kavita Chowdhry, "ISI Aiding Narcotics Smuggling into India," *India Today*, 20 February 2009.
26. Central Bureau of Narcotics, http://cbn.nic.in/html/operationscbn.htm, accessed on 24 March 2009.
27. Andrew Prosser, "Nuclear Trafficking Routes: Dangerous Trends in Southern Asia," Centre for Defence Information, 22 November 2004, www.cdi.org/PDFs/TraffickingSmuggling.pdf, accessed on 2 February 2009.
28. Ibid.
29. "Call Centres Under Narcotics Bureau Lens," *The Financial Express*, 20 May 2008.
30. Statement by the INCB President at CND 52nd session, 16 March 2009—Agenda Item 7B 2008, Report of the International Narcotics Control Board, http://www.incb.org/incb/index.html, accessed on 29 March 2009.

31. Michel Chossudovsky, "The Spoils of War: Afghanistan's Multibillion Dollar Heroin Trade," 05 April 2004, http://www.globalresearch.ca, accessed on 18 March 2009.
32. Central Bureau of Narcotics, n. 26.
33. Narcotics Control Bureau, http://narcoticsindia.nic.in/ accessed on 24 March 2009.
34. "DEA History," US Drug Enforcement Administration, http://www.usdoj.gov/dea/history.htm, accessed on 20 March 2009.
35. Philip Shenon and Stephen Engelberg, "Eight Important Days in November: Unraveling the Iran-Contra Affair," *The New York Times*, 05 July 1987.
36. "World at Risk," Report of the Commission on the Prevention of WMD Proliferation and Terrorism, 02 December 2008, available at http://www.globalsecurity.org/wmd/library/report/2008/wmd-prolif-terror-commission.htm, accessed on 26 March 2009.
37. United States Department of State Publication Office of the Coordinator for Counterterrorism, "Country Reports on Terrorism 2007," April 2008.
38. Ibid., Chapter 3, p. 171.
39. Ibid.

5

'GROUND ZERO': VICTIMS AND TARGETS

Swapna Kona Nayudu

> *Fascism is not defined by the number of its victims, but by the way it kills them.*
>
> —Jean Paul Sartre

Joining the Dots: Terrorist Attacks in Urban India

The demolition of the Babri Masjid in Ayodhya on 06 December 1992 gave way to an overtly militant culture of political fencing in India. The sentiments invoked by this event were further provoked by riots at the end of that year and heightening tensions that led to the serial bomb blasts in Bombay on 12 March 1993. These events together mark a watershed in the history of violence in post-independent India, given the scale and intensity of their impact. The bomb blasts in Mumbai took more than 200 lives and injured about 1,200 others, with bombs going off simultaneously in numerous locations around the city. The state's security forces were ill-equipped to deal with the design, methods and outcome of the terror attack that made a strong impression on public memory.

By successfully carrying out the blasts in Bombay (now Mumbai), the terrorists had exposed the weaknesses of the systems of intelligence, policing and security in the country's commercial capital. But, more importantly, they had found a way to exploit the faultlines within India's social fabric in an unprecedented manner.

This new phenomenon of urban terrorism had claimed its victims and infiltrated its targets, securing a national, regional and global audience to this violent act.

The targeting of places of importance and the resultant indiscriminate killing of many innocent men and women are not expressions of discontent but an attempt to destroy the "other", referring to an identity removed from one's own and seen as distinct, and even conflicting. Terrorists play on the conflicting identities that populate India's cities. The theatre of this new manner of warfare is not on India's borders, mountains or in its rural areas. Instead, it is in the centre of public consciousness – in India's largest cities, thronged by its teeming millions. Thus, the threat of this new terrorism is inherently more urgent in its nature, more direct in its approach and less likely to be ignored. This has become clear as India's cities have been similarly targeted in various other incidents. In the 1990s, attacks on India's hinterland had been numerous, but over the last decade, more metropolitan centres have found themselves targeted.

By targeting cities, the new terrorists were situating themselves away from older forms of terrorism – they were targeting a completely different demography that was part of the more accessible India, contributor to its globalised economy and exposed to the many international currents sweeping their way through the country. In all these bombings, the patterns of victimisation were always similar – intended to achieve maximum impact, the terrorists targeted public places, hoping to cause the maximum possible damage.

In one incident, on 11 July 2006, seven serial bombs went off in Mumbai at different points on the western line of the suburban railway network.[1] Mumbai's local trains were chosen as suitable targets because of their indispensability to the general public in Mumbai. This was effective as 209 people lost their lives and others were injured. The severity of the attack had a long-lasting effect, further compounded by the events of 07 July 2007 in London and by the memory of the earlier terror attacks of 13 March 2003 in Mumbai, which had also targeted the rail network, although on a much smaller scale. The pattern of this kind of terrorism resounded globally, gaining an audience that looked in shock and fear at these successive acts of violence.

While the rhetoric of an international nexus planning these blasts has been strongly accentuated, it is also true that communal tensions in India give rise to sectarian violence that aggravates the menace of this 'new terrorism.' The explosions in Malegaon on 08 September 2006 caused the deaths of at least 32 people and injured over 100, most were Muslim pilgrims.[2] The targeting of people in places of worship while they were praying is also illustrative of how, in some sense, the patterns of victimisation have not changed all that much. Whether targeting people at their place of worship or in public transport, the victims are all non-combatant civilians with overlapping and mixed identities. In particular incidents, specific communities were targeted, but largely the killing was indiscriminate. When it wasn't diffused in its choice of victims, it was extremely particular, pinpointing specific individuals to be targeted (such as in political assassinations). But mostly, urban terrorism, even though it is a fairly recent phenomenon, has followed patterns of victimisation similar to the older forms of terrorism.

An exception to the pattern of old terrorism was the attack on the Indian Parliament in Delhi in December 2001, attributed to the Lashkar-e-Tayyeba (LeT), the Pakistan-based Inter-Services Intelligence (ISI)-supported terrorist outfit. By targeting a heritage monument that houses India's national legislature, the militants achieved the objective of shocking the nation and gaining a response in the form of a military stand-off between India and Pakistan along the Line of Control (LoC). The targeting of the Parliament building was allegedly a response to the Kargil conflict of 1999 through a direct assault on the most evident symbol of the Indian state. The targeted were public office-holders in the seat of legislature of the world's largest democracy. This attack marked a departure from hitherto witnessed terrorist attacks. It was direct, specific and successful in causing an immediate political upheaval.

From 2001 to 2007, numerous terrorist incidents took place in India, both in small towns and in large cities. The only distinguishing trait between them and earlier incidences of terrorism was the scale at which these were carried out and the urban targets they chose. They were also becoming more frequent. Mumbai and Delhi were regularly targeted and the undercurrent of tension was palpable. In one incident, the capital was targeted on 29 October 2005 in three successive explosions, resulting in the death of 62 people and approximately 200 other casualties.[3] This did not mean, however, that terrorism in the rest of India had waned. On the contrary, terrorist activity has seen an alarming rise as various terrorist groupings are making their presence felt in different parts of India.

But the nature of terrorist attacks in India has intensified since 2007. India has always had sporadic incidents involving political, religious and other kinds of violence in the heartland and in more frequent incidents on its periphery. But the scale of the attacks in Mumbai and in Delhi has been unprecedented. The terrorist attacks that occurred in Hyderabad, Bangalore, Jaipur, Guwahati and Ahmedabad were indicative of the percolation of this large-scale new brand of terrorism to other cities in India that had hitherto experienced petty crime, communal riots and associated violence but nothing on the scale of the terrorist attacks of 2007 and 2008.

On 25 August 2007, Hyderabad witnessed bomb blasts in an amusement park and a crowded market area restaurant in which 44 people were reported dead. Moreover, 19 other bombs were also unearthed from across the city soon thereafter, leading to a wave of panic across the state of Andhra Pradesh and in other metros around India.[4] But heightened security did not prevent the Jaipur blasts of 2008, where, on 13 May, nine synchronised bombs went off almost simultaneously in six different spots, leading to 63 deaths and more than 216 casualties. On 25 July 2008, in a similar pattern, Bangalore saw nine bomb blasts that went off in different parts of the city, killing two and injuring 10.[5] Within 24 hours, 16 bomb blasts hit Ahmedabad in over an hour, killing 45 and resulting in more than 200 casualties.[6] A series of five synchronised bomb blasts took place on 13 September 2008 at various locations in New Delhi. The first bomb exploded at 6:10 pm and four other blasts followed in quick succession, ending with at least 30 people killed and over 90 injured. On 30 October 2008, 18 bombs went off in markets in Guwahati city and the surrounding area of western Assam, causing at least 84 deaths and 470 injuries.[7]

All these blasts were intensely public—going off in pressure cookers, in trains, on the road, in markets and amongst the common populace. Some were attributed to the LeT and a previously unknown Islamic militant group called the Indian Mujahideen took responsibility for the Jaipur blasts. While the motivations remain debatable and the perpetrators are speculated upon, the pattern of targeting Indian urban centres where the damage to the Indian psyche will far outdo the loss of life and property is easily discernible.

Tracing the Target: Patterns of Victimisation

In all the above mentioned incidents, the patterns of targeting and victimisation are made up of three stages – the threat and actual use of violence, the immediate effects of this threat or act and the resultant long-term social consequences. These three stages are interchangeable, depending on the motives of the attack. This gives rise to two scenarios: in the first, the victims are fixed – particular political figures or other public figures of importance, through whom the target is a larger audience that would be shocked and fearful in the aftermath of the attack. Once the victims have been identified, the attack is carried out to cause large-scale collateral damage that would intensify the significance of the attack. Once the attack has sunk into the psyche of its immediate audience, it percolates into the larger social consciousness, leading to the deepening of social schisms. The terrorist attack, thus, secures its objectives. The attack on the Parliament in 2001 is an example of this type of attack. Other methods that could be used are kidnapping, assassination and execution of public figures.

The second scenario is built around the target itself and intended to enhance the symbolic value of an attack by choosing its victims on the basis of their identities – national, racial, religious, socio-economic, etc. While these victims are not chosen on an individual basis, they are supposed to illustrate the vulnerability of a certain identity, thus, playing into the psychology of the larger society of which these people are a part. Once the criteria for victimhood has been identified, the killing of these people is largely indiscriminate. The same is true for the targeting of geographical places as well – heritage monuments, public places, schools, hospitals – all are the nerve centres of a nation and striking these is likely to have the most impact. Once identified as valuable, the building or area is under the threat of violence. While this is reminiscent of Naxalite, Maoist, guerrilla or anti-state terrorist activity in post-colonial India, the new wave of terrorism can be differentiated by the scale of its operations and the urban nature of its targets. The bomb blasts in Mumbai in 1993 are examples of this kind of terrorist attacks.

In both scenarios, it is clear that the targets of the violent acts are not only its victims but also the audience that reacts and responds to this act, with more violence or the deepening of rifts. As terrorism is the act of violence or its threatened use, to create fear and distort normality in a nation's everyday life through the damage it inflicts, in both scenarios, the objectives are met by securing a reaction from the target audience to the attack. The immediate victims of the violence then represent the means to an end. Thus, while the Muslims praying in the mosque at Malegaon were victims of the blasts that occurred there, other Muslims around Malegaon, Maharashtra, India or around the world are the indirect targets of this attack. This is further amplified when they are provoked to react in a certain manner in order to magnify the immediate damage of the bomb blast.

The conceptualisation of victimhood and identification of targets in 'new terrorism' can be further distinguished by understanding the functioning of the new terrorist's mind. While a terrorist seeks validity in a political or social setting and demands it through the threat or use of force, the new terrorist chooses to destroy the political or social setting in question, constructing, instead, a new environment, one that is convivial to his ideologies. Therefore, the targets or victims are not intended to demonstrate the urgency of a demand or the gravity of a situation, but to reverse the situation itself. Convinced that the path to reconciliation is impossible, the new terrorist is not keen on negotiation. As a result, the targets he chooses and the victims of his actions are the consequences of a nihilistic plan of action – where the end objective is to annihilate, not just threaten. New terrorism is not a means to an end, but the end itself.

With this kind of *modus operandi*, this 'new terrorism' is closest to war – the last resort where all else has failed. The targets and victims of war are far from the targets and victims of terrorism in its conventional sense. 'New' terrorists, thus, indulge in violence, which would be considered excessive and indiscriminate, when compared to the actions of their predecessors.[8] This can be illustrated by the targeting of hospitals, where apart from other patients admitted to the hospital, in the case of a terrorist attack, the survivors from one scene of a terrorist attack could become victims in another. Thus, the dehumanising of the victims goes one step further. This is visible in the targeting of the Cama Hospital in the recent attacks in Mumbai on 26 November 2008.

When terrorists choose their victims and targets, it is done with the intention of achieving maximum impact. In domestic and international settings, terrorists mostly choose political targets such as public buildings, political figures and groups, and the military and police. But terrorist acts may also be aimed at private targets, especially if the terrorist has more than one objective to secure. The loss of life and the destruction of property can be aimed at achieving total destruction or as a part of a larger regional or global movement. In either scenario, "For the nihilistic terrorist, with no other aims than the destruction of persons, property or symbols of authority, an urban setting is perhaps most desirable. Here is where the targets are most varied and abundant; here is where the impact of a destructive act is most widespread."[9] The blasts in Hyderabad, which targeted a restaurant not owned by the state and an amusement park that was a public facility, are indicative of this two-fold targeting.

The definition of terrorism itself can be founded in the effects it has on its victims and on its target audience. When an act of violence is carried out in such a way that it maximises the severity and length of the psychological impact on the people affected by it, it can constitute an act of terrorism. Political violence in an asymmetrical conflict that is designed to induce fear, terrorism is essentially a political tactic. It is differentiated from war by its intentional and specific selection of civilians, non-combatants as direct targets. But it is also considered largely "illegitimate", authorised neither by the government nor by international law. While this might be a highly controversial and subjective definition of terrorism,[10] in the phenomenon of 'new terrorism', legitimacy acquires additional importance. This is because 'new terrorism' doesn't intend to legitimise its cause through violent actions, and doesn't involve itself in a debate on legitimacy.[11] The new terrorist decides that the other side is illegitimate and proceeds on that assumption. Targets and victims, thus, bear the unrestrained brunt of this ideological rigidity. As mentioned above, there is no scope for negotiation in this new brand of terrorism.

Target Mumbai – 26/11 and Its Discontents

This theorising on the nature of 'new terrorism' resonates with the terrorist attacks that took place in Mumbai on 26 November 2008. In many ways, 26/11 constitutes what new terrorism has come to mean. The chosen targets and the patterns of victimisation of the attacks indicate how the phenomenon of new terrorism has found its defining point in these attacks, particularly in the context of India. The choice of the city is telling, since more than any other city in India, Mumbai offers a plethora of targets, both human and material. It is home to India's socio-economic elite, public officials of importance and attracts many non-locals, such as tourists. It is also the country's commercial and industrial hub. Businessmen and foreign investors constitute a large part of the targeted victims of this attack. Considered a soft target, Mumbai is also the venue of other vulnerable and symbolic places of importance. The terror attacks, thus, found multiple convenient victims in Mumbai.

The logic of the 26/11 Mumbai attack is best understood by examining its target selection. The Taj Palace Hotel, Oberoi Trident Hotel, Chhatrapati Shivaji Terminus Railway Station, Leopold Café, Cama Hospital and Nariman House offer a different array of targets. While the reconnaissance and planning of the attack betrayed sophistication, the selection of these targets also demonstrated an extremely professional and deliberate plan of action. The Taj Palace Hotel is a long standing city landmark and attracts foreign guests and local elite and the Oberoi Trident is a popular venue for the city's upper crust. The attacks caused the death of approximately 40 people at the Taj and about 30 people at the Oberoi. By targeting the hotels, the terrorists had two main groups of victims—first, a large number of foreigners present in the hotel at any given time; and second, the more affluent section of society that constitutes a large section of the hotel's clientele. This was the first time in the history of terrorism in India that both these sections had been targeted, singularly or collectively. Also, by storming the hotels, the terrorists had achieved two objectives – the internationalisation of the attack by the targeting of foreigners on Indian territory, and the globalisation of the attack by the media coverage of the same.

To further particularise the targeting, Americans and Britons had been singled out (by asking for their passports and asking others for their nationalities), leading to speculation that this was in response to the American War on Terror in India's extended neighbourhood. The simultaneous targeting of Jews in Nariman House that houses a Jewish centre led to the gruesome death of a rabbi and his family. This was the first time that Jews had been targeted in India, leading immediately to the issuing of security warnings to Israelis travelling to India in the ensuing holiday season.[12] The targeting of Nariman House also shows how this attack did not stem from a conflict entirely internal to India. Jews have traditionally not been a prosecuted or alienated minority in India and have rarely been a significantly vocal minority demanding rights or participating in political agitation. So, the extension of an international conflict into an Indian location of a terrorist attack shows how new terrorism operates on a scale hitherto unaccounted for in Indian security calculations.

One of the methods of disseminating the effects of a terror attack has always been the media. Unfortunately, these channels of awareness and information also become carriers of panic, throwing the world into frenzy and causing the indirect targets of the terror attack to multiply. This form of 'new terrorism', in fact, seeks to exploit that effect. As experienced with the 9/11 and the 26/11 attacks, new terrorism entails a prolonged urban confrontation that exposes the inability of security forces to cope with the volatility of the terrorists due to the completely unexpected nature of the attack. This leads to viewers becoming witness to the protracted fighting. The difficulty of overcoming the terrorists, the sensitivity of the situation and the fearlessness of the terrorists (especially in the case of suicide bombers/fighters) become all too evident, further exacerbating the psychological impact of the terrorist attack. Even though they are eventually successful in eliminating the terrorists, initially, the security forces have to grapple with combating them. This is covered extensively by news channels. Thus, the careful choice of targets leads to guaranteed prime time coverage, reaching audiences across the world, causing panic and so, indirectly multiplying the number of targets. 'New terrorism', therefore, is as much, if not more, broadcast-based as it is dependent on the immediate damage of a bomb blast.

In the coverage of 26/11, less attention was focussed on the firing at the Leopold Café, which witnessed 10 deaths, or at the Chhatrapati Shivaji Terminus (CST) Railway Station, where 58 people lost their lives. Clearly, while targeting a selection of poor labourers, hawkers, small-scale businessmen and their families, the firing was indiscriminate. Images of Ajmal Kasab were available across the Internet and on television screens worldwide as the sole survivor and source of information on the motivations and planning of the terrorist attack. Short videos of him and a fellow terrorist spraying CST with bullets were played repeatedly to show how the killing was truly indiscriminate.

But the obvious economic inequality between those present at the Taj and the Oberoi, on the one hand, and at CST and Leopold, on the other, has already become a point for debate – angry analysis of the media coverage of the terrorist attacks points out to the attention that the Taj and the Oberoi received in comparison to the coverage of CST. Counter arguments point to the prolonged nature of the encounters at the hotels, as opposed to the other targets. In any case, the attacks caused a social upheaval. Lack of well-equipped security personnel and the failure of intelligence were not as much a concern after incidences of terrorism in the rest of the country as they became in the case of Mumbai. Jaipur or Guwahati did not lead to the fall of the political leadership or the investigation of security structures. The reaction to the Mumbai terrorist attack is symptomatic of future targeting of victims. Clearly, choosing the most secure sections of society incites fear in such a way that it has an immediate and urgent reaction.

The death of top police officers in the event of this terrorist attack adds a new dimension to this episode. This attack was the first in which numerous high-profile victims were targeted or lost their lives in collateral damage. In the past, while political assassinations targeted certain high-profile public figures, never did a group of high-profile victims die as a result of the same attack. Hemant Karkare, chief of the Anti-Terror Squad, and two other top-ranking officials, Vijay Salaskar and Ashok Kamte, lost their lives in the midst of the violence. Salaskar was a well-known encounter specialist and Karkare had been courting media attention because of his role in the investigation of the Malegaon blasts.[13] The death of these officers had a severe impact on the public's psyche – symbols of security, their deaths signified the fallibility of safety nets in India while also having a tangible effect on the counter-terrorist operations in the city. The immediate effect of this targeting unanticipated by the terrorists themselves was the confusion and angst amongst the law enforcement officials in the city, lack of coordination between the bureaucracy and the police and the eventual embarrassment of the government. As Bruce Hoffman puts it, "This furthers their (the terrorists') aim of trying to undermine popular confidence in the government's ability to protect its citizens."[14]

The government's ability to deal with the magnitude of this incident is debatable, not only because of the lack of political will or deficiency in the state's security apparatus, but also because of the transnational nexus of such terrorist attacks. South Asia has suffered numerous incidences of terrorist violence in the past few years, especially in this last year itself. Terrorism is so pervasive across South Asia that the region accounts for 87 percent of all attacks globally that led to casualties, according to a study by the US government's National Counterterrorism Centre in early 2008.[15] The patterns of targeting in this new form of terrorism show how it is borderless, and in a way, much more international than its precedents were. In 1992, Boutros Boutros Ghali had noted, "The time of absolute and exclusive sovereignty has passed; its theory was never matched with reality."[16] This is also increasingly true of actions by non-state actors indulging in the menace of terrorism. The targets have become less predictable and more diffused as terrorism has become more the tool of amorphous groups of people with an ideological or religious motivation rather than state-sponsored violence.

The targeting of Indians outside India became visible in the attack on the Indian embassy in Kabul, Afghanistan, on 07 July 2008 that killed 58 people and injured 141.[17] In another trend of targeting, when the attack in Mumbai that targeted foreign nationals is placed in the context of the attacks on Indians elsewhere, the linkages become evident – the message of new terrorism in the context of India seems to be that the Indian people and Indian cities, particularly landmarks and places of importance are not safe and will be targeted. The methods used for attacking these targets are also internationally sourced – terrorists across the world are adopting the tactics of one another, relying not on ideological leanings alone, but also on technological efficiency. Thus, it is quite possible that techniques witnessed in areas of chronic conflict like Kashmir or the Northeast will soon make their way to cities in the heart of India, if they haven't already. New terrorism targets people and places, not to establish control over them but to demoralise and destroy them.[18] As a political strategy, the victimisation of soft targets in the midst of an Indian metropolitan centre surely is more effective than making claims on the territory of an Indian state along the border.[19] We can, thus, discern the strategic logic of new terrorism in the choice of its targets.

This is also evident in how Mumbai was a marked departure in scope from other recent terrorist attacks in India that targeted local people rather than foreigners and hit single rather than multiple targets.[20] The collateral damage of these attacks also shows how unlike the use of force to generate fear only as a coercive method in the past, 'new terrorism' views and exploits fear as a consequence. Hence, the threat of violence is minimal – in 'new terrorism', actions happen first, followed by panic and widespread social upheaval. Long-term effects of the attack will include a blow to the economy as foreign investors rethink the security of their assets in India. Tourism will also suffer a major setback. However, in a more damaging consequence, this crisis could feed the violence that can arise from extreme economic inequality and racial and religious conflicts, giving rise to a cycle of conflict.

In Conclusion: Damage Control and the Consequences of New Terrorism

American President Barack Obama has already signalled the shifting focus to South Asia's conflicts. But other South Asian conflicts might not be far removed from the wars in Iraq and Afghanistan. Going by the threat of fundamentalist terrorism and its international nature, the victimisation of India, its nationals and property, inside and outside the country, is an alarming prospect. A combination of internal sources of terrorism combined with the spectre of global discontent played out on Indian soil may be on a scale India is not equipped to deal with. Particularly, the "dense and conflictive spaces of cities"[21] make for tempting targets, necessitating ways to combat urban warfare on a larger scale.

Most importantly, this new kind of terrorism doesn't creep in on society; it engages in a brazen frontal assault and cashes in on its vulnerabilities. It gives rise to the popular perception that the country is under aggression, opening up spaces for political debate founded not on well-developed political analysis, but on knee-jerk reactions in a state of panic. Thus, an act of 'new terrorism' secures its objective of being a catalyst that sets off a chain reaction, causing a domino-like effect on the unravelling of socio-political structures. Subsequently, there is disenchantment with the political leadership and structures of governance. The general population of a country or a city, thus, disengages from the process of political reconciliation, preferring instead to disassociate from the government, which comes to be viewed as weak and ineffective. The only way to counter this downward spiral is for governments to identify possible targets and accommodate their security within the framework of traditional national security. The victimisation of a country's citizens constitutes a direct threat to its national security, in whatever form it may take place. Indeed, to re-paraphrase Clausewitz, terrorism is the continuation of policy by other means.

Thus, the threat or actual execution of 'new terrorism' depends almost entirely on the targets it chooses. While securing these probable targets might be a long-term project, in the short- and mid-term, it is essential to identify them, not only to minimise physical victimisation as a consequence of a terrorist attack, but to minimise social alienation that could lead to terrorism in the first place. While the scope and ambition of new terrorism might distinguish its targets from older forms of terrorism, it is essentially the outlet of an ideological divergence that might or might not be reconciled. An attempt to address the motivations of this new terrorism might prevent future victims.

Notes

1. "Scores Dead in Mumbai Train Bombs," *BBC News*, 11 July 2006, http://news.bbc.co.uk/2/hi/south_asia/5169332.stm, accessed on 05 February 2009.
2. "Timeline: Major Attacks in India Since 2003," *Reuters*, 25 July 2008, http://www.reuters.com/article/topNews/idUSB68384820080725?sp=truc, accessed on 05 February 2009.
3. "Delhi Blasts Death Toll at 62," *AFP*, 31 October 2005, http://www.news24.com/News24/World/News/0,,2-10-1462_1826434,00.html, accessed on 05 February 2009.
4. "Death Toll in Hyderabad Serial Blasts Rises to 44," *IBN Live*, 26 August 2007, http://ibnlive.in.com/news/death-toll-in-hyderabad-serial-blasts-rises-to-41/47450-3.html, accessed on 05 February 2009.
5. "For the First Time in 280 Years," *The Times of India*, 14 May 2008, http://timesofindia.indiatimes.com/articleshow/3037795.cms, accessed on 05 February 2009.
6. "Ahmedabad Blasts: Toll Rises," *NDTV*, 26 July 2008, http://www.ndtv.com/convergence/ndtv/mumbaiterrorstrike/Story.aspx?ID=NEWEN20080058856&type=News, accessed on 05 February 2009.
7. "At Least 61 Killed and Over 470 Injured in 18 Blasts in Assam," *Associated Press of Pakistan*, 30 October 2008, http://www.app.com.pk/en_/index.php?option=com_content&task=view&id=57515&Itemid=2, accessed on 05 February 2009.
8. Audrey K Cronin, "Behind the Curve: Globalization and International Terrorism,' *International Security*, Vol. 27, No. 3, Winter 2002/2003, p. 41.
9. Michael Stohl, *The Politics of Terrorism* (Florida: CRC Press, 1988), p. 54.
10. Often illustrated in the saying, "One man's terrorist is another man's freedom fighter."
11. Carsten Bockstette, "Jihadist Terrorist Use of Strategic Communication Management Techniques," George C Marshall Centre for European Security Studies, *Occasional Paper Series*, Vol. 20, December 2008, pp. 1-28.
12. Ryan Clarke, "The Indigenisation of Terrorism in India," *S Rajaratnam School of International Studies Commentaries*, Vol. 2008, Issue 137, 26 December 2008.
13. "Witness Account of Karkare, Kamte and Salaskar's Death," *The Indian Express*, 29 November 2008, http://www.indianexpress.com/news/witness-account-of-karkare-kamte-and-salaskars-death/392181/, accessed on 06 February 2009.
14. Bruce Hoffman, "Insurgency and Counterinsurgency in Iraq," 2005, http://www.rand.org/pubs/occasional_papers/2005/RAND_OP127.pdf, accessed on

06 February 2009.

15. Seth G Jones, "The Backlash Against Terror," *Ethics Newsline*, 08 December 2008, http://www.rand.org/commentary/2008/12/08/EN.html, accessed on 06 February 2009.
16. Boutros Boutros-Ghali, quoted in Mark Duffield, *Development, Security and Unending War: Governing the World of Peoples* (London: Polity, 2007), p. 44.
17. Katie Paul, "Proxy Attack?," *Newsweek*, 08 July 2008, http://www.newsweek.com/id/145071, accessed on 06 February 2009.
18. Rollie Lal, "Terrorism in India is Not Just an Internal Threat," *Financial Times*, 30 September 2003, http://www.rand.org/commentary/2003/09/30/FT.html, accessed on 06 February 2009.
19. Brian Michael Jenkins, "Outside View: Mumbai's Terrifying Logic," *Middle East Times*, 09 December 2008, http://www.metimes.com/Security/2008/12/09/outside_view_mumbais_terrifying_logic/6b60/, accessed on 06 February 2009.
20. Alan Cowell and Mark McDonald, "Amid the Horror: Who are the Attackers?" *International Herald Tribune*, 27 November 2008, http://www.iht.com/articles/2008/11/27/asia/group.php, accessed on 06 February 2009.
21. Saskia Sassen, "The New Wars and Cities: After Mumbai," *Open Democracy*, 29 November 2008, http://www.opendemocracy.net/article/the-new-wars-and-cities-after-mumbai, accessed on 06 February 2009.

6

ENHANCING BORDER SECURITY AND BORDER MANAGEMENT

Ravi Tuteja and Mansi Mehrotra

India occupies a strategic position in Southern Asia. The mainland coastline is about 5,422 km. If island territories are included, it is 7,600 kms touching 12 states and union territories (UTs) alongwith land borders of 14,880 km running through 92 districts in 17 states,[1] bordering seven countries including Afghanistan in the northern part of the state of Jammu and Kashmir (J&K). However, at present, the border with Afghanistan falls in the Pakistan Occupied Kashmir (POK).

India's nation building challenges and internal security are linked with border security and border management. Apart from preventing and containing inter-state conflict on the borders, border security and border management involves: thwarting illegal border crossing; preventing smuggling of contraband goods like arms, drugs and explosives; and stopping cross-border terrorism and infiltration. This has made border management a complicated and challenging task requiring resolute and concerted action on the part of intelligence, administrative, security and regulatory agencies. Such an undertaking requires serious and committed political will. Thus, it is necessary to adopt a holistic, multi-disciplinary and integrated approach in formulating a comprehensive strategy towards improvement of border management for national security in times of war and peace.

Until now, land border management had been of prime importance due to wars in the past with Pakistan and China. However, recent history shows that terror outfits, as a result of global networking, have acquired advanced techniques and technological capabilities to challenge national security. Consequently, the concept of border security needs a reassessment in the light of mounting non-conventional threats that expose the vulnerabilities of India's land, air space and maritime borders to cross-border terrorism. The Purulia incident of 1995, the acquisition of aircraft by the Liberation of Tamil Tigers Eelam (LTTE), the 9/11 incident in the US, and other incidences of plane hijacking make air defence important. The Mumbai carnage of 2008 and repeated incidents of Somalian piracy demonstrated the dangers from the seas.

Impediments to Effective Border Management

The major encumbrances that have rendered border management ineffective are: lack of understanding among the decision-makers about military issues; and deployment of multiple forces in the same area of operation. Absence of coordination amongst military, paramilitary and police forces that are involved in border management has led to lack of accountability towards encroachment. Other issues include poor intelligence due to absence of institutionalised information sharing arrangements; absence of information sharing mechanisms among the army, air force and navy; disputed and unsettled boundary issues; porous borders; difficult terrain; insufficient strength in terms of equipment and manpower; lack of proactive approach by decision-makers; and minimal presence of the Coast Guard in coastal areas. These difficulties have kept the borders vulnerable and have, in turn, facilitated problems of infiltration, illegal immigration, drugs and arms smuggling, cross-border terrorism, counterfeit currency and support to the internal separatist movements by external actors.

To overcome the above mentioned impediments, Prime Minister Atal Bihari Vajpayee had constituted a Group of Ministers (GoM), to review the national security system in its entirety and, in particular, to consider the recommendations of the Kargil Review Committee and formulate specific proposals for implementation. The GoM was led by then Minister of Home Affairs, L K Advani. The report came out with significant recommendations to safeguard national security against any armed intrusion, entry of narcotics, illegal migration, terrorism and arms smuggling. The GoM decided that some of the recommendations that required greater deliberation should initially be addressed by four Task Forces, one each in the area of Intelligence Apparatus, Internal Security, Border Management and Management of Defence. While some recommendations have been implemented, much remains to be done to make border management more effective.

Land Border Security

According to the MoD,[2] the length of India's land borders with its neighbours is Bangladesh: 4,351 km; China: 4,056 km; Pakistan: 3,224 km; Nepal: 1,751 km; Myanmar: 1,643 km; and Bhutan: 700 km.

India-Bangladesh

The notoriously porous India-Bangladesh border is referred to as the "problem area". The major security concerns of India from Bangladesh are illegal migration, smuggling of contraband goods and trans-border movement of insurgents.

While expressing concerns about illegal migration from Bangladesh, Union Home Minister P Chidambaram has admitted illegal migration as a major challenge to homeland security.[3] Recently, religion too has become a cause for concern in the Northeast. Islamist militancy has started consolidating itself since Bangladeshi infiltration remains unchecked and illegal immigration continues to be a sensitive issue, misused for political purposes.

There are 12 to 15 Muslim extremist organisations working in the region. The purpose of these organisations is to spread Islamic fundamentalism in the entire northeast. It is reported that, the Harkat-ul-Mujahideen (HUM) and Harkat-ul-Jehad (HUJ) are directly raised by the Pakistani Inter-Service Intelligence (ISI) and these are the most fanatical in their ideology. There are specific concerns about members of the Harkat ul-Jihad-al-Islami (HuJI), which operates in both Bangladesh and Pakistan, and has been blamed for attacks in the cities of India in recent years. There are also worries about potential strikes by separatists targeting West Bengal and Assam, who are believed to have camps in Bangladesh.

Presently, the Border Security Force (BSF)[4] is in charge of manning the Indo-Bangladesh borders. There have been frequent clashes between the BSF and the erstwhile Bangladesh Rifles (BDR)[5] over encroachment, enclaves and adverse possessions.[6] The border forces are left to deal with the problems on a day-to-day basis due to the political and diplomatic failures in resolving the issue.

Other hurdles that keep the security fragile on the Indo-Bangladesh border include security personnel who have no coherent system to deal with the massive inflow of migrants. Dual immigration laws such as the Illegal Migrants Determined by Tribunal (IMDT) Act, 1983 followed in Assam makes it easy for illegal immigrants to claim their rights in India. The rivulet changes its course each monsoon season, thus, making the border fencing difficult and border management poor. In addition, there are many villages on the zero line that make the fencing unfeasible as the fence may pass through the houses and villages, thus infringing on international regulations.

The GoM recommended that in order to prevent any illegal infiltration from Bangladesh, temporary permits need to be given to the migrants on humanitarian grounds. In addition, complete fencing of the border has been made mandatory.

It is only through a serious dialogue at the political and diplomatic levels that one can resolve the issue of enclaves and adverse possessions. It is important to give clear direction and authority to the BSF to stop further infiltration. Above all, there is a need for amendment of the IMDT Act and enforcement of the Foreign Nationals Act, 1946.

Since much of the illegal cross-border activities take place at the behest of the Pakistani ISI, which has also spread its nefarious activities into Bangladesh, India needs to build closer cooperation with Bangladesh at the diplomatic and economic levels. It cannot be expected that the BSF and the Bangladeshi border security force will work out strategies to deal with organised criminal activities in the border areas.

On the diplomatic front, India needs to resolve pending issues with its eastern neighbours, especially the question of enclaves and adverse possessions. In order to check political and economic instability in Bangladesh, India needs to come up with proper and timely assistance. Politically, this can be done by assisting Bangladesh in state-building. Economically, both countries can work towards establishing a free trade zone and transit facilities.

A twin approach, social and diplomatic and military-to-military confidence building measures, can go a long way in stemming the institutionalisation of terrorism in Bangladesh, which would have a direct effect on India's security. In fact, this could be a basis for a South Asian Task Force to deal with terrorism in the region, suggested by none other than the Bangladesh Prime Minister when India's External Affairs Minister, Pranab Mukherjee, visited Dhaka in February 2009.

India-China

India and China share a long border, punctuated by Nepal and Bhutan. However, a large number of disputed regions lie along this border including Aksai Chin in the western region, which is close to Xinjiang[7] and Tibet, and Arunachal Pradesh in the eastern sector.

China has helped anti-government groups in India's Northeast in the past. However, there are no reports that suggest continued Chinese support to the Northeast militant groups. Yet, presently, there are substantial intelligence reports which suggest that owing to the current Bangladeshi government's policy to control and eliminate operations of the Indian militant groups, some leaders of ULFA, an outlawed organisation, have crossed over into China via Bhutan and established contact with the Chinese Army.[8]

Although presently there is no account that suggests any direct infiltration or terrorist activities taking place from the China border, prospective future infiltration from the eastern border cannot be ruled out. Despite the tough terrain that makes mobility difficult, future security threats may arise, particularly in a situation where extremist organisations manage to acquire a strong toehold. Security will remain fragile principally because of the disputed borders and because of the harsh weather conditions that keep this sector unmanned and porous.

It should also be noted that despite the war between India and China in 1962, mutual suspicion and traditional rivalry, India is one of the very few countries, apart from the US and Russia, with whom China has formalised a dialogue mechanism on counter-terrorism. India and China have even conducted joint anti-terror exercises. The first such military exercise ("Hand-in-Hand, 2007") was held at Kunming in the Yunnan province of China in December 2007. Another exercise was held in the mountainous terrains of Belgaum, Karnataka, in which Chinese troops from the 1st Company of the Infantry Battalion of the Chengdu Military Area Command and Indian Army troops from 8 Maratha Light Infantry Battalion participated in the joint military exercise. Such endeavours can be a stepping stone for building mutual trust and strategic partnership.

Presently, the western sector of the Line of Actual Control (LAC) in Ladakh and Himachal Pradesh come under the Northern and Western Commands. The middle sector along the Uttrakhand border is under the Central Command. It is manned by the Special Frontier Force that reports to the Cabinet Secretariat and the Indo-Tibetan Border Police (ITBP), which comes under the Ministry of Home Affairs. In the eastern sector, the Sikkim borders are manned by the infantry battalions of the Indian Army and the Arunachal Pradesh, Nagaland, Manipur and Mizoram borders are manned by the Assam Rifles (AR), which is a Ministry of Home Affairs force.

However, the borders between India and China remain susceptible to cross-border terrorism and infiltration as the borders are porous and not clearly demarcated. The Border Peace and Tranquillity Agreement (1993) and the agreement on Confidence Building Measures in the Military Field (1996) between India and China were expected to reduce the operational commitments of the army from having to permanently man the difficult LAC with China.[9] But little progress has taken place. The LAC with China offers an illustrative example of the lack of coordination in border management.[10] The division of command hinders promptness in action and relationships between the commanders and their subordinates. On the Chinese side, the entire Sino-Indian border is manned by the Border Guard division of the Chinese People's Liberation Army (PLA) under a single PLA commander of the Tibet Autonomous Region.

Thus, in order to prevent future security threats arising from cross-border terrorism and infiltration, the GoM had recommended that the borders must be clearly demarcated. Additionally, it is important to put up tall pylons or pillars at a distance of about one to two kilometres without prejudice to the position of either side on their respective claim lines, which can withstand the harsh weather conditions. This will help both countries to monitor and prevent the movement of terrorists, infiltrators and illegal imports across either side of the border. These recommendations have remained on paper due to diplomatic failure and lack of initiatives by the concerned agencies. The GoM has also suggested the need for establishing one single command for promptness in action. However, no effort in this direction has been made.

India-Pakistan

The international boundary between India and Pakistan is referred to as International Border (IB). The IB goes across Punjab, Rajasthan and Gujarat on the Indian side and Punjab and Sindh provinces on the Pakistani side. Further, the Line of Control (LoC) separates Indian administered Jammu and Kashmir from POK. Additionally,

Pakistan is also involved in other territorial disputes with India on Siachen Glacier and Sir Creek.

The security concerns on the Indo-Pakistan border include issues related to infiltration; inadvertent crossings; smuggling of arms, narcotics and fake currency; and illegal construction on either side of the International Border.

The entire border with Pakistan is manned by the BSF except for the LoC in J&K, which is the responsibility of the army. The primary responsibility of the army is to ensure the physical integrity of the LoC against encroachment by the Pakistan Army and to minimise trans-LoC infiltration by armed terrorists, usually aided and abetted by the Pakistan Army and the ISI.

The terrain on India's western border makes it difficult and challenging to guard. The biggest impediment is the mutual distrust and traditional rivalry between the two countries that prevents information sharing and keeps the border security and border management fragile.

To overcome the security threats, the GoM recommended border fencing and floodlighting of the entire border. It is also important to develop patrolling tracks. Most of the area has been fenced and floodlights have been installed. However, the topography restricts complete fencing and floodlighting along the borders.

Also, it is important to review the tactical deployment of the border guarding forces and patrolling arrangements. It is mandatory to strengthen security and checking arrangements at Attari given that there are reports that the Samjhauta Express is being used for gun running and drug-trafficking. Border security should be checked by suitable and stern legal actions against people caught in gun-running, drug-trafficking and illegal immigration across Rajasthan border.

India-Nepal

Nepal shares its borders with the Indian states of Uttaranchal, Bihar, Uttar Pradesh, West Bengal and Sikkim. The Indo-Nepal border is unique in the sense that people of both the countries can cross it from any point, despite the existence of border check posts at several locations. There are six transit points for a third country to have trade with Nepal, for which entry and exit visa is required to cross the border.

The border region of Bihar consists of eight districts. The porous Bihar-Nepal border makes it easy for unlawful activities to take place along the border areas. Before the formation of the Maoist government in Nepal, the Bihar police had arrested many Nepalese Maoists in the border districts of West and East Champaran, Sitamarhi, Sheohar and Madhubani. In fact, the Maoists had established their training camps in the forests of Bagha in the West Champaran district, which has emerged as a safe haven for the Nepalese insurgents. In Uttar Pradesh, Baharaich and Maharajganj have emerged as a shelter for the Maoists.

The Maoists of Nepal, with the help of the Pakistani ISI, have well-established linkages with Indian left wing extremist (LWE) organisations, primarily with the Communist Party of India (Maoist) and are members of the Revolutionary Internationalist Movement (RIM). India alleges that the ISI is using the Pakistan Embassy in Kathmandu to indulge in anti-Indian activities. According to a report, "Nepal has become a preferred haven for Dawood Ibrahim's associates and terrorists being actively backed by Pakistan after committing crimes in India."[11]

There are also some reports about the Nepalese Maoists' links with insurgent groups active in India's Northeast, such as ULFA, Kamtapur Liberation Organisation (KLO), Gurkha National Liberation Front (GNLF) and Gurkha Liberation Organisation (GLO).

Presently, the Sashastra Seema Bal (SSB) is responsible for manning the Indo-Nepalese border. The force is under the Ministry of Home Affairs.

The entire area of Bihar, Chhattisgarh, Jharkhand, Andhra Pradesh, Orissa and Madhya Pradesh has been identified in Maoist literature as the Compact Revolutionary Zone (CRZ).[12] The porous Bihar-Nepal border, poor governance, lack of rule of law and incapability of the police force provide a context for these

LWE groups to operate without much difficulty. Further, the 1950 Indo-Nepal Treaty had kept the borders between the two countries unattended. With the coming of the Maoists in Nepal, gradual efforts were made to step up vigilance along this border, as India fears the southward spread of Maoist ideology.

The GoM suggested an urgent need to upgrade the SSB on the border. The existing police stations in the border areas should be suitably upgraded and strengthened with sufficient numbers of trained personnel for crime investigation, intensive village surveillance, adequate intelligence gathering and assisting in organising anti-smuggling raids/ambushes. Immigration Check Posts (ICPs) should be increased to cover all transit points and should have Land Customs Stations (LCS) integrated with them, with adequate facilities for the integrated posts to function from. Reciprocal measures for the cars coming from Nepal to India should be adopted. A unified/joint command for coordination of intelligence, as well as for operational activities needs to be formed. Demarcation of the border should be completed and the Joint Working Group should meet more frequently. The scope for cooperation in border area development should be enlarged and an agreement on mutual legal assistance should be finalised. Many of these suggestions still await implementation.

India-Myanmar

The 1,643-km-long unfenced India-Myanmar border has become a regular route for international gun-runners, besides a corridor for separatists operating in India's Northeast. The Northeastern states of Assam, Manipur, Mizoram, Nagaland and Arunachal Pradesh share borders with Myanmar. Due to their ethnic connections, insurgent groups from the Northeast of India not only receive shelter in Myanmar but also operate bases from there. In fact, the insurgency-related problem in the Northeast has been present from pre-independence times. At least a dozen separatist groups active in India's Northeast are said to have well-entrenched bases in parts of Sagaing division along the river Chindwin in northwest Myanmar.

Most of the weapons of the rebel groups of the Northeast, including AK-47 and Type 56 assault rifles, mortars, 40 mm rocket launchers, pistols, revolvers and grenades, come via Bhutan, Bangladesh, and the Arakans—a mountainous area in Myanmar—from parts of Thailand and Cambodia. In November 2001, the Myanmarese junta claimed to have arrested some 200 rebels from Manipur, besides seizing up to 1,700 assorted weapons, including Chinese assault rifles and rocket launchers.[13] The cooperation between various terrorist organisations of Northeast India with terrorist organisations of Myanmar led to the formation of the Indo-Burmese Revolutionary Front (IBRF).

Myanmar failed in its efforts to crack down on insurgent camps due to their remoteness and has, therefore, sought assistance from India for improving infrastructure and upgradation of military facilities.[14]

Presently, the army and some units of Assam Rifles are entrusted with the responsibility of guarding the country's border with Myanmar. Indian and Myanmarese troops have, of late, been engaged in a joint fight against terrorism. However, the border security management with Myanmar remains operationally inactive. The absence of the Myanmar Army, combined with the difficult terrain, makes this border extremely challenging to manage.

To prevent infiltration, the GoM Report suggested that additional forces with the Assam Rifles for performing counter-insurgency duties and border management related activities should be considered. The plan to construct a road running parallel to the Indo-Myanmar border should be implemented and periodic survey and inspection of boundary pillars, by both sides, is likely to prevent any encroachment. Nonetheless, much more needs to be done on the eastern border.

India-Bhutan

In the 1990s, the ULFA and National Democratic Front of Bodoland (NDFB) established several camps in the forests on the Indo-Bhutan border in return for their support in terrorising the

Nepali-speaking Lhotshampas to leave Bhutan. The linkages with several officers and personnel of the Royal Bhutan Army (RBA) and police helped them sustain as they provided the rebel groups of the Northeast with rations, logistic support as well as aid and contacts for money laundering.

In December 2003, as a result of counter-terrorism initiatives between New Delhi and Thimpu, the Royal Bhutan Army and the Special Frontier Force launched a military campaign against the terrorist outfits in Bhutan. Many terrorist camps were destroyed in the operation. Presently, it is suspected that terrorists are trying to make retaliatory attacks against Bhutan.

The BSF shares the responsibility with the SSB in guarding the Indo-Bhutan border. The borders have been relatively quiet after the Royal Bhutanese Army drove out the Bodo and ULFA insurgents from its territory some years ago. Presently, the insurgent groups of the Northeast are finding it difficult to maintain their camps under the new Bangladeshi government. It is assessed that some of these terrorist groups are now trying to shift their base to Bhutan.

The Indo-Bhutan border is porous and a major portion remains unguarded by the security personnel on the Bhutanese side, which makes it easy for the insurgent groups to find safe havens in Bhutan. The Bhutanese are not active on the issue of border security as they do not feel any threat from India. In addition, they do not want to create any tension with the Northeastern insurgent groups as the Bhutanese have to cross Assam in order to connect to eastern Bhutan that is divided by the Black Mountains.

The GoM Report suggested that it is important to strengthen police, intelligence machinery and administrative arrangements on both sides of the border to ensure regular and effective monitoring of the activities of insurgent groups along the border and to take adequate measures for an effective and capable counter-insurgency network. It is important to regulate the movement of Bhupalis along the Bhutan border and check the Bangladeshis, presenting themselves as Indians, seeking jobs and employment in Bhutan.

Border Area Development Programme Schemes

A. Education

- Primary school building (additional rooms)
- Middle school building (additional rooms)
- Secondary/Higher Secondary School buildings(additional rooms)
- Development of play fields
- Construction of hostels/dormitories
- Buying of school dresses/books
- Adult education
- Public libraries and reading rooms
- Development of human resources through vocational and technical education
- TV/Dish antennas
- Books/journals

B. Health

- Provision of medical equipments of basic/elementary Type. X-Ray, ECG machines etc. can also be purchased.
- Provision of equipment for Dental clinic.
- First aid kit for midwives.
- Construction of public toilets and bathroom
- Setting up of mobile dispensaries in rural areas by Govt. /Panchayati Raj Institutions.
- Health Awareness Programme
- Eye camps
- RCH programme
- Blood Banks
- Control of Malaria, Filaria, Leprosy, AIDS etc.

C. Agriculture and allied sectors

- Animal Husbandry
- Pisciculture
- Sericulture
- Poultry farming
- Farm forestry, horticulture, pastures, parks and gardens in government and community lands or other surrendered lands.
- Desilting of ponds in villages, towns and cities.
- Construction of public irrigation (Minor work) and public drainage facilities.
- Construction of common gobar gas plants, non-conventional energy systems/devices for community use and related activities.

- Construction of irrigation embankments, or lift irrigation or water table recharging facilities.
- Minor irrigation works
- Anti-erosion works (only construction of small bunds etc.)
- Water conservation programmes
- Social Forestry, JFM
- Use of improved seeds, fertilizers and improved technology.
- Veterinary aid Centres, artificial insemination Centres and breeding Centres.

D. Infrastructure
- Rural Sanitation
- Solar Street Lights
- Solar household lights
- Electrification
- Strengthening of existing roads (only links road)
- Construction and strengthening of kutcha roads, part road, Approach roads, link roads.
- Drinking water facility – construction of tubewells, water tanks.
- Repair and maintenance of existing roads.
- Public Distribution System and its improvement (in terms of Infrastructure).
- Industries – Handlooms, tiny units, handicraft, furniture making.
- Construction of culverts/bridges and roads.
- Drain & gutters.
- Footpaths, pathways and footbridges.
- Provisions of civic amenities like electricity, water, pathways, public toilets etc. in slum areas of cities, towns and villages and in SC/ST habitations.
- Provision of common work sheds in slums and for artisans.
- Bus sheds/stops for public transport passengers.
- Repair and maintenance works of any type other than special repairs for restoration/up gradation of any asset.
- Development of infrastructure for weekly haats/bazaars and also for cultural activities etc. in border areas.
- Construction of buildings for local bodies for recognized District or State Sports Associations and for Cultural and Sport Activities or for hospitals (provision of multi-gym facilities in gymnastic centers, sports association, physical education training institutions, etc.)

E. Social Sector
- Construction of community centers
- Rural Sanitation
- Anganwadies, Creches
- Cultural Centres/Community Halls
- Construction of common shelters for the old or Handicapped
- Training for youth for self employment and skill upgradation
- Setting up of small industries using local inputs.

Source: Border Area Development Programme, Ministry of Home Affairs (Department of Border Management)

Maritime Security

The United Nations Convention on the Law of the Sea (UNCLOS) of 1982 had expanded India's jurisdiction as a coastal state through the concept of the Exclusive Economic Zone (EEZ) of 2,013 million sq km. After the delimitation of the continental shelf, the area of responsibility of maritime agencies will increase to 2.9 million sq km, which would be almost equal to India's entire landmass.[15] However, India is yet to ratify its maritime boundary with Bangladesh and Pakistan. If the sea borders are not properly demarcated and protected, well financed and internationally supported illicit elements can exploit the porous borders and drugs and arms smuggling, movement of terrorists, sea bunkering, counterfeit currency, poaching, human trafficking and illegal migration can threaten national security.

India's maritime security has assumed a new dimension in the post 26/11 era. It demonstrated the maritime capability of the terrorist elements for transporting arms, ammunition, explosives and men for facilitating land-based terrorist operations.

Several terrorist organisations in the Indian Ocean littoral are known to possess merchant fleets of various types. Bin Laden's terror ships, termed the "phantom fleet", are a cause of concern for the international community. Although the LTTE of Sri Lanka has been dismantled, it has potential for regrouping. At one time, the LTTE had a well-developed capability for maritime terrorism. They had an entire fleet engaged in dubious maritime trade. Lloyds of London lists 11 merchant ships belonging to Asian front companies that were managed by Kumaran Pathmanathan of the LTTE.[16]

The United Nations Conference on Trade and Development (UNCTAD) Report, 'Review of Maritime Transport 2000', notes that world sea-based trade recorded its fourteenth consecutive annual increase, and Asia's share of imports and exports was 26.1 percent and 18.8 percent respectively. Thus, the prospects for sea-borne trade are set to rise dramatically. Unfortunately, along with this rise in traffic, the variety and intensity of threats, including piracy, maritime terrorism, drug-trafficking, gun-running, human smuggling, pollution, accidents and inter-state conflicts are also expected to show a proportional rise.[17] Thus, with the increase in the maritime trade, the problems of infiltration and smuggling of contraband goods have swelled, particularly because the containers are sealed and they often pass through the ports without undergoing adequate security checks. In fact, Al Qaeda has used shipping containers to infiltrate across borders. The Container Security Initiative (CSI), which does not cover any port in the Indian Ocean, is a step towards overcoming this challenge. However, "While one of the CSI conditions is that officials of the US Customs and Border Patrol will be posted at JNPT (Jawaharlal Nehru Port Trust),[18] this will be a reciprocal step where India can also post its officials at US ports."[19] So far, India has acceded to the Rome Convention for the Suppression of Unlawful Acts Against the Safety of Maritime Navigation (1988).

Somali pirates along the Gulf of Aden have shown the vulnerability of merchant ships in the high seas. These acts of piracy, not amounting to terrorism, continue to take place. The increasing commercial activities make it the most preferred destination for pirates and terrorist elements like the LTTE, Al Qaeda, Lashkar-e-Tayyeba (LeT) and other groups using the sea route to attack targets. All over the world, navies are adopting new techniques to tackle this menace. The Indian Navy, thus, cannot ignore this part.[20]

Additionally, the Indian Navy had in the past provided escort to American warships travelling through the Strait of Malacca (to take part in 'Operation Enduring Freedom' in Afghanistan). Thus, the security of sea lanes requires all-inclusive strategies encompassing, sometimes, conflicting national interests of the concerned states. In spite of serious maritime security threats, traditional maritime international law does not take cognisance of maritime terrorism.

The baffling security scenario of the Lakshadweep Island due to close proximity to Sri Lanka, smuggling of contraband, terrorists from across the border sneaking through sea routes and the absence of any worthwhile surveillance had impelled the Director General of the Coast Guard to moot the idea of a marine police force in December 1996 during the Sixth Standing Committee meeting of the Island Development Authority. Except for the Andaman and Nicobar group of islands, the nation does not have a separate marine police wing in other coastal states of India.[21] The Lakshadweep government has since put up a case for a marine police force on the same lines as for the Andaman and Nicobar Islands in October 1999. Ten years down the line, it is yet to materialise.

The major obstruction to maritime security arising from terrorism and infiltration is that currently there is a plethora of organisations, policies and enforcement measures relating to maritime security issues. This results in overlapping of jurisdiction and an inability to provide quick decisions or respond effectively to fast evolving situations. Currently, as many as 12 ministries and eight departments of the central government are involved in maritime-related policy formulation and implementation, as are nine coastal states and four union territories, with defence left to the navy and the coast guard. Thus, the major challenges to maritime security will not only include the surveillance and security of the extended maritime zone, an increase in domestic shipping tonnage, enhanced effectiveness of both major and minor ports, but also the strengthening of regulatory and enforcement mechanisms in India's maritime zones.[22]

Presently, the Indian Navy and Coast Guard are responsible for maritime security. The Coast Guard came into being on 01 February 1977 to ensure safety of life and property at sea. "The term Coast Guard is strictly a misnomer in maritime security affairs. It is not a guard on duty along the coast. The duty of the coast guard is ideally to prevent a threat from reaching the shore. A serious study into the concept of borders will indicate that the concept is different at sea. The duties of the coast guard are generally seaward of the coastline and extend up to 200 nautical miles perimeter of the EEZ where the maritime zones terminate, unless extended further in future."[23] The Coast Guard assists the Indian Navy in surveillance of the maritime zones that include the Palk Strait, the Gulf of Mannar, the coast of Maharashtra and Gujarat and other island territories. The coast guard is also responsible for curbing the influx of refugees and terrorists, prevent poaching and smuggling of contraband goods.

The Indian Navy also has a Marine Commando Force (MARCOS) with a total strength of around 2,000, guarding the coastal areas.[24] The MARCOS can sabotage enemy vessels, harbour installations, conduct reconnaissance, raids and even counter-terrorist operations in a maritime environment.[25] They can operate in beaches, coastal, jungles and ravines areas. Being divers, they can reach hostile shores swimming underwater.

India has been spearheading a multilateral naval exercise, designated 'Milan', since the mid-1990s, which is conducted every year off the Andaman and Nicobar Islands. In addition, bilateral and multilateral exercises involving search-and-rescue drills, exchange of information, anti-submarine warfare, advanced mine counter-measures and anti-terror tactics have been held between regional navies from time-to-time. In December 2002, the Malabar series of exercises by the US and Indian Navies were revived. The exercise is carried out each year and has also involved ships from Sri Lanka, the Maldives and Mauritius.[26] The last such exercise was held off the coast of Japan in April-May 2009 where the Japan Maritime Self-Defence Forces also participated along with Indian Navy and the US Navy.[27]

Coastal security was also addressed by the GoM in its report. Its recommendations included the upgradation of the Coast Guard and the establishment of specialised marine police in all coastal states and island territories. These are currently under implementation. However, the implementation of the GoM recommendations on the creation of a separate maritime police wing is long overdue.

According to Vice Admiral P S Das, "to overcome the shortcomings arising from maritime security, India's maritime doctrine must encompass four basic capabilities: maximisation of power in the littorals; control of the battlespace; command, control, surveillance, reconnaissance, intelligence and communications; and sustainment of forces at sea."[28] There should be an increase in the number of personnel, along with the pay and allowances benefits. The navy and Coast Guard may set up joint operations rooms at regional levels and compatibility between them in terms of weapons, equipment and training should be ensured.

A worldwide system of tracking and monitoring the movements of all ocean-going ships and larger navies should train the smaller navies to be able to do their bit for maritime counter-terrorism.[29] Maritime operations are basically commercial activities, and, therefore, the security regime has to factor this into its operations.[30] Sanitising the coastal waters at least up to a distance of 200 nautical miles from the coast, if not more, will thwart insurgency.[31]

Prevention should also include information networking, port security, coordination and joint patrol, regional cooperation, gathering and collation of information, notification of relevant organisations, promulgation of anti-piracy law, actions on interception, and criminal investigation against the offender.

Security of Air Space

Air space security is referred to as the technique and method used in shielding airports and aircraft from criminals, including hijackers, terrorists, insurgents and smugglers. The air security strategy has to be in concurrence with the national security and counter-terrorism policy. Thus, the objective of airport security will be to safeguard the passengers, crew, ground personnel, the general public and the airport infrastructure against unlawful acts according to the International Civil Aviation Organisation (ICAO) Standards and Recommended Practices as laid down in the Chicago Convention.

Presently, the security of Indian airports is managed by the Central Industrial Security Force (CISF), a paramilitary organisation, under the regulatory framework of the Bureau of Civil Aviation Security. In addition, the Airport Security Unit (ASU), a unit trained to counter unlawful interference with civil aviation, is deployed at every airport. Further, every airline has an aviation security force which is a separate department. The use of metal detectors, X-ray machines and backscatter X-ray scanners help in screening the travellers and detecting if they are carrying either weapons or items that could be used as weapons on board aircraft.

Throughout the world, there have been a few dozen airports that have instituted a version of a "trusted traveller programme". Proponents argue that security screening can be made more efficient by detecting the people that are threats, and then searching them. They argue that searching trusted, verified individuals should not take the amount of time it does. Critics argue that such programmes decrease security by providing an easier path to carry contraband through.[32] However, there is negligible prevention to check terrorists using different or fake passports to travel. For example, Paresh Barua, leader of ULFA, has been using a Bangladeshi passport to travel. Additionally, plastic surgery has made it easy for insurgents to change their appearance and get new passports.

The restaurants and kiosks at airports have started using plastic utensils instead of utensils made of glass to prevent these from being used as weapons. Non-passengers are not allowed inside the airports or sanitised areas, including airport ramps and operational spaces.

Aircraft carrying cargo still remain vulnerable as only a small proportion of air cargo is inspected. Additionally, airport employees can easily bypass security checkpoints when entering secure areas.

Thus, airport security needs to provide the first line of defence by making it difficult for would-be attackers to bring weapons or bombs into the airport.

India's concern over security of air space arose particularly after the Kandahar hijacking (1999). Further, between 1998 and 2001, the LTTE had managed to procure surface-to-air missiles from different sources (including the Pakistan-based terrorist group Harkat-ul-Mujahideen) and used them effectively.[33] The build-up of its air arm by the LTTE merited a reassessment of the security threat arising from the air as the terrorist organisation had attained potential for air strike.

There are possibilities that abandoned airstrips in the country could be used as bases by terrorists planning suicide strikes using small aircraft. In 2008, Indian Defence Minister AK Antony summoned the military chiefs to warn them to be prepared for attacks from the air and the sea in the wake of growing criticism over security after the Mumbai attacks.

With regard to airport security, much has been done. However, it will be difficult to prevent people travelling on fake passports. Securing the borders from air attacks by the terrorist groups will require enhanced air defence surveillance capability through procurement of additional low level transportable radars and additional radars, aerostats and airborne warning and control system (AWACS); the procurement of an integrated air command and control system must be expedited; measures must be adopted to counter the threat of intrusion from unmanned aerial vehicles (UAVs); and there is also a need to integrate civil and Indian Air Force resources for their optimum utilisation in this direction.

Conclusion

Indian borders are regarded as "hot borders". This requires India to have a proactive policy rather than a reactive policy to the issue. To have secure borders, there is a need to demarcate land and maritime borders with our neighbours. It is also important to have a separate department for border management to be created within the Ministry of Home Affairs that would deal solely with border security and border management. Additionally, separate and exclusive forces need to be created for border management and the code of "one border, one force" and the "single point control" may be adopted that will enforce the principle of accountability. Consequently, all paramilitary forces managing unsettled borders, particularly the LoC and LAC, should operate directly under the control of the army and there should be lateral induction from the army to the paramilitary forces so as to enhance their operational effectiveness. However, the BSF should have the responsibility for all the settled borders and the border guarding forces should have the responsibility bearing on internal security like preventing illegal immigration, carrying out anti-smuggling activities, checking infiltration and collection of intelligence.

India is situated between the "Golden Crescent" and the "Golden Triangle", the two famous drug peddling regions. Terrorist groups often work hand-in-hand with drug cartels. It is important to take strict measures to deal with the entry of narcotics, illegal immigrants, terrorists and arms by making strict laws to punish the criminals, by sanitising the border and by erecting border fencing, along with motorable roads close to the fence.

It is also necessary to establish closer relations with the border population to protect them from subversive propaganda. Consequently, the concept of village voluntary forces (VVF) should be promoted in the border districts and efforts should be made to facilitate legitimate trade. However, it is imperative to prevent unauthorised settlements along the borders and to initiate special development programmes.

There is a need for advancement in surveillance technology, particularly aerial and satellite imagery, which can help maintain a constant vigil and record along the LoC and LAC. In this regard, the integration of all national radar resources of the army, navy and air force must be progressed at a faster pace. In addition, it is mandatory to upgrade the country's technical, counter-intelligence, economic intelligence gathering and electronic capabilities, including coastal radar and interceptor boats. It would be advantageous to set up a specialised marine police in all coastal states and island territories. The police force should be appropriately trained and equipped with boats and weapons. In addition, there is a need to strengthen the BSF Water Wing in Gujarat and West Bengal. Fishermen watch groups may also be set up in each of the coastal states. Further, close cooperation and coordination between the navy and Coast Guard, in both war and peace-time, is required.

The unresolved border issues, a high level distrust with China and Pakistan, and porous borders with Nepal, Myanmar, and Bangladesh make it essential to develop effective and efficient land border management. Not taking adequate measures would make the task of anti-national forces that much easier. Finally, promoting regional cooperation, friendly relations with neighbouring countries and information sharing can provide for sound border management.

Notes

1. "Managing Borders of the Country," *Sainik Samachar*, Vol. 48, No. 21, 01 November 2001, http://mod.nic.in/samachar/nov1-01/html/ch6.htm, accessed on 10 February 2009.
2. Gurmeet Kanwal, "India's Borders," *Indian Defence Review*, Vol. 231, http://www.indiandefencereview.com/2008/10/indias-borders.html, accessed on 10 February 2009.
3. "Bangladeshis Have no Business to be in India," *The Times of India*, http://economictimes.indiatimes.com/News/PoliticsNation/Bangladeshis_have_no_business_to_be_in_India_says_PC/articleshow/3965314.cms, accessed on 10 February 2009.
4. Presently, Bangladesh Rifles (BDR), the force that used to guard the India-Bangladesh border on the Bangladesh side, has been disbanded after the February 2009 mutiny by the BDR men.
5. There are 111 Indian enclaves within Bangladesh and 51 Bangladeshi enclaves in India. In addition, there are 34 tracts of Indian land under the adverse possession of Bangladesh and 40 pieces of Bangladeshi land in India's adverse possession.

The enclaves were the result of the treaty between the Kingdom of Koch Bihar and the Mughals. During the 1947 partition, Koch Bihar was merged to India and Rangpur became part of East Pakistan, now Bangladesh. Soon after the independence of Bangladesh, both India and Bangladesh agreed to exchange the enclaves, but the issue could not be resolved. The residents of the enclaves live in extremely dire conditions with lack of social, economic, security and medical facilities. Although the residents of the respective enclaves can go to their countries after showing their identity cards and seeking permission from border guards, the people on both sides feel harassed and neglected by their respective government.

6. Uighurs form the majority in Xinjiang. Their ultimate ideological goal is the regrouping of all Muslims under a single state, the Caliphate. This Islamist network, which spans Central Asia, operates within an "Islamist corridor" that overlaps drug trafficking routes and facilitates the movement of militants, weapons and explosives. See Hayder Mili, "Xinjiang: An Emerging Narco-Islamist Corridor?" *Terrorism Monitor*, Vol. 3, Issue 8, http://www.jamestown.org/single/?no_cache=1&tx_ttnews%5Btt_news%5D=30287, accessed on 10 February 2009.
7. In the recent reports, police and intelligence officials said there could be up to 50 ULFA militants now holed up in China's Yunnan Province led by 'Lt' Partha Jyoti Gogoi. "ULFA Eyeing China for Shelter, Commander in China-Myanmar Border," *Thaindian News*, 29 November 2008, http://www.thaindian.com/newsportal/south-asia/ulfa-eyeing-china-for-shelter-commander-in-china-myanmar-border_100112644.html, accessed on 10 February 2009.
8. Ten meetings of the Sino-Indian Joint Working Group (SIJWG) and five of an expert group have taken place to determine where the LAC lies.
9. Gurmeet Kanwal, "Indian Border Security: Poor Management in Evidence," Institute of Peace and Conflict Studies, Issue Brief No. 55, October 2007, accessed on 10 February 2009.
10. "India, Nepal Vow to Fight Terrorism," *The Times of India*, 13 September 2004.
11. The CRZ was organised by the Nepal and Indian members of the Naxalite (the popular term for left wing extremism in India. It originated in Naxalbari, hence, the term "Naxal", in the state of West Bengal in the late 1960s) Movement, in a meeting at Siliguri in the Indian state of West Bengal during August 2001.
12. "India to Strengthen Vigil on Border with Myanmar," *India News Online*, 08 March 2002, http://news.indiamart.com/news-analysis/india-to-strengthen--

4145.html, accesssed on 10 February 2009.

13. Anuj Chopra, "Why India is Selling Weapons to Burma," *The Christian Science Monitor*, 23 July 2007, http://www.csmonitor.com/2007/0723/p04s01-wosc.html, accessed on 10 February 2009.
14. Group of Ministers (India), "Reforming the National Security System," http://mod.nic.in/newadditions/chapter-v.pdf, accessed on 10 February 2009.
15. "Killing of Sea Bird not a Big Blow to LTTE Shipping Operations," *The Sunday Times*, 18 February 1996, http://sundaytimes.lk/960218/oped/mil.htmt, accessed on 10 February 2009.
16. P K Ghosh, "Maritime Security Challenges in South Asia and the Indian Ocean: Response Strategies," Paper prepared for the Centre for Strategic and International Studies, 'American-Pacific Sealanes Security Institute Conference on Maritime Security in Asia', Honolulu, Hawaii, 18-20 January 2004, pp. 2-3.
17. JNPT is a pilot project which was picked because 58 percent of container traffic moves out of India from this port.
18. "In US, India Will Seal Sea Security Deal to Avoid Al Qaeda Dirty Bombs," *India Daily*, 10 February 2005, http://www.indiadaily.com/editorial/1572.asp, accessed on 10 February 2009.
19. Anil K Satapathy, "Maritime Terrorism: A New Challenge for Indian Navy," 12 March 2008, http://www.zeenews.com/exclusive/2008-12-03/488177news.html, accessed on 10 Feb 2009.
20. R S Vasan, "Creation of Marine Police Wings in the Maritime States of India," South Asia Analysis Group Paper No.1405, 06 June 2005.
21. "Dimensions of National Security: The Maritime Aspect," excerpted from the 11th Admiral R D Katari Memorial Lecture organised by the Delhi Charter of the Navy Foundation, http://mod.nic.in/samachar/dec15-01/html/ch2.htm, accessed on 10 February 2009.
22. Prabhakaran Paleri, *Role of the Coast Guard in the Maritime Security of India* (New Delhi: Knowledge World, 2004), p. 129.
23. V P Malik, "The Role of the Army in Maritime Counter-Terrorism," in Swati Parashar (ed.), *Maritime Counter-Terrorism: A Pan-Asian Perspective* (New Delhi: Dorling Kindersley, 2008), p. 20.
24. Maritime Commandos, *The Indian Navy Today*, http://www.bharat-rakshak.com/NAVY/Marines.html, accessed on 10 February 2009.
25. Ghosh, n. 16.
26. For details, see "India, Japan, US Foster Relationships During MALABAR," http://www.defencetalk.com/india-japan-us-foster-relationships-during-

malabar-18716/, accessed on 15 May 2009, accessed on 10 February 2009.

27. P S Das, "A View from the Sea," in Jasjit Singh (ed.), *Air Power and Joint Operations* (New Delhi: Knowledge World, 2002), p. 243.
28. Madhvendra Singh, "Maritime Counter-Terrorism: Navies of the World Unite," in Parashar, n. 24, pp. 7 & 9.
29. J N Roy, "The Role of the Police in Maritime Counter-Terrorism," in Parashar, n. 24, p. 29.
30. K R Singh, *Maritime Security for India* (New Delhi: New Century Publication, 2008), p. 50.
31. For details, see Bruce Schneier, "An Easy Path for Terrorists," http://www.schneier.com/essay-051.html, 24 August 2004 and Samidh Chakrabarti and Aaron Strauss, "Carnival Booth: An Algorithm for Defeating the Computer-Assisted Passenger Screening System," *First Monday*, Vol. 7, No.10, 2002.
32. R Hariharan, "LTTE Uses Air Power to Make Statement," *The Hindu*, 28 March 2007.
33. "LTTE Threat: India to Mobilise Additional Air Assets," Rediff.com, http://www.rediff.com/news/2007/may/08ltte.htm, accessed on 10 February 2009.

7

Strengthening the Combat Arm

S M Singh

The magnitude of our shared responsibilities should make our disagreements look small lest we will live in world of coercion.

– Anon

Introduction

India's security concerns are vast, varying from peace, economic development and social justice, to preservation of strategic autonomy and sovereignty of the country. India has six major religions, 52 major tribes, 6,400 castes and sub-castes with 1,654 minor/major languages. As per the Terrorism Index of Vulnerability for 186 countries (April 2007), Pakistan is at No 3, United States at No 4, Philippines at No 5, Afghanistan at No 6, Iraq at No 8, India at No 9, the United Kingdom and Sri Lanka are at No 10. Terrorism is a dynamic phenomenon with an ever changing dimension, scope and intensity of violent actions. Tackling terrorism would need a holistic approach with due integration of all players/members and articulation of comprehensive policies, that can adequately grapple with challenges arising from an unstable but rising economy, growing ethno-religious divides, lack of education or rise of educated unemployed to the accommodation of an increasing number of deprived and marginalised.

India, as a nation-state, requires a potent, agile and responsive national security apparatus that can meet the demands of its size, strategic location, and the prevailing security environment. India shares about 15,000 km of its land borders with seven countries. With 7,600 km of coastline, India has a maritime boundary with five countries. These realities exacerbate the problems of governance, especially due to external abetment of terrorism, internal divisive forces and other destabilising activities.[1] While reviewing the security apparatus and associated organisations, it would also be necessary to address the policies and functioning of India's political philosophy, police, legal system, bureaucracy and crime control establishments, including intelligence. In order to ensure peace and stability, it is imperative to optimally manage the combat forces and agencies responsible for peace and stability. Although India has reformed its higher defence organisation and management, there is lack of integration and coordination.[2]

To date, as per the Ministry of Home Affairs (MHA), there are 34 organisations responsible for disruptive activities in India.[3] The number is constantly on the rise and this excludes the sleeper cells and internationally organised groups.

In the new age of terrorism, India's security is not only dependent on the Governmnet of India and its various branches but on every single citizen of the country, in India or living abroad. It is our absolute duty to know, be aware of and use, our resources to help these agencies in order to help protect this country. We need to manage our resources and strengthen our entire system to safeguard the interests of every single Indian citizen, irrespective of his religious belief, colour, education, status, social motivation or language. Leaders must take interest in matters related to national security through structured briefings, informal interactions, workshops/seminars and debates during parliamentary sessions.

National security management recedes into the background in times of peace and is considered too delicate to be tampered with in times of war and proxy war. The Kargil experience, and the continuing proxy war, wherein 26/11 was only its most recent and blatant incident, justify a thorough review of the national governance and security system in its entirety. The Kargil Review Committee (KRC) also recommended an independent body of credible experts and think-tanks, national commissions or task forces to conduct studies pertaining to national security, in a holistic manner. The KRC and Group of Ministers (GoM) recommendations brought out four Task Forces – intelligence, defence management, internal security and border management – to be effective and efficient tools in governance.[4]

The causes of dilution of the security apparatus to function effectively are many and they lead to erosion in the discipline/ moral values of agencies dealing with internal security and stability. Inappropriate legislative, legal and administrative powers hamper the controlling abilities of the concerned organisations and, thus, contribute to the increased nature of violence and anti-national activities.[5]

National Security Environment: Salient Features

India is strategically located in relation to both continental Asia as well as the Indian Ocean region. India's geographical and topographical diversity, especially on its borders, poses unique challenges for our armed forces in terms of both equipment and training. India's peninsular shape provides a coastline of about 7,600 km and an exclusive economic zone (EEZ) of over two million sq km. The island territories in the east are 1,300 km away from the mainland, and physically much closer to Southeast Asia. Peninsular India is adjacent to one of the most vital sea lanes stretching from the Suez Canal and Persian Gulf to the Strait of Malacca through which much of the oil from the Gulf region transits. This is an area which has attracted superpower rivalries in the past and continues to see heightened activity of extra-regional navies on account of current global security concerns. India's size, strategic location, trade interests and security concerns extend from the Persian Gulf in the west to the Strait of Malacca in the east and from the Central Asian Republics in the north to near the equator in the south. In view of this, it is essential for the country to maintain a credible land, air and maritime force to safeguard its security interests.

Against the backdrop of democracy, secularism, social and economic development, India's internal security objectives could be as follows:

- Ensuring internal security as defined by law and enshrined in the Constitution.
- Protecting and preserving people and property against any unlawful threat.
- Protection against societal instability, religious and other forms of radicalism and extremism emanating from within and outside the country.
- Protection against use or threat of weapons of mass destruction.
- Development of technologies and allied equipment having a bearing on India's internal security.
- Promoting cooperation and understanding with neighbouring countries on internal security.
- Pursuing strategic dialogues related to internal security and development with regional and extra-regional nations.
- Promoting good governance, thereby ensuring peace, prosperity and confidence of people.

Factors Influencing the Security Environment in 2020

The factors which are likely to influence the security environment in 2020 are as follows:[6]

- The twin revolutions of rising expectations and information and communications will continue.
- The fundamental ideological conflict between India and Pakistan is unlikely to be resolved without a major socio-political change in Pakistan.
- Territorial disputes with neighbours that have defied resolution for 50 years may not lend themselves to an early solution.
- Religious extremism and radical politics will continue to have an adverse impact on our core values.

- Rising dependence on energy imports will make us increasingly vulnerable, economically, as well as diplomatically.
- Public opinion, both domestic and international, and the media will be increasingly important forces in international affairs.
- The international order is likely to evolve into a polycentric configuration, with its centre of gravity shifting increasingly to Asia, which will include seven out of the ten largest economies and six out of the eight nuclear weapon states.
- The increasing economic and military strength of China may pose a serious challenge to India's security unless adequate measures are taken.

Future Threats: Threats to a society or a nation in the age of new terrorism are becoming more complex, pronounced and quick to manifest, causing serious destruction and disruptions, including psychological impact. The nature of such threats could take forms as given below:

- Ideological extremism.
- Enhanced operation capabilities.
- Organisation networks.
- Trans-national associations.
- Non-state actors.
- Increased weapon lethality
- Mass casualties.
- Economic disruption.
- Exploited media.

Force Restructuring: Why is it Necessary?

The perceived security environment and future threats mandates a review of national force structures in order to effectively meet external and internal threats.[7]

One of the crucial elements of such an approach should be to understand the dynamics of support networks and factors such as ideological motivation, financial inducements and various illegal entities that form such a network. There is also a need to review the response mechanism of the security forces, including their skill, attitude, preparedness and coordination with other relevant agencies. The changing profile of terrorism as enabled by globalisation and evident in the seamless connectivity between some terrorist groups and other types of non-state actors suggests that there is a need to restructure forces to combat acts of terrorism. Meticulous planning, the ability to address multiple targets simultaneously with the tools of modern technology, along with the undermentioned factors demand suitably organised and equipped forces:

- Global networking of terrorist organisations.
- Multiple dimensions with respect to funding, support and information.
- Global propaganda through a variety of agencies e.g. TV networks and the Internet.
- Innovative planning, selection of targets and disregard to personal safety.
- Changing social expectations i.e. human rights and fundamental freedoms.

Besides, the changing profile of terrorism, there is also a need to understand the terrorist planning cycle (TPC) for comprehensive force structuring, force application and related policies. A TPC involves the following stages:

- Aim.
- Overall policy on terrorism.
- Broad target selection.
- Intelligence and surveillance.
- Specific target selection.
- Pre-attack surveillance and planning.
- Attack rehearsals.
- Coordination with support elements (if applicable).
- Action on objective.
- Escape and evasion.

Strengthening the combat arm of the nation, especially the police force, in view of the changing nature, area, and magnitude of threat, is necessary. The police force needs to undergo significant modernisation if it is to cope with the challenge of local and international terrorism. The simultaneity of action demands a coordinated response from security, legal, financial and administrative authorities. It is imperative to educate and manage the information hungry environment, and shaping of the perception of the masses and the international community. We need to ensure greater involvement of the public and the political leaders. Therefore, the security apparatus of the country should be made responsive, combat-oriented, motivated, accountable, legally and politically correct, versatile, and physically and mentally mobile, with facilities for continuous and updated, if not-real time, flow of intelligence.

Organisations so tailored, on a priority, would minimise fresh terrorist incidents. Meanwhile, expeditiously tackling previous cases would create an environment of deterrence and security. This, however, would also demand a responsive public, especially when there are large inadequacies in administration. While discussing force restructuring, it is imperative to educate and sensitise the political leadership and organisations with regard to the security implications and effects of terrorism, as also and how, if controlled, it will benefit the nation.[8] It is time to be morally right as responsible citizens of a transforming nation or else, future generations will never forgive us.

Similar Organisations of Other Nations may be Examined: France has two unique mechanisms not found in any other country and which we need to consider like the Estate-Major Particular (EMP) and the Institute des Hautes Etudes de Defense National (IHEDN). The former is an elite group of high-ranking military officers located in the president's office to advise him. The latter is a prestigious think-tank whose findings are not publicised but made available to the French NSC equivalent.[10]

Legislative Support to Institutionalise the NSC: The NSC has been established under an executive order. Its approval, functioning and continuity need to be sanctioned by an Act of Parliament like in the USA. Some of the legislative clauses that need to be incorporated with reference to our past experiences of national security decision-making are:[11]

- The Prime Minister must consult the NSC.
- NSC Directives must be as per decisions of the PM for accountability and legality.
- NSC Directives must be signed by the PM.

Hence, it is recommended that the NSC should have direct control of intelligence agencies. Representatives of armed forces at intelligence and operational levels must be in the NSAB Committee. Necessary legislative support from the PM's Office for due accountability is an imperative.[12]

Unified Command Concept: In Assam and Jammu & Kashmir there are civil–military joint organisations named as Strategic and Core Groups. The former being headed by the chief minister of the state and the latter by the military commander. The joint organisations are functioning well and effectively. The same model can be adopted by states on internal security matters.

Review and Strengthening of Combat Organisations: In view of the existence of a large number of security organisations, it may not be prudent to raise yet another organisation i.e. National Intelligence Agency (NIA), which essentially is a post-attack investigative agency lacking in 'teeth' i.e. executing powers. It may be prudent to incorporate the National Security Guards (NSG) and Advance Research Centre (ARC) with the NIA as an interim measure along with a legal component for expeditious decisions through 'fast track' provisions. Such an amalgamation must be done through an 'ordinance' We may need to audit the efficacy of the National Technical Research Organisation (NTRO) and may incorporate with the NIA like the Multi-Agency Centre (MAC) for purposes of greater accountability. This will also help to make up the manpower and equipment deficiencies. The NIA should be given charge of investigating all terror-related activities like funding, *hawala* transactions, fake currency, drug-trafficking and misuse of communication equipment like cyber net and satellite phones.[13]

At the execution level, the Special Investigation Team (SIT), Anti Terrorist Squad (ATS)/Special Operations Group (SOG)/ Special Task Force (STF)/Greyhounds/COBRA need to adopt better procedures of cohesion, coordination, and integration, and to understand their vulnerabilities. The potential of these organisations must be exploited for the right cause rather than for settling political scores. There could be various models for command and control. Certain basic essentials for these are:[14]

- Representatives from the MoD, Integrated Defence Staff (IDS) and MHA (as appropriate).
- Empowered decision-making/taking body.
- A nominated list of personnel on the panel to take decisions, if required.
- Nodal point (operation centre) with adequate redundancy for meetings, with video conferencing facility and other communication facilities.
- Information technology (IT) set-up with integrated information reference facility at the centre and state levels.
- Joint operations centre with suitably qualified/equipped staff on 24 x 7 basis.
- Security hardened establishments, irrespective of designation/ status of office bearers.

There are seven central police organisations (CPOs) involved in internal security and maintenance of law and order as part of the MHA security apparatus. Besides these, the 28 states and seven union territories (UTs) also have their police/security organisations. Furthermore, the MoD too has various organisations to support the cause of internal security, stability and maintenance of law and order. There are 17 divisions under the MHA that are responsible for peace and stability, either directly or indirectly.[15] A large set-up can only delay the decision-making process and given that today is the world of information technology, software and solutions/option, delays cannot be acceptable since they could cause destruction, as was seen in Mumbai on 26 November 2008. The inference is obvious: an organisation which is compact, coordinated and responsive, flat and not hierarchical, bereft of red tape and bureaucratic and political strings is the need of the hour. Finally, such an organisation should be all encompassing, be it in intelligence, execution, administration (including medical), legal, training and investigation elements.

An organisation which could meet the above requirements will have to be a national level force, with deputations at the state level and having national, regional and international language experts. Such an organisation would have to have stability and continuity for the staff to be responsive. It may be named the Internal Security Agency (ISA) with a Joint Operations Centre (JOC), having the following wings:

- Research Wing (including electronic surveillance for communication and non-communication activities), along with forensic and criminology sections.
- Cyber Wing (to include cyber and space).
- Intelligence and Investigation Wing (including imaging facility).
- Psychological Operations Wing.
- Combat Wing (including mobility resources.)
- Legal Wing.
- Monitoring Wing (especially current activities) with language experts and related software.
- Finance and Audit Wing.
- Training Wing (including historical section having lessons from various operations).
- A Medical Cell for rehabilitation purposes.
- Administration Wing.

The Internal Security Force (ISF) will also have a vigilance and monitoring committee, with representatives from each wing, having interchangeable appointments. The organisation will need to have a Rehabilitation Wing to look after the welfare and reemployment of people who are boarded out on medical grounds. The organisation will also need to continuously review the interests of staff relating to pay and allowances, domestic stability, career protection (excluding discipline cases), age criteria, extension of service, etc. as part of its human resources (HR) policy. A similar model should be organised for the state security apparatus and named State Security Guards (SSG) with provision for deputations/ cross attachments amongst the ISF and SSG. The procedure for requisitioning of defence forces needs to be reviewed and suitable provisions must be incorporated for utilisation of their service in monitoring, execution, training, advisory, post-incident revival and recovery before routine governance is put in place.

Coordination and Integration: There is no institutionalised mechanism for coordination or objective-oriented interaction between the agencies and consumers at different levels. Similarly, there is no mechanism for tasking the agencies, monitoring their performance, accountability, responsibility and reviewing their records to evaluate their quality. Nor is there any oversight of the overall functioning of the agencies. These are all standard features the world over. In the absence of such procedures, the government and the nation do not know whether they are getting value for money. The development of country/regional specialisation, along with associated language skills is, therefore, an imperative.

Uniformed forces, other than forces under the MoD, are larger in numbers but due to different names/organisations, they appear lesser and smaller. There is a large amount of duplication of such human resources in utilisation and management. It may be prudent to review these organisations. An idea worth considering may be to integrate all forces and organisations, including intelligence agencies, to report to a single office under a single ministry [i.e. either MoD or MHA, with deputations from the Ministry of External Affairs

(MEA)]. Under the ministry, there could be forces grouped in two categories i.e. National Armed Forces (NAF) having the Defence Services, Special Frontier Force and Border Security Force as one entity; and the rest under a second category of Internal Security Force (ISF) comprising the Central Reserve Police Force (CRPF) including Rapid Action Force (RAF)/Rapid Operations Force (ROF), Indo-Tibetan Border Police (ITBP), Central Industrial Security Force (CISF), Sashastra Seema Bal (SSB), etc. The resources so formed will provide good potential and flexibility for security tasks. To effect seamless integration and coordination, the NAF and ISF will function under the NSC and be represented by their respective chiefs. Suitable representatives could be nominated to cater for any contingency/absence of nominated persons. The NSC will be a group of ministers, defence chiefs and bureaucrats functioning under the PM. Every member will be accountable for all decisions. Great advantages to the country will accrue from reorganisation, such as maximisation of existing resources, including manpower, simple and direct command and control, and greater transparency with due accountability.[16]

The combat arm, today, is ill structured and without adequate technology and training to deal with the varied threats in relation to internal security. There is general agreement that in the light of the new situations of proxy war and large scale terrorism that the country faces, the role and the tasks of the paramilitary and police forces have to be redefined, particularly with reference to command and control and leadership functions. They need to be trained to much higher standards of performance and need to be better equipped to deal with terrorist threats. The possibility of adopting an integrated manpower policy for the armed forces, paramilitary forces and the central police forces merits examination.

Border management has become immensely more complex over the years. It is now being handled by the Assam Rifles, the Border Security Force, SSB, and the Indo-Tibetan Border Police. Border fencing in Punjab and Jammu and Kashmir (J&K) has produced positive results. Along the Indo-Bangladesh border, vested interests have come in the way of effective border management.[17] If the country is to acquire increased capabilities for area surveillance, the present structure, arms, equipment and procedures for border patrolling must be reviewed. The issue needs a detailed study in order to evolve force structures and procedures that ensure improved border management in order to bring about a reduction, if not elimination, of the inflow of narcotics, illegal migrants, terrorists and arms.

Police Reforms

Existing Police Force: According to the MHA Annual Report 2007, as on 31 December 2007, there were about 25 lakh policemen under central and state governments, including a total of 474 Battalions (Bn) of paramilitary forces and CPOs (viz BSF – 157 Bns, CRPF –185 Bns, ITBP – 45 Bns, SSB – 41Bns and AR – 46 Bns). In 1970, a scheme of India Reserve (IR) Bns was introduced when a need was felt for capacity building in the states to deal with emerging problems. The government approved the raising of additional 35 IR Bns during the period 2007-08 to 2009-10.[18] As per a survey, India's police force is grossly inadequate i.e. 142 policemen per one lakh people – one of the lowest in the world.

The report published by the National Crime Records Bureau compared the crime rate from 1953 to 2006. The report noted that burglary declined over a period of 53 years by 38 percent (from 1,47,379 in 1953 to 91,666 in 2006), whereas murder has increased by 231 percent (from 9,803 in 1953 to 32,481 in 2006). Kidnapping has increased by 356 percent (from 5,261 in 1953 to 23,991 in 2006), robbery by 120 percent (from 8,407 in 1953 to 18,456 in 2006) and riots by 176 percent (from 20,529 in 1953 to 56,641 in 2006).[19]

In today's environment, the police is suffering from a poor image in the eyes of the public. The reasons for this are as follows:

- Indifferent attitude.
- Unnecessary use of force.
- Hostile reception at police stations.

- Bias.
- Lethargic in reaching the scene of crime.
- Indifferent attitude to information.
- Misuse of official machinery and position.
- Harassment and extortion.
- Unjustifiable arrests.
- Improper investigations.
- Ineffective in matter of property and related crimes.
- Third degree methods employed in handling suspects.

There are also politico-administrative and departmental hurdles, some of which are listed to be addressed while formulating policy on police reforms:

- Feeling of victimisation.
- Poor human rights policies.
- Poor standard of training.
- Lack of public support.

Sanctioned and Actual Strength of Police Forces

Sl. No.	States/UTs.	Total	
		Sanctioned	**Actual**
1.	Andhra Pradesh	92,106	NR
2.	Arunachal Pradesh	6,108	5,239
3.	Assam	55,952	46,541
4.	Bihar	74,188	52,075
5.	Chhattisgarh	36,987	25,412
6.	Goa	4,540	4,178
7.	Gujarat	72,723	53,451
8.	Haryana	52,109	50,524
9.	Himachal Pradesh	14,722	12,033
10.	Jammu & Kashmir	68,125	NR
11.	Jharkhand	51,081	40,663
12.	Karnataka	76,997	57,509
13.	Kerala	43,111	39,022
14.	Madhya Pradesh	76,365	NR

15.	Maharashtra*	1,82,195	NR
16.	Manipur	16,771	13,339
17.	Meghalaya	9,347	8,550
18.	Mizoram	7,874	7,233
19.	Nagaland	31,407	31,305
20	Orissa	45,156	38,752
21	Punjab	71,859	63,641
22	Rajasthan	71,664	51,051
23	Sikkim	3,522	2,854
24	Tamil Nadu*	98,683	NR
25	Tripura	25,504	19,367
26.	Uttar Pradesh	1,66,126	1,50,134
27.	Uttarkhand	20,896	14,591
28.	West Bengal	82,593	65,944
29.	A&N lands	2,901	2,750
30	Chandigarh	4,628	4,395
31	D&N Haveli	208	185
32	Daman & Diu	246	226
33.	Delhi	62,420	66,275
34	Lakshadweep	349	302
35	Pondicherry*	3,246	NR
	All India	16,32,651	9,27,541**

* As on 01.01.2006

** All India total of actual excludes the States of Andhra Pradesh, Jammu & Kashmir, Madhya Pradesh, Maharashtra, Tamil Nadu & Pondicherry

NR – Data not received

Source: "States/CPFs Police Strength," Bureau of Police Research and Development (BPR&D), 01 January 2007, p. 35

Suggested Reforms: The police is an important instrument in the management of administrative grievances, to maintain peace in society and to take care of any aberrations in human behaviour which could be in contravention of societal norms. In the present scenario, the police is feared or best avoided as much possible due to its image of corruption, inhumane attitude and non-professionalism.

The police organisation at the Centre and state levels should have two sets of components: one, to be people friendly and approachable, and the other, the armed component for maintenance of law and order. The former should generate confidence and trust amongst the public, which would not only facilitate safety, security and tranquillity, but would also generate goodwill and intelligence of varied kinds, which in turn would provide timely indicators of any misadventure by anti-social/anti-national elements.

The Combat Wing should be organised at the state and Centre levels to undertake tasks/manage situations which affect the peace and harmony. All assistance to their operations will be provided by the 'people-friendly' police who essentially would be 'beat-policemen' monitoring and gathering inputs of any anti-social/national nature.

The Police Reforms at first instance must replace the vintage Police Act of 1861 by a new Police Act. The old Police Act does not dwell on the accountability of the police to the community, does not mention any statement of mission of the police, nor is there any emphasis on the public responsibility of the police in a democratic society. The idea is not to make the police more powerful through the proposed reforms, but to make the police forces clearly accountable to the people and the law enforcement work, conscious of their duty to protect human rights by functioning in a non-partisan manner, to work with a spirit of service and to be people-oriented, and to build up a force which would be in a position to protect the democratic fabric of the Constitution. While reviewing the Police Act and formulating a new Act, the following aspects must be considered:

- Training of police cadres to be done in general and thereafter specialisation with regular refresher courses and an evaluation-based philosophy.
- The age profile of the Anti-terrorist Force personnel needs a review i.e. a younger profile will be more beneficial.
- Recruitment of personnel should be done with better education qualification, psychological and fitness standards.

- Selection/training should include IT related knowledge/ training.
- The age profile of personnel at field level should be such that the personnel can respond suitably to the situation
- The police needs to be apolitical. In fact, its purpose must be to maintain peace, law and order and harmony, without political interference/involvement.
- At the functional level, the policemen should have a buddy or a team system, for knowledge/situational back-up as well as safety and security of the cadres.
- There is a necessity to make the police organisation more accountable to the public. The ethos and ethics need a thorough review.
- The promotion policy should be such that only qualified and capable persons can grow in the organisation. Also, the caste-based reservation/promotion should be discontinued to make the system efficient and credible.
- Regular refresher capsules are a must in view of the changing nature and techniques of crime.
- Legally, there should be no suspension for defaulters on disciplinary grounds; in fact, defaulting individual should simply be removed from the service after the due process.
- The Law and Order wing should be separate from the Investigation Wing.
- The functional assets are required to be improved.

Similarly, various policy and legal provisions in respect of central police organisations and paramilitary forces must be reviewed, approved and applied.

Training: It is the bedrock of any organisational performance. The training of police personnel could be categorised under basic, special, orientation, or refresher courses. Basic orientation and refresher training could be done under the state training establishments, whereas the specialised training could be under the Centre – including refresher courses in specialised categories.

The training academies in the States and at the Centre need to be reorganised as state-of-the art institutions for new courses, mid-career programmes and in-service courses, besides workshops, seminars and orientation capsules. The establishments must also be made responsible for tests/evaluation, qualification at various ranks. The evaluation progress must incorporate specialised courses pertaining to intelligence collection, collation, and analysis, interrogation, forensic, cyber and info warfare, network-centric communication, crime, jungle warfare, counter-terrorism, maintenance of law and order and riot control. There could be super specialisation in white collar crimes, DNA finger printing techniques, explosives and firearms, crime scene management, media interaction and reporting, credit card frauds, toxicology and detection of poison in food articles, neutron activation analysis (NAA) techniques, handling of nuclear, biological, chemical (NBC) agents, ballistics gun shot residue (GSR) analysis, computer forensics, sleeper cell detection and crime against women. Besides these, the training capsules on winning hearts and minds could also be planned.

The syllabi or scope needs to be reviewed regularly at a joint organisation composed of police and military establishments like the Bureau of Police Research and Development (BPR&D) including the Psychological Department. The major advantage will be coordination and refinement in performance/outcome. BPR&D will be interacting with the MoD establishment for coordination and integration of training. This is critical because any organisation that seeks to be professionally updated requires constant monitoring, and, hence, the personnel should be put through regular examination/performance tests.

Weapons, Equipment and Mobility: The department of police certainly needs to upgrade the inventory of weapons and equipment like automatic assault rifles e.g. MP-5, AK47, collapsible ladders, bullet-proof jackets and helmets, explosives to make holes in concrete structures, stun grenades, long range sniper rifles and light anti-material rifles along with suitable communication systems, equipment to identify friend or foe and see through capability at night and under smoke. In fact, a suitably equipped force can nip anti-national situations in the bud. Swift means of mobility through rail, road and air is an imperative to make the force effective at the place of incident.

Police Cyber and Communication Network: Network-satellite/land-based systems need to be established with adequate redundancy at national and state levels. The facility needs to be duly integrated for communications, real-time exchange/online sharing of data, with digitised maps for spotting, tracking, guidance, planning and crime-related information.

Anti-terror Laws

The Parliament has passed the National Investigation Agency Bill 2008 and amended the Unlawful Activities (Prevention) Act (UAPA) with broad unanimity. The amendments may provide some relief to law enforcement agencies but a comprehensive legal framework is still lacking to defend against, prevent, and punish the perpetrators of terrorism. A stable, comprehensive, all India anti-terrorist legislation, having adequate safeguards against abuse needs to be put in place where nobody is excused or has immunity. The anti-terror law should aim at widening its network to tackle various facets of terrorism. The new Act should include treating confessions before the police as evidence. The Administrative Reforms Commission's 8th Report of June 2008 on 'Combating Terrorism-Protecting by Righteousness' also known as the Moily Committee Report needs to be incorporated without any politico-bureaucratic tampering.[20]

It may be interesting to note that there has been an overall drop in conviction from 20 percent to 5–10 percent, despite the ever increasing crime rate. This reflects inadequacies or criminalisation and politicisation of the legal system. In India, there is a requirement of enacting a 'law' which is without political colour, and is efficient and effective, with the provision that any one misusing the law will also be subjected to punishment.

Provisions are required for quicker interrogation, minimum period of remands/jail while undergoing interrogation/trial, and immediate notification to relatives of arrests and whereabouts of the suspect/accused. Issues related to religion or ethnicity having linkages to the act of terror are to be duly incorporated. Laying down of responsive and acceptable timelines is essential for any kind of law to be effective.

Under the Unlawful Activities (Prevention) Act (UAPA), the period of detention without bail has been increased from 90 days to 180 days as the investigating agencies face difficulties in completing the probe within the stipulated 90 days time-frame. However, there is another side to this point. "Security concerns should never be used to jeopardise people's basic human rights," says Asia Pacific Programme Deputy Director at Amnesty International, Madhu Malhotra.[21] The flaws within the Indian police system allow torture to routinely happen and it often casts doubt on the confessions made voluntarily. In the UK, where confessions to the police are admissible, provided they are not coerced or induced, the question of admissibility is decided in a separate 'mini trial' within the trial. Only those confessions that fall under elaborate judicial principles are admissible in the trial. Even in the US, any confessions made in violation of procedures or made under duress are not admissible. The danger associated with allowing police confessions is that this may lead to police complacency and inadequate investigations. The confessional statement often becomes the *piece de resistance* of the police case and works as an excuse to ignore the need for collecting other evidence.

The new law is meant for Indians involved in terror acts. A few suggestions to make anti-terror laws more effective and efficient are as follows:

- It may be prudent to treat those who abet anything related to disturbances and having linkages with terrorism under this law, without exception.
- Foreigners should be denied bail until they are proven innocent.

- The legal provisions under UAPA should be legally correct rather than beneficial to an individual or an organisation, as being experienced, wherein ruling governments through various committees should draft and approve policy provisions and their scope of application.
- Fast track courts should be created for early disposal of cases.

Although the UAPA has taken into consideration the existing resolutions of the United Nations' Security Council for banning any militant organisation or freezing its assets, presently it extends the ban on any outfit which has already been prohibited by the world body. The amended UAPA suggests that if there is any Indian national involved in a terror-related case, he/she cannot be released on bail or on his/her own bond unless the public prosecutor has been given an opportunity of being heard on the application for such release.

The why, how, when and where of anti-national agencies and application of law must be suitably defined. Various aspects which need to be covered under the laws are as follows:

- Scope of law i.e. all issues directly or indirectly related to terrorism.
- Interrogation and Investigation.
- Arrests/apprehensions.
- Immunity against what and to whom.
- Punishment, bail and bail denial policy.
- Imprisonment and fast track litigation process.
- Career/job protection of people involved in investigations.
- Provisions to seal accounts.
- Policy for abetters and cyber crimes.
- Policy with regard to demographic changes: people and authorities.
- Resettlement of displaced people.

Conclusion

In view of factors influencing the national security environment and changing contours of future threats, i.e. ideological extremism and enhanced operational capabilities having trans-national networked terrorist organisations, it is imperative to review the higher control organisation, including the existing forces, in totality. It may be prudent to examine the internal security set-up of other nations. Constitutional, legal and administrative reforms are absolutely essential to counter future threats.

The security threats to the country can be minimised/neutralised by seamless integration and coordination of all resources, encompassing legal and administrative functions, combined with good governance, inclusive development, accountability and a vigilant citizen and media. A responsible leadership having mental clarity and vision with the ability to take decisions in the interest of the public and the nation can defeat terrorism in any form.

Notes

1. Government of India, Ministry of Defence, "Assistance to Civil Authorities," http://mod.nic.in/assistcivilauth/welcome.html, accessed on 23 February 2009.
2. Ravi Nanda, *India's Security: Changed Perspectives* (New Delhi: Lancer, 2005), p. 153.
3. Government of India, Ministry of Home Affairs, "Banned Organisations," http://www.mha.nic.in/uniquepage.asp?ID_PK=292, accessed on 23 February 2009.
4. Kargil Review Committee, *From Surprise to Reckoning: Kargil Review Committee Report* (New Delhi: Sage, 2000), pp. 253-54.
5. Vijay Kapoor, "Good Governance: Key to Stablity and Economic Development of the Nation," in P C Dogra (ed.), *Threat to Security: How Secured is India from Within* (New Delhi: Manas, 2007), p. 54
6. S P Gupta, *India Vision 2020: The Report* (New Delhi: Government of India, 2004), p. 88.
7. Nanda, n. 2, p. 155.
8. Ibid., p. 166.
9. Subhash Kapila, "India's National Security Council: A Critical Review," South Asia Analysis Group, 10 May 2000, http://www.southasiaanalysis.org/papers2/paper123.html, accessed on 23 February 2009.
10. Ibid.

11. Ibid.
12. Ibid.
13. "Overhauling the Police," *India Today*, 19 January 2009, p. 44.
14. Nanda, n. 2, p. 167.
15. Government of India, Ministry of Home Affairs, "Organisational Setup," http://www.mha.nic.in/uniquepage.asp?Id_Pk=277, accessed on 23 February 2009.
16. Nanda, n. 2, p. 151.
17. Ibid., p.167.
18. Government of India, Ministry of Home Affairs, "Police Forces," *Annual Report 2007-08,* p. 77.
19. Government of India, National Crime Records Bureau, "Crime in India - Snapshots 1953-2006," http://ncrb.nic.in/CII2006/cii-2006/Snapshots%20 1953-2006.pdf, accessed on 23 February 2009.
20. Government of India, Second Administrative Reforms Commission, "Combating Terrorism: Protecting by Righteousness," Eighth Report, June 2008.
21. "India: New Anti-Terror Laws Would Violate International Human Rights Standards," *Amnesty International*, http://www.amnesty.org/en/for-media/press-releases/india-new-anti-terror-laws-would-violate-international-human-rights-stan, accessed on 05 February 2009.

8

CREDIBLE INTELLIGENCE

S C Meston

Introduction

Timely, complete and credible intelligence is a critical requirement for national security in general, and for counter-terrorism operations in particular. Due to the complexities involved in its collection and analysis, intelligence is mostly incomplete, untimely, not credible or overloaded with unnecessary information. It also suffers from ambiguity in interpretation caused by individual or organisational biases and distortions.

Many intelligence agencies are involved in acquiring and disseminating intelligence, providing analysis of the ground situation, key players and their collaborators, their dispositions and likely intentions. Analysis of likely intentions is the most tedious and difficult, as also the most contentious, task.

Presently, India has a large number of intelligence agencies but lacks an apex body to effectively integrate their diverse expertise and capabilities. We need to be able to work horizontally rather than confine ourselves in a cylindrical approach.

Intelligence Agencies

The primary function of the Research and Analysis Wing (R&AW) is collection of external intelligence, counter-terrorism and covert operations. In addition, it is also responsible for obtaining and analysing information about foreign governments, corporations, and persons in order to advise the policy-makers.

The IB (Intelligence Bureau) is responsible for collecting intelligence within India and also executing counter-intelligence and counter-terrorism tasks. The IB comprises employees also from law enforcement agencies, mostly from the Indian Police Service and the military. In addition to domestic intelligence responsibilities, the IB is particularly tasked with intelligence collection in border areas.

The Defence Intelligence Agency (DIA) was established post Kargil 1999, to coordinate the intelligence activities of the three defence services and act as a single point of contact for the armed forces with the Joint Intelligence Committee (JIC).

The National Technical Research Organisation (NTRO) is dedicated to the collection of technical intelligence (TECHINT). While the exact nature of the operations conducted by NTRO is classified, it deals with research on imagery and communications, using various platforms. Beginning with R&AW's Aviation Research Centre (ARC) assets, NTRO is rapidly expanding and strengthening its intelligence capabilities. The NTRO is now one more agency that has been added to the already existing organisations engaged in collection of technical intelligence. The IB, R&AW and the Signals Intelligence Directorate continue to maintain autonomous TECHINT units.

Besides these, the state police forces, the CPOs (central police organisations), and paramilitary forces have their own set-up to acquire intelligence.

Coordinating Agencies

The Joint Intelligence Committee (JIC) under the Cabinet Secretariat is responsible for coordinating activities between R&AW, IB and DIA and analysing intelligence inputs received therefrom. With the establishment of the National Security Council (NSC), the role of the JIC has been merged with the NSC. As a part of the third tier of the NSC, the JIC consists of experts on several issues, who analyse intelligence inputs and coordinate the functioning of intelligence agencies. The NSCS (National Security Council Secretariat) provides secretariat support to the work of the NSC, SPG (Strategic Policy Group) and NSAB (National Security Advisory Board). The SPG, headed by the Cabinet Secretary and consisting of the professional heads of the ministries concerned with national security and the chiefs of the intelligence agencies and the armed forces, works out policy/decision options and submits them to the NSC for consideration.

To have an overall hub for counter-terrorism efforts, a plan to create the Multi-Agency Centre (MAC) was proposed by the high-level Kargil Committee. MAC, along with state-level subsidiaries called SMACs, runs and operates a national counter-terrorism database, to identify operational priorities, and build the capabilities needed to execute them. In turn, MAC has to be fed by state-level police-intelligence Joint Task Forces. Ground-level intelligence work would have been carried out by Inter-State Intelligence Support Teams reporting to MAC. MAC was conceived on the pattern of the US National Counter-Terrorism Centre, and is responsible for the joint analysis of intelligence flowing from different quarters and coordinating relevant follow-up actions.

Post-26/11 the NIA (National Investigation Agency) was raised with the purpose of achieving convergence and synergy of multiplicity of agencies. According to Ajit Doval, former head of IB, the NIA, as the name suggests, is purely an investigating agency for post strike investigation. It does not bring us anywhere closer to preventing a strike. On the contrary, it adds one more stand-alone platform with no structural integration or operational unification. As a post-event investigation agency, at its best, it might marginally increase conviction rates or ensure enhanced punishment to a few *jehadis*. Working at a suicidal level of motivation, the *jehadis* may find it amusing. Had this agency existed before the Mumbai carnage, none of the shortcomings that came to light would have been minimised. It would not have ensured improved intelligence integration or action oriented dissemination, better preemptive or preventive response, etc. Rather than ending the turf war, there would have been one more agency involved. They might be interrogating Ajmal Kasab, a little better but the real masterminds would have still remained beyond their reach and jurisdiction. Legal actions are important but, at the end of the day, the war against terrorism would neither be won nor lost in the courts of law.

US 'War on Terror' has not weakened Al Qaeda (Global Poll) Participants (23,937 adult citizens from 23 countries)

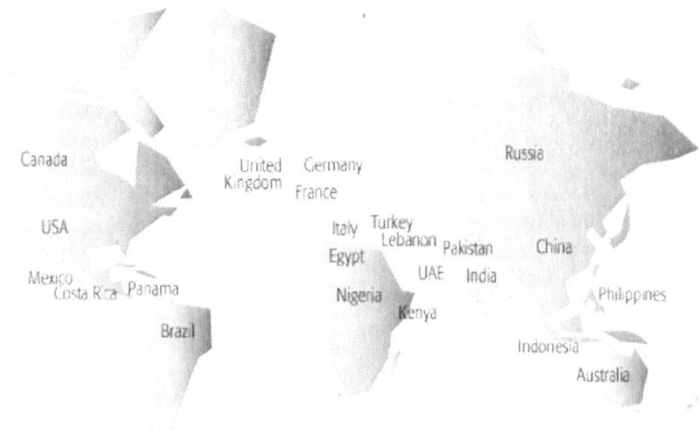

Results

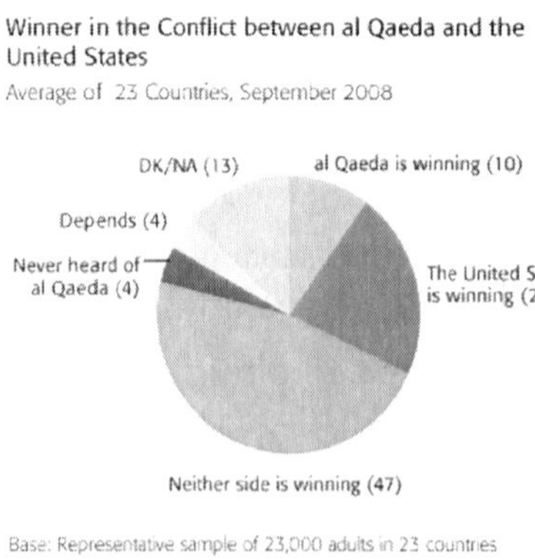

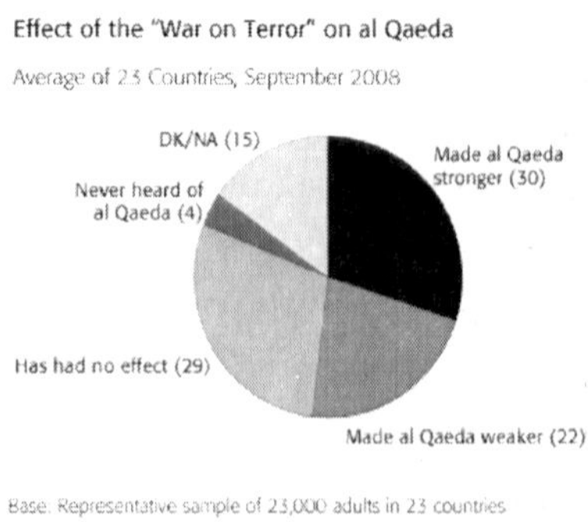

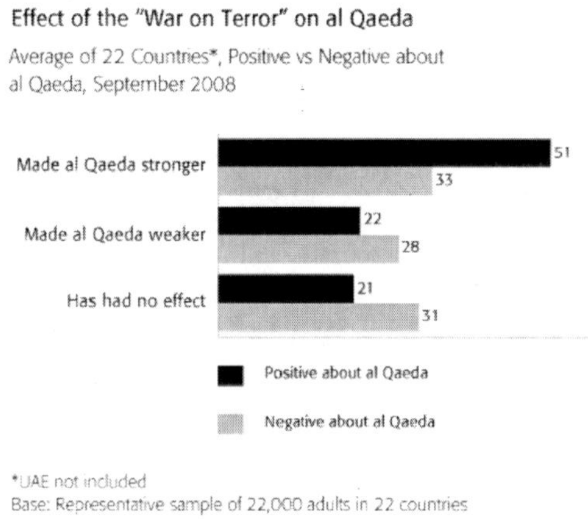

Source: BBC World Service, GlobeScan and Program on International Policy Attitudes, University of Virginia, 8 July-12 September 2008, http://www.globescan.com/news_archives/bbc_al_qaeda/

Weaknesses

The Cabinet Secretary, who presides over the SPG meetings and takes the necessary follow-up action, has very little control over the functioning of the JIC. The JIC is headed by one of the deputy national security advisers (DNSA), an officer of the rank of Secretary to the government. He/she is accountable to the NSA and not to the Cabinet secretary.

The nature of organised crime has changed significantly in scope and dimension. Collaboration between terrorists, local criminals, narcotics distributors, arms smugglers and divisive elements in society is commonplace. Intelligence targeting of these elusive and dangerous criminals is a difficult task, especially as it involves trans-national and trans-state networks running across many borders. There are voids in intelligence sharing between national and state agencies. Data banks, if being maintained, are not known to neighbouring or affected states. "Reluctance, and even refusal, to share information" that could prevent attacks "sends a message to terrorists that they can breach Indian security, that they can come in here and do anything."[1]

MAC is staffed only by a skeleton crew of Intelligence Bureau personnel. While MAC does operate a database, powered by bare-bones computer systems designed in-house, it has no real-time links to the state police forces. A few SMACs are in existence, one in each metropolitan centre, again run by a skeleton staff. Due to inadequate staffing, there is no sign of the development of the comprehensive database on terrorists on which the entire counter-terrorism information grid was to be built. Senior intelligence officials have pointed out that the interrogation reports of 16,000 Islamist terrorists caught between 1991 and 2005 could prove to be a goldmine of actionable intelligence.[2]

Recommendations

We need to have a unified structure. The US model of having a Director, National Intelligence and National Counter-Terrorism Centre could be considered after due deliberations at the highest level, with suitable modifications to meet our requirements. Gaps in our system suggest the need for counter-intelligence coordination at the highest level between the national level and local security agencies and with the states. Unless we improve and refine our structure, the quality and functioning of our entire internal intelligence apparatus will remain acutely vulnerable to further terrorist penetration and attacks. It may be noted that after the US reforms in the intelligence structure post-9/11, no further terrorist attack has taken place on the US soil.

A suitable structure could be evolved where the intelligence gathering community, important decision-makers and the responders could be co-located. A National Counter-Terrorism Centre (NCTC) can be established under a Cabinet Minister Counter-Terrorism (CT). It should have three distinct agencies. First, a Chief of National Counter-Terrorism Intelligence (CNCTI) to coordinate terrorist-related intelligence from all intelligence agencies. The MAC could be reconstituted to form this organisation. Second, a Counter-Terrorism Advisor (CTA), reporting directly to the Cabinet minister (CT) for decision-making, besides also providing relevant inputs to the NSA. The third agency should be the responders i.e DG NSG, police and army (when summoned). Such organisations should also exist in the affected states where representatives of CNCTI, CTA, DG NSG, army and police are based. This would ensure synergy and optional coordination. At each level, certain experts who are skillful negotiators should be incorporated, anticipating hostage crisis scenarios.

We must know 'what do we want to know' and 'what do we do' to seek it. This can best be worked out by having a regular intelligence gathering strategy under CNCTI. Accordingly, intelligence targets can be identified, selected and specified, with judicious tasking and allocation of resources from all intelligence agencies implying a mix of all.

A nationalised intelligence data bank is required, which should be accessible to all intelligence agencies and state police through networking, under the stewardship of NCTC. Such a bank presently is only within the purview of MAC.

There is also a need for a holistic view of restructuring of our intelligence agencies to ensure synergy and timely action. Our present structures seem to be flawed. All intelligence agencies should undertake an in-house analysis. All systems must be complementary and substantially supplemented and supported by inputs from other agencies, duly functioning in tandem. The cylindrical approach within each intelligence agency is important, but a simultaneous horizontal approach also needs to be advocated, keeping the national interest always supreme. All intelligence agencies must share information with each other rapidly. Presently, each agency is forwarding information to the highest bosses and not simultaneously sharing it horizontally with other agencies' action responders. Timely information provides adequate response time for comprehension of the situation and its associated fallouts, thereby evolving an appropriate response option. There is a requirement for greater interaction between producers and consumers. All intelligence agencies should share a common mission of working together and collectively share credit or blame, rather than looking for scapegoats.

Traditional methods and techniques of seeking information require urgent upgradation. The manpower requirement of all agencies needs to be made up at the earliest, with good levels of motivation and incentives. Recruitment should be open to all walks of life, including private sectors. Staffing issues of MAC need to be addressed on priority.

Military intelligence should also conduct land-based human intelligence (HUMINT) operations, especially focussed on target countries. They should be permitted to acquire external operational and tactical intelligence for all target countries. Military intelligence capabilities should be upgraded with unmanned aerial vehicles (UAVs). External intelligence should not remain the sole charter of R&AW. Basic principles of intelligence are to use the maximum possible agencies and sources. This also helps in collaborating information gained. Multiplicity of sources is not being followed. We must establish multiple channels at both strategic and operational levels. Credible covert operations should be planned and executed and kept absolutely secretive. Even the idea of thinking about covert operations as a nation should not be made public and discussed in forums to weigh the pros and cons of such a strategy.

Information today is easily available from 'open domain' sources such as private/national/international news channels, Internet, journals, newspapers, seminars, etc. We need to spot young talent as part-time workers on the pay rolls of various intelligence agencies with high incentives who could collate such information and give it to the intelligence agencies. It may be noted that a housewife in the UK in early 2000 had provided valuable information from an Al Qaeda site on a proposed terrorist attack in India. The intelligence agencies, therefore, need to focus on specific main intelligence issues rather than utilising their resources, time and effort on seeking easily available information from the 'open domain'. All possible sources of information should be tapped. Many institutions like the Centre for Land Warfare Studies (CLAWS), Institute for Defence Studies and Analyses (IDSA), United Service Institution of India (USI) and academic universities have ongoing exchange visit programmes with many countries. During such formal and informal interaction, information flows out. The same should be analysed and forwarded to NSC or CNCTI, as applicable.

Our intelligence philosophy has been drawn up from 'Chanakyaniti' period and the 'British Raj' culture of 'snooping around' with the mere purpose of gaining personal and political intelligence by spying on each other. This intelligence focus has to change to a 'strategic' intelligence culture. Our present focus is too much on past intelligence, which actually is 'news'. Today, focus is required on anticipatory and predictive intelligence.

Armed forces personnel, with a flair for intelligence, need to be deputed to R&AW on a permanent basis. Ex-Servicemen should also be suitably employed. It is felt that due to such organisations being manned by police personnel, the tendency is to address an issue with a 'policeman approach' because he has grown up in a 'law and order environment'. Therefore, he tends to view the intelligence problem with a law and order approach, as a matter of habit inculcated over the span of his service profile.

Diverting our intelligence resources to corroborate media inputs which are being reported upon simultaneously by so many news channels, should not be resorted to. We should judiciously resort to seeking further information so that suitable options can be generated for any responses that may be required.

We should carry out effective technical surveillance and jam terrorist communications during physical engagements. In the case of the 26/11 Mumbai attack, the terrorists were in communication with their mentors based in Pakistan, for approximately a total period of 16½ hours. The communication was made in spurts over the entire duration. Though we effectively got the records of the conversation, we could have jammed their network and made them 'blind'. By not blinding them, the results were catastrophic. The positive side is that we were provided records by the US for submitting evidence to Pakistan.

Weapons of mass destruction and nuclear and missile technology falling into the hands of terrorist groups is a distinct possibility. Obtaining this kind of intelligence is the biggest challenge and should be catered to in our intelligence thought process and action.

Conclusions

Various inadequacies in our intelligence system have been highlighted. The same can be overcome by reorganisation and reconstitution of MAC, beefing up the present staff strength, and widening the recruitment base to include qualified technical personnel and experts from all other fields and private sectors. The proposed National Counter-Terrorism Centre should be a centre for joint intelligence and operational planning, duly staffed by personnel from various agencies. This should serve as the primary organisation for analysing and integrating all terrorist related intelligence as acquired by different intelligence agencies. Horizontal flow/exchange of information should be a continuous process amongst all agencies and states. The shared knowledge bank on existing and suspected terrorists, including international terror groups and their goals, strategies, capabilities and networks of contacts and support should be constantly updated and known to all the concerned agencies. Optimally gathered, judiciously analysed and wisely shared intelligence can be the most effective tool in the country's fight against terrorism. It is imperative that the government pays adequate attention to this challenge.

Notes

1. Wilson John, "India's Intelligence Services Struggle with War on Terrorism," *Terrorism Monitor*, Vol. 6, No. 6, 24 March 2008.
2. "Intelligence bodies rush to avoid Mumbai blame: experts," http://www.google.com/hostednews/afp/article/ALeqM5iIbZhKPTDqTwZzDpRXweEDt-22iw, accessed on 11 January 2009.

9

Countering Terrorism Through International Cooperation

Monika Chansoria

The ghastly terror attacks on Mumbai on 26 November 2008 stand out as a defining moment and turning point in India's war against terrorism. Despite having faced Pakistan-sponsored terror and dealt with it for nearly three decades, the nation today is faced with an absolute urgency to formulate and consequently, implement an effective counter-terrorism strategy.

Transnational terrorist networks and groups have established widespread support infrastructures beyond the borders of a single nation. Cross-pollination among them further makes it extremely complex to identify and consequently separate them. Hence, there is a need for nations to collaborate closely at the multilateral, regional and bilateral levels to tackle these terrorist outfits. An effective tool in this endeavour, particularly in the case of India, would irrefutably be the augmentation of international cooperation through coordination of efforts on regional and international levels in order to strengthen the global response to the challenge of terrorism.

Multilateral Arrangements

United Nations

The United Nations (UN) has constantly struggled to arrive at a unanimously acceptable definition of terrorism for decades. The first attempt towards an internationally acceptable definition was made under the League of Nations, but the convention drafted for the purpose in 1937 never came into function. Since then and till date, the UN member states have no agreed definition of terrorism. However, the General Assembly Resolution 49/60 titled, "Measures to Eliminate International Terrorism", contains a provision describing terrorism and comes close to a definition: "Criminal acts intended or calculated to provoke a state of terror in the general public, a group of persons or particular persons for political purposes are in any circumstance unjustifiable, whatever the considerations of a political, philosophical, ideological, racial, ethnic, religious or any other nature that may be invoked to justify them."[1]

Following the 9/11 terror attacks on the United States, UN Security Council (UNSC) Resolution 1373 adopted on 28 September 2001, was envisaged as an international counter-terrorism measure aimed at monitoring efforts by states to implement a wide range of counter-terrorism measures mandated by the resolution. The resolution was adopted unanimously by the UN Security Council under Chapter VII of the United Nations Charter, and, therefore, is binding on all UN member states. The resolution aims at placing barriers on the movement, organisation and fund-raising activities of terrorist groups, with the UN member states encouraged to share their intelligence on terrorist groups in order to assist each other in combating international terrorism. The resolution also calls on all states to adjust their national laws so that they can ratify the existing international conventions on terrorism, stating that all states "should also ensure that terrorist acts are established as serious criminal offences in domestic laws and regulations and that the seriousness of such acts is duly reflected in sentences served."[2]

As part of UN Resolution 1373, a Counter-Terrorism Committee (CTC) was established to monitor the implementation of the resolution. Through its capacity-building and global coordination initiatives, the CTC has become a significant element in the worldwide campaign against terrorism. UN Resolution 1535 reorganises and consolidates the committee's support staff under a new Counter-Terrorism Executive Directorate (CTED) established in 2004 to provide the CTC expert advice and to facilitate technical assistance to countries in addition to promoting closer cooperation and coordination both within the UN and among regional and inter-governmental bodies. Since its inception, the committee has worked with states to identify gaps in their counter-terrorism capabilities and find the necessary technical assistance to fill these gaps. It has also taken on new tasks, including serving as the central clearing house for the exchange of information and coordination among over 60 international and regional organisations. The new directorate was found better equipped to respond more quickly and flexibly to request for assistance from states and international organisations and to better facilitate the exchange of counter-terrorism information.

This measure followed the adoption, in January 2004, of Resolution 1526 aimed at strengthening the ability of Resolution 1267 of October 1999, which imposed an air embargo and a freeze on the assets of the Taliban (then in power in Afghanistan) for refusing to extradite Osama bin Laden. The CTC were expanded and modified between 2000 and 2006, including in UN Resolution 1333 of December 2000, the addition of measures against individuals associated with Al Qaeda, which led to the 1267 Committee also being referred to as the Al Qaeda and Taliban Sanctions Committee. The sanctions now comprise a freeze on assets, an arms embargo and a travel ban against designated individuals and entities associated with Al Qaeda, Osama bin Laden and/ or the Taliban, wherever they may be located.[3] Gradually, following numerous concerns and a wave of court cases around the world, steps have been taken to improve the clarity of UN procedures on adding to and removing names from the so-called consolidated list of individuals and entities suspected of terrorist links. However, some still argue that these procedures do not pay adequate attention to respecting fundamental human rights.

There is strong support amongst some members to hold a general debate on terrorism, which is not directly linked to the Council's counter-terrorism committees or to a specific terrorist event. In fact, in light of the terrorist attacks in Mumbai, such a debate would be more timely than ever. However, there have been growing concerns about the slow pace in the implementation of the UN global counter-terrorism strategy and insufficient cooperation between member states and the UN. Post-26/11, there is an ever-growing demand for the member states to coordinate information sharing that would be instrumental towards devising a comprehensive anti-terror strategy. This highlights the need for a coordinated approach so as to increase transparency in the steps being taken by states, international and regional organisations, including civil society, in addressing the threat of terrorism. The UN should play a more proactive role by making sure that coherence between the work of the Security Council's Counter-Terrorism Committees and the UN Global Counter-Terrorism Strategy comes through effectively. The UN Global Counter-Terrorism Strategy was adopted by member states on 08 September 2006 in the form of a resolution that could be termed as a unique global instrument to enhance national, regional and international efforts to counter terrorism by means of a wide array of measures ranging from strengthening state capacity to handle counter-terrorist threats, to better coordinating United Nations counter-terrorism activities. However, the effectiveness of these mechanisms would eventually depend upon transparent coordination among international, regional and sub-regional organisations where they share best practices in counter-terrorism capacity-building.

International Conventions/Protocols to Counter Terrorism

1. 1963 Convention on Offences and Certain Other Acts Committed On Board Aircraft
   - Applies to acts affecting in-flight safety;
   - Authorizes the aircraft commander to impose reasonable measures, including restraint, on any person he or she has reason to believe has committed or is about to commit such an act, where necessary to protect the safety of the aircraft; and
   - Requires contracting States to take custody of offenders and to return control of the aircraft to the lawful commander.

2. 1970 Convention for the Suppression of Unlawful Seizure of Aircraft
   - Makes it an offence for any person on board an aircraft in flight to "unlawfully, by force or threat thereof, or any other form of intimidation, [to] seize or exercise control of that aircraft" or to attempt to do so;
   - Requires parties to the convention to make hijackings punishable by Requires parties to the convention to make hijackings punishable by "severe penalties"
   - Requires parties that have custody of offenders to either extradite the offender or submit the case for prosecution; and
   - Requires parties to assist each other in connection with criminal proceedings brought under the Convention.

3. 1971 Convention for the Suppression of Unlawful Acts against the Safety of Civil Aviation
   - Makes it an offence for any person unlawfully and intentionally to perform an act of violence against a person on board an aircraft in flight, if that act is likely to endanger the safety of the aircraft; to place an explosive device on an aircraft; to attempt such acts; or to be an accomplice of a person who performs or attempts to perform such acts;
   - Requires parties to the Convention to make offences punishable by "severe penalties"; and
   - Requires parties that have custody of offenders to either extradite the offender or submit the case for prosecution.

4. 1973 Convention on the Prevention and Punishment of Crimes Against Internationally Protected Persons

- Defines an "internationally protected person" as a Head of State, Minister for Foreign Affairs, representative or official of a State or international organization who is entitled to special protection in a foreign State, and his/her family; and
- Requires parties to criminalize and make punishable "by appropriate penalties which take into account their grave nature" the intentional murder, kidnapping or other attack upon the person or liberty of an internationally protected person, a violent attack upon the official premises, the private accommodations, or the means of transport of such person; a threat or attempt to commit such an attack; and an act "constituting participation as an accomplice".

5. 1979 International Convention against the Taking of Hostages
   - Provides that "any person who seizes or detains and threatens to kill, to injure, or to continue to detain another person in order to compel a third party, namely, a State, an international intergovernmental organization, a natural or juridical person, or a group of persons, to do or abstain from doing any act as an explicit or implicit condition for the release of the hostage commits the offence of taking of hostage within the meaning of this Convention".

6. 1980 Convention on the Physical Protection of Nuclear Material
   - Criminalizes the unlawful possession, use, transfer or theft of nuclear material and threats to use nuclear material to cause death, serious injury or substantial property damage.
   - Makes it legally binding for States Parties to protect nuclear facilities and material in peaceful domestic use, storage as well as transport; and
   - Provides for expanded cooperation between and among States regarding rapid measures to locate and recover stolen or smuggled nuclear material, mitigate any radiological consequences or sabotage, and prevent and combat related offences.

7. 1988 Protocol for the Suppression of Unlawful Acts of Violence at Airports Serving International Civil Aviation, supplementary to the Convention for the Suppression of Unlawful Acts against the Safety of Civil Aviation (Extends and supplements the Montreal Convention on Air Safety)

- Extends the provisions of the Montreal Convention to encompass terrorist acts at airports serving international civil aviation.

8. 1988 Convention for the Suppression of Unlawful Acts against the Safety of Maritime Navigation
   - Establishes a legal regime applicable to acts against international maritime navigation that is similar to the regimes established for international aviation; and
   - Makes it an offence for a person unlawfully and intentionally to seize or exercise control over a ship by force, threat, or intimidation; to perform an act of violence against a person on board a ship if that act is likely to endanger the safe navigation of the ship; to place a destructive device or substance aboard a ship; and other acts against the safety of ships.

9. 1988 Protocol for the Suppression of Unlawful Acts Against the Safety of Fixed Platforms Located on the Continental Shelf
   - Establishes a legal regime applicable to acts against fixed platforms on the continental shelf that is similar to the regimes established against international aviation.

10. 1991 Convention on the Marking of Plastic Explosives for the Purpose of Detection
    - Designed to control and limit the used of unmarked and undetectable plastic explosives (negotiated in the aftermath of the 1988 Pan Am flight 103 bombing);
    - Parties are obligated in their respective territories to ensure effective control over Parties are obligated in their respective territories to ensure effective control over "unmarked"
    - Generally speaking, each party must, inter alia, take necessary and effective measures to prohibit and prevent the manufacture of unmarked plastic explosives; prevent the movement of unmarked plastic explosives into or out of its territory; exercise strict and effective control over possession and transfer of unmarked explosives made or imported prior to the entry into force of the Convention; ensure that all stocks of unmarked explosives not held by the military or police are destroyed, consumed, marked, or rendered permanently ineffective within three years; take necessary measures to ensure that unmarked plastic explosives held by the military or police are destroyed, consumed, marked or rendered permanently ineffective within fifteen years; and,

ensure the destruction, as soon as possible, of any unmarked explosives manufactured after the date of entry into force of the Convention for that State.

11. 1997 International Convention for the Suppression of Terrorist Bombings
    - Creates a regime of universal jurisdiction over the unlawful and intentional use of explosives and other lethal devices in, into, or against various defined public places with intent to kill or cause serious bodily injury, or with intent to cause extensive destruction of the public place.

12. 1999 International Convention for the Suppression of the Financing of Terrorism
    - Requires parties to take steps to prevent and counteract the financing of terrorists, whether direct or indirect, through groups claiming to have charitable, social or cultural goals or which also engage in illicit activities such as drug trafficking or gun running;
    - Commits States to hold those who finance terrorism criminally, civilly or administratively liable for such acts; and
    - Provides for the identification, freezing and seizure of funds allocated for terrorist activities, as well as for the sharing of the forfeited funds with other States on a case-by-case basis. Bank secrecy is no longer adequate justification for refusing to cooperate.

13. 2005 International Convention for the Suppression of Acts of Nuclear Terrorism
    - Covers a broad range of acts and possible targets, including nuclear power plants and nuclear reactors;
    - Covers threats and attempts to commit such crimes or to participate in them, as an accomplice;
    - Stipulates that offenders shall be either extradited or prosecuted;
    - Encourages States to cooperate in preventing terrorist attacks by sharing information and assisting each other in connection with criminal investigations and extradition proceedings; and
    - Deals with both crisis situations (assisting States to solve the situation) and post-crisis situations (rendering nuclear material safe through the International Atomic Energy Agency (IAEA).

14. 2005 Protocol to the Convention for the Suppression of Unlawful Acts against the Safety of Maritime Navigation
    - Criminalizes the use of a ship as a device to further an act of terrorism;
    - Criminalizes the transport on board a ship various materials knowing that they are intended to be used to cause, or in a threat to cause, death or serious injury or damage to further an act of terrorism;
    - Criminalizes the transporting on board a ship of persons who have committed an act of terrorism; and
    - Introduces procedures for governing the boarding of a ship believed to have committed an offence under the Convention.

15. 2005 Protocol to the Protocol for the Suppression of Unlawful Acts against the Safety of Fixed Platforms Located on the Continental Shelf
    - Adapts the changes to the Convention for the Suppression of Unlawful Acts against the Safety of Maritime Navigation to the context of fixed platforms located on the continental shelf.

Source: United Nations: Action to Counter Terrorism - http://www.un.org/terrorism/instruments.shtml

Regional Cooperation

ASEAN-India

The Association of Southeast Asian Nations (ASEAN) comprising Indonesia, Malaysia, the Philippines, Singapore, Thailand, Brunei, Cambodia, Laos, Myanmar, and Vietnam has comprehensively reviewed ASEAN-India cooperation, since New Delhi's rapid engagement with the region began in 1992, when it became a sectoral dialogue partner with the ASEAN Regional Forum (ARF). ASEAN's leading role and centrality in all ASEAN-related architecture facilitated India's rapid development of ties with the region. ASEAN and India have common interests in managing trans-boundary issues such as maritime security, counter-terrorism and disaster relief. Crucially,

India drew together ASEAN's support for countering terrorism in the region by signing the ASEAN-India Joint Declaration for Cooperation to Combat International Terrorism adopted on 08 October 2003 in Bali, Indonesia.[4] The signatories undertook steps to strengthen cooperation at the bilateral, regional and international levels to combat terrorism in a comprehensive manner, including the following:

- Continue and improve intelligence and terrorist financing information sharing, including the development of more effective counter-terrorism policies and legal, regulatory and administrative counter-terrorism regimes
- Enhance liaison relationships amongst national law enforcement agencies to engender practical counter-terrorism regimes.
- Provide assistance on transportation, border and immigration control challenges, including document and identity fraud to effectively stem the flow of terrorist-related material, money and people.

In efforts to strengthen counter-terror ties, Prime Minister Manmohan Singh inked the "ASEAN-India Partnership for Peace, Progress and Shared Prosperity" with leaders of ASEAN countries at the ASEAN Annual Summit in November 2004 where the forum sought India's help for training the forces of ASEAN member states in dealing with anti-terrorism operations. So far, the security relationship with ASEAN has not included active training and joint exercises pertaining to counter-terrorism, although at bilateral levels, India has joint working groups on counter-terrorism with many member countries.

SAARC

The South Asian Association for Regional Cooperation (SAARC) has been making efforts to study ways to counter terrorism in the region. Towards this end, a working group has specifically been functioning since 2007 to analyse terror funding in the region. The eight-nation regional grouping has also called for urgent conclusion of a Comprehensive Convention on International Terrorism—an initiative with which India has been very closely associated. Nonetheless, according to Mahmoud Hmoud, member of the International Law Commission, negotiating a Comprehensive Convention on International Terrorism would be an arduous and intense process since the legal regime to be created by this instrument must deal with significant legal and political consequences. If genuine political will exists to conclude the Comprehensive Convention, there is no absence of legal answers that can guarantee an effective law enforcement instrument against international terrorism, without infringing on legal rights and positions under international law.[5]

In fact, a working document on the draft Comprehensive Convention on International Terrorism has already been submitted by the Government of India which realises the need to undertake effective measure to prevent acts of terrorism and to ensure that perpetrators of terrorist acts do not escape prosecution and punishment by providing for their extradition or prosecution. In fact, the newly-elected Bangladesh Prime Minister Sheikh Hasina has initiated a plan to form a joint South Asian task force through which all the eight member states would remain united in containing terrorism by jointly devising ways and means to identify terrorists and their outfits operating in the region.

An Additional Protocol to the SAARC Regional Convention was adopted at the 12th Summit in Islamabad in which the member states committed themselves to prevent and suppress the financing of terrorists by criminalising the acts of the provision, acquisition and collection of funds for such acts. In the case of South Asia, it would be imperative to mention that addressing the issue of terrorism collectively in the region comes with a key impediment—the fact that pockets in South Asia are both the source and victim of terrorism. Therefore, the forum finds it extremely difficult to arrive at a consensus while formulating and consequently implementing an anti-terror strategy smoothly in the region since incorporating both India and Pakistan in such a strategy would be an uphill task given the high levels of suspicion between the two, especially in the aftermath of the Mumbai carnage. The platform of SAARC, thus, would be an intricate and complex launching pad as far as anti-terror policy and operations are concerned since 'terrorism' is both a point of agreement and contention, given the fact that the Mumbai attacks were plotted and directed from Pakistani soil.

Bilateral Initiatives

United States

India has collaborated very closely with the United States in counter-terrorism initiatives. The rise in India's strategic prominence vis-à-vis the US was a key factor when Indo-US counter-terrorism cooperation began in 2000 and resulted in the establishment of the US-India Counter-Terrorism Joint Working Group (CTJWG) in January 2000 as a confidence-building measure. However, the 11 September 2001 terror attacks on the United States changed Washington's perception of transnational terrorism entirely, and the ensuing Global War on Terror spearheaded by the United States stands testament to the same.

India pledged its support to the US and offered substantial assistance to Washington in its counter-terrorism efforts in Afghanistan. This significantly included "the use of numerous Indian military bases, an offer that was never made even to the erstwhile Soviet Union, which functioned as New Delhi's patron during the last decades of the Cold War."[6] In addition, India also provided satellite imagery of Afghanistan to the US before the initiation of the US-led Operation Enduring Freedom. The Indian Navy contributed significantly to the US effort during this operation by escorting vessels carrying cargo for military operations through the Strait of Malacca and the Andaman Sea.[7] Through the CTJWG mechanism, India and the US have exchanged information, training material, and methods related to interrupting terrorist financial networks, institutional and law enforcement steps to strengthen homeland security, border management and surveillance techniques, aviation security and disaster management in the event of a terrorist incident involving weapons of mass destruction.[8]

In 2001, the two countries launched the Indo-US Cyber Security Forum to focus on cyber security, cyber forensics and related research towards enhancing cooperation between law enforcement agencies of both countries in dealing with cyber crime. As part of the agreement, ongoing cooperation between India and the US National Institute of Standards and Technology was expected to expand to new areas, including harmonisation of standards. The CTJWG has met nine times since its inception and "proved to be a useful mechanism for exchange of information, intelligence sharing, anti-terrorism training programmes and for strengthening institutional links between crime prevention agencies in the two countries."[9] The US-India counter-terrorism initiatives have progressed well. These initiatives include the following:

- Exchange of information and assessments on the international and regional terrorist situation.
- Strengthening of intelligence and investigative cooperation.
- Qualitative upgradation and expansion of anti-terrorism training programme for Indian law enforcement officials.
- Signing of a Mutual Legal Assistance Treaty.
- Launching of a bilateral Cyber Security Forum, with a wide-ranging programme of action to address challenges of cyber terrorism and information security.
- Introduction of military-to-military cooperation on counter-terrorism to supplement the initiatives of the US-India Defence Policy Group in this area.
- Working together on multilateral initiatives on terrorism, including on the implementation of UNSC Resolution 1373.
- Initiation of dialogue and cooperation in homeland/internal security, terrorist financing, forensic science, transportation security and border management.
- Undertaking of concrete steps to detect and counter the activities of individual terrorists and terrorist organisations of concern to the two countries.

Since 2002, the Service-to-Service joint training exercises have expanded significantly, with India and the United States undertaking a broad spectrum of joint military exercises, including greater military-to-military ties and company-level joint counter-insurgency training of army units.[10] In addition, several US Army personnel have undertaken jungle terrain training at the Counter-Insurgency and Jungle Warfare School, Vairengte, in the Northeastern Indian state of Mizoram. Lately, the major areas of cooperation have expanded to greater intelligence sharing, an upgraded Anti-Terrorism Training Assistance Programme (ATAP) for Indian law enforcement officials, the launching of a cyber security forum to focus on cyber terrorism and information security, improving border monitoring, counter-terrorism equipment sales, counter-narcotics, money laundering and the ratification and implementation of the Treaty on Mutual Legal Assistance.[11]

Moreover, India and the US have collectively also supported the UN Global Counter-Terrorism Strategy and have pursued the draft UN Comprehensive Convention on International Terrorism. Cooperation in the area of law enforcement includes programmes developed by Diplomatic Security Anti-Terrorism Assistance (DSATA), the Department of Homeland Security, the Federal Bureau of Investigation (FBI) and the Drug Enforcement Administration (DEA). Under DSATA, joint training of security and law enforcement officials has been conducted in India and in the United States (Washington DC, Louisiana and New Mexico). The programmes provide both equipment and training in explosives investigation and counter-measures, hostage negotiation, counter-terrorism legislation and counter-terror police training.

The Department of Homeland Security initiated the Container Security Initiative (CSI) in January 2002 to promote improved port and nuclear security. The CSI envisages screening of all containers at foreign ports by US Customs officials in concert with their host-nation counterparts before the cargo containers are shipped to US ports. India has been contemplating joining the CSI since 2003 and many rounds of Indo-US discussions have been held in this regard. The primary obstacle so far had been concerns expressed by intelligence and customs agencies regarding stationing of US officials in Indian ports, including their possible intrusion into local port jurisdiction, enforcement and strategic imports. For many years, containers from India bound for the US were routed through Colombo as there were many reservations in India about the provisions of CSI. However, it has been reported as recently as February 2009 that Jawaharlal Nehru Port Trust (JNPT) in Mumbai has been cleared by the government to be a CSI-compliant port that would allow shipping of containers without any transhipment through another port.[12]

Similarly, the FBI has expanded cooperation with its Indian counterparts, providing training on combating cyber-crime, drug-trafficking and counter-terrorism. Since 2004, the FBI has been conducting a course on "surveillance and detection" for Indian police officers under its ATAP and, in addition, it also ran an "Evidence Recovery Preservation and Exploitation" course to train India's Central Bureau of Investigation (CBI), police and National Security Guard personnel to collect evidence in case of mass casualty attacks, as have been witnessed in Jaipur, Hyderabad, Bangalore and Ahmedabad.[13] Also, according to Indian media reports, the US had shared intelligence with the Indian government weeks before the bombing of India's embassy in Kabul on 07 July 2008.[14]

While the US legal framework for counter-terrorism is perceived as placing a restriction on individual freedom, the United States views India's counter-terrorism efforts as being hampered by "outdated and overburdened law enforcement and legal systems."[15] The Indian system of court procedures has been depicted as being sluggish and prone to corruption, where terrorism trials take years to complete.[16] Counter-terrorism expert B Raman has echoed this view and states:

> The strategy for counter-terrorism includes four crucial aspects—prevention through timely intelligence, physical security to thwart terrorist attacks if intelligence fails, crisis management if physical security too fails and deterrence through investigation and

> prosecution. The weakest link in India's counter-terrorism capability is deterrence through legal action against terrorists and their organisations. Here, India's investigative and prosecution agencies are required to fight against terrorism with the normal laws of the land, which were enacted long before terrorism emerged as a major threat to national security.[17]

This reality needs to be understood and addressed in spite of the fact that India continues to rank among the world's most terror-afflicted countries.

Even though post-9/11 Pakistan yet again emerged as a critical ally in the US-led operations in Afghanistan, given its geo-strategic location and linkages with the Taliban, sooner or later, Washington would have no option but to point at Pakistan as the centre of terror activity not just in South Asia but globally. While publishing its 2006 Country Reports on Terrorism, the US Administration designated three Pakistan-based militant groups—Harkat-ul-Mujahideen, Jaish-e-Mohammed (JeM) and Lashkar-e-Tayyeba (LeT)—as "Foreign Terrorist Organisations" and further included the Harkat-ul-Jehad-al-Islami (HuJI), Hizbul Mujahideen and Jamaat-ul-Mujahideen as "Groups of Concern".

In the past, India has expressed dissatisfaction with what it views as inconsistencies and backsliding in US public statements concerning the Pakistan-based terrorist threat to India. However, following the Mumbai terror attacks on 26/11, the US pressure on Pakistan to ban the frontal organisation of the LeT and Jamaat-ud-Dawa (JuD) helped to assuage Indian concerns. In fact, State Department spokesman Sean McCormack was asked to provide clarification to a statement by the defence minister of Pakistan wherein he stated that Islamabad had to ban the Jamaat because if it had not done so, it would have been branded a terrorist state. Although, McCormack denied this by saying that Pakistan acted because "it saw it in its interest to do so," the American pressure on Islamabad has been evident.

The future course of counter-terrorism cooperation between Washington and New Delhi should focus on the following:

- Increase intelligence sharing to foster intelligence-liaison relationships, given that 90 percent of the success in counter-terrorism is dependent on timely intelligence;
- Washington and New Delhi should maintain and provide joint access to databases of anti-terror information;
- The level and frequency of the US-India Counter-Terrorism Joint Working Group meetings ought to be raised; and,
- Cooperative efforts to include counter-terrorism in the field of maritime coordination should be expanded.

However, the worsening security scenario in Pakistan and Afghanistan is further goading the leadership in Islamabad to retain the edge and command a bargaining position with Washington. On its part, India needs to keep up the international pressure (especially that of the US) on Islamabad and make sure that this time around Pakistan actually takes tangible action against the radical terror outfits operating from its soil. As former Secretary of State Condoleezza Rice said in New Delhi on 03 December 2008, "India and the United States have been cooperating... but we're going to do it in a more intensive and urgent manner."[18] In the foreseeable future, President Barack Obama's biggest foreign policy challenge would undoubtedly be Pakistan. According to former US National Security Advisor, Stephen Hadley, "Pakistan's increasingly turbulent border region poses threats not just to the US mission in Afghanistan, but also to India, as evidenced by the recent Mumbai terrorist attacks, as well as to urban areas of Pakistan itself, and to the world beyond."[19]

Israel

Israel expressed the hope that the Mumbai terror attacks would infuse a new sense of urgency into counter-terrorism cooperation with India and allow the transfer of strategies and tactics and not just arms and equipment to help Indian security agencies to prevent or respond faster to such crises in future. It would be apt to state that the possibility of collaborating closely with Israel continues to remain doubtful given the nature of domestic political sensitivity within India. Moreover, some security experts and military officers in Israel came down critically against New Delhi given the manner in which the Indian forces responded during the three-day siege in Mumbai, particularly the encounter at Nariman House, a Jewish centre where six Jews were killed.

At best, India could learn from the Israeli experience in coping with terrorism especially from South Lebanon. Some key aspects of Israel's counter-terrorism strategy are that it is offensive, emphasises prevention especially through intelligence, and is supported by stringent laws and psychological measures. In the aftermath of the disaster of the Yom Kippur War, the Israelis crucially included the Analysis Division with Mossad and Shabak—a lesson that should be absorbed by India.[20] The Israeli intelligence structure is based on a bottom up approach with the intelligence structure as follows:

- AMAN: Military intelligence branch of the Israeli Defence Forces.
- MOSSAD: Responsible primarily for external intelligence.
- Shin Bet (SHABAK): Responsible for internal security, including the Israeli-occupied territories.
- LEKEM: Scientific Affairs Liaison Bureau.

Although New Delhi and Jerusalem set up a Joint Working Group on Counter-Terrorism in 2001, the panel has remained more of an annual meeting forum while cooperation on the ground has focussed on India sourcing unmanned aerial vehicles and ground sensors from Israel to curb infiltration on the Line of Control (LoC) in Kashmir. These steps, in addition to the fence erected along the LoC, which also uses several Israeli gadgets, have gone a long way in reducing infiltration. Therefore, there has been recognition of the importance of technology in counter-terrorism and India's import of weapons systems and surveillance equipment from Israel is proof of the same. India needs to closely cooperate with Israel, especially on the issue of sharing information vis-à-vis *jehadi* groups and should lose no time in reaping the dividends of this initiative.

The commando-style attacks across Mumbai by highly trained terrorists have made it imperative for India to change its strategy vis-à-vis preparedness to deal with the changing tactics of the terrorists, according to Israeli security experts. They opine that one of the key lessons of 26/11 is the need for a change in the basic approach of the Indian security forces, be it the army, special forces such as the National Security Guards (NSG) or marine commandos and indeed, the local police. "Modern terrorism has become very complicated... These days there are hybrid threats where terrorists operate more like a modern army and less like a guerrilla group and we have to understand their motives and define terrorism anew," asserts Gidi Netzer, an Israel-based international expert on counter-terrorism and conflict-crisis management.[21] The India-Israel Joint Working Group on Counter-Terrorism should be utilised more effectively, including discussions on domestic counter-terrorism measures, combating terrorist financing, transfer of weapons to terrorists, the threat of narco-trafficking and cooperation at both bilateral and multilateral forums.

China

The post-Mumbai terror attack period witnessed the first-ever Sino-Indian military combat exercise on Indian soil to jointly counter terrorism and insurgency with the larger aim of evolving a collaborative security mechanism among Asian powers to tackle the growing menace of transnational terrorism. The exercises are a result of a Memorandum of Understanding (MoU) signed between India and China in May 2006, which stipulated that the two countries would hold joint military exercises and join forces in counter-terrorism operations.

Consequently, joint counter-terror exercises were conducted from 06 to 14 December 2008, in Belgaum, Karnataka. A 137-strong Chinese Army contingent from the 1st Company of the Infantry Battalion of the Chengdu Military Area Command and Indian Army troops from 8 Maratha Light Infantry battalion undertook joint tactical manoeuvres and drills, interoperability training and joint command post procedures, which finally culminated in a simulated joint counter-terrorism operational exercise.[22] It may be recalled that the military ties between the Indian and Chinese armed forces have been building since December 2007, when the first-ever joint counter-terrorism exercise Hand-in-Hand between the two armies was held at Kunming. However, according to counter-terrorism expert B Raman:

> Operational cooperation in counter-terrorism and counter-piracy between the navies of the two countries is of far greater relevance as compared to cooperation between the Indian and Chinese armies, since no India-based terrorist group is operating in Chinese territory and vice versa. On the contrary, Chinese territory and nationals have been subjected to attacks not only by the Uighurs, but also by indigenous Pakistan-based Jihadi terrorist organisations.[23]

India has shared evidence about the involvement of Pakistan-based elements with China, seeking Beijing's influence in persuading Islamabad in bringing the perpetrators of the 26/11 terror attack to justice. Foreign Secretary Shiv Shankar Menon gave details of the Mumbai terror strikes to Chinese Vice Foreign Minister He Yafei who was sent to India as a special envoy to defuse tensions between India and Pakistan. China and India have both been advocates of continued strengthening of the multilateral counter-terrorism cooperation within the UN framework, including capacity-building measures in counter-terrorism and investing more resources in developing countries so as to aid them to fight terror. Both New Delhi and Beijing have experienced the scourge of Islamic radical extremist terror groups – India in the case of Kashmir, and elsewhere across the nation, and China in the Xinjiang province. Thus, the two could forge closer collaboration in the fields of intelligence sharing and counter-terror exercises. Initially, the Chinese government had been rather silent with respect to responding to the Mumbai terror attacks, and, in fact, the Chinese state-controlled media had even made its pro-Pakistan tilt visible by echoing Islamabad's position on the issue. Regrettably, the Chinese stance has not changed much since then and China still refuses to condemn outright its ally, Pakistan.

Japan

Affirming their common commitment to fight terrorism, Japan and India, including the Japanese Maritime Self-Defence Force's replenishment activities in the Indian Ocean, constitute an important part in the international community's effort to eradicate terrorism.[24] In this regard, New Delhi could pick up vital lessons from Japan's contribution to the fight against terrorism, especially in the Indian Ocean region. With Coalition forces engaged in activities such as Operation Enduring Freedom (OEF), International Security Assistance Force (ISAF), Provincial Reconstruction Team (PRT) in Afghanistan and OEF-Maritime Interdiction Operations (OEF-MIO) in the Indian Ocean, Japan has been conducting refuelling of vessels participating in the OEF-MIO from 2001 to 2007 under the Anti-Terrorism Special Measures Law and from February 2008 under the Replenishment Support Special Measures Law. Improved and frequent joint maritime exercises with Japan could prove beneficial for India.

Russia and UK

India and Russia closely share concerns on the growing threat of cross-border terrorism. Russian President Dmitry Medvedev and Indian Prime Minister Manmohan Singh reaffirmed their commitment for strengthening bilateral cooperation against terrorism in the aftermath of the 26/11 terror strikes on Mumbai. In fact, the Russian president was the first head of state to visit India following the Mumbai massacre and affirmed, "We stand ready for cooperation in all areas with a view to preventing such acts of terrorism, investigating the recent attack and establishing a global system of protection against terrorism."[25]

Russia has viewed with concern the rise of Islamic radicalism and extremism in Central Asia and in the former Soviet provinces. Moscow and New Delhi have agreed to intensify bilateral cooperation in anti-terror efforts within the framework of the Indo-Russian Joint Working Group on Combating International Terrorism (JWGCIT), including strengthening measures to curb financing of terror as a part of the counter-terrorism strategy. The two nations have also been working closely on the growing threat of the use of cyber-space by terrorists in their activities.[26] In order to step up efforts to curb financing of terror, India and Russia have signed an agreement on cooperation between their financial intelligence units.[27] It would be prudent to understand that in the aspect of counter-terrorism cooperation with India, the Russian policy-makers find themselves in a better position than their American counterparts. Washington has long confronted the difficult challenge of performing the balancing act of improving security ties with India while simultaneously sustaining good bilateral relations with Pakistan in order to facilitate its war on terror; Moscow does not have to placate Islamabad on this count.

Along with Russia, India is closely cooperating with Great Britain—a nation that shares a "strategic partnership of equals" with India, in the words of British Prime Minister Gordon Brown. India and Britain have agreed to establish a new bilateral dialogue to end terrorist financing by means of the Indo-UK Joint Working Group on Counter-Terrorism. Moreover, the two countries have expanded their existing counter-terrorism cooperation further in the fields of civil aviation security and crisis management. Multilaterally, Britain has extended support to India's initiative for the adoption of a Comprehensive Convention on International Terrorism at the UN. Post-26/11, the cooperation between Indian and British intelligence agencies should be further strengthened in addition to seeking the UK's influence in putting pressure upon Pakistan to act against the terrorist outfits operating on its soil and persuading Islamabad to bring the perpetrators to book.

Pakistan

India needs to keep up the international pressure on Pakistan and stress upon initiatives on the floor of the United Nations and beyond to specify and ban terrorist and *jehadi* outfits that are operating within and out of Pakistani territory, especially the ones that are the prime accused in the Mumbai 26/11 attacks. Pakistan should be held accountable for terrorist networks operating from its soil, especially the LeT. Even though New Delhi has found success in getting the United Nations Security Council to ban the Jamaat-ud-Dawa and proclaim Hafiz Saeed and Zaki-ur Rehman Lakhvi as terrorists, India needs to go all out to secure the arrest of the JeM chief, Maulana Masood Azhar. Azhar figures in India's most wanted list for being the key perpetrator and the mastermind of the Jammu and Kashmir Assembly attack and Indian Parliament attack in 2001.

According to Ashley Tellis at the Carnegie Endowment for International Peace, "Pakistan today, is clearly both part of the problem and the solution to the threat of terrorism...."[28] In fact, the 9/11 Commission had highlighted Pakistan's deep involvement with international terrorism and recommended a long-term US commitment to provide comprehensive support to Pakistan. The Pakistani establishment has been demanding US aid worth billions of dollars from subsequent Administrations, in the name of reform and modernisation of the *madrasas* so as to prevent their misuse for *jehad*. Unfortunately, there have been no tangible results that are visible on the ground and continued terror attacks against India are proof of the same. The present leadership under President Zardari too is blatantly exploiting the presence of Al Qaeda and the Taliban in the territory so as to remain in a commanding position to bargain. According to analysts, the Pakistan military considers the Taliban as their strategic asset in the Af-Pak region and, thus, it does not seem too likely that they would be transparent in operations "against" these groups leading to their complete wipe out.

Islamabad's intention at cracking down on these extremist radical outfits has always been placed under a shadow of doubt given the fact that there is continuing caginess and denial in Pakistan's response. Time and again since 26/11, it has gone back and forth on statements and assurances in what seem to be obvious efforts to shield terror outfits that are breeding on its soil. India, therefore, needs to take on all these individuals and organisations by moving to the UNSC. In fact, their listing by the UNSC will force Pakistan to meet New Delhi's demand for the extradition of some of the accused. India must accelerate building up pressure on Pakistan, not just bilaterally, but also through the world community. Thus, even though the need for Pakistan to cooperate on the issue of tackling terrorism in the region is immense, the chances of it being certifiable remain bleak.

Afghanistan, Bangladesh and Maldives

Afghan President Hamid Karzai's visit to New Delhi in January 2009 exclusively focussed on counter-terror cooperation and stability in the aftermath of the Mumbai attacks. President Karzai is believed to have shared Afghan intelligence on the antecedents of LeT operatives and their possible links with the Taliban. The scope of cooperation in this context with Afghanistan is immense and should be urgently explored in areas ranging from covert intelligence operations to possible military tie-ups.

In the particular case of Bangladesh, India wants Dhaka to act decisively against the over 100 suspected terror-training camps and hideouts of the Northeastern insurgent outfits within its borders, apart from carrying out a crackdown on the HuJI. The recent spate of terror strikes across Indian cities, including the bombings at Jaipur, Varanasi, Faizabad, Ajmer and Lucknow point towards HuJI as a key suspect. The HuJI, established in 1992, with reported assistance from Osama bin Laden's International Islamic Front, operates in Bangladesh from the coastal area stretching from across the port city of Chittagong down south through to the Myanmar border. The HuJI cadres allegedly also infiltrate frequently into the eastern borders of India to maintain contacts with other terrorist and subversive outfits of the region, notwithstanding the fact that

Bangladesh government had officially banned the HuJI in October 2005. In addition, the US State Department labelled the HuJI as a Foreign Terrorist Organisation (FTO) as recently as March 2008 and accordingly all the US financial institutions were required to freeze assets held by the HuJI.[29] Besides, it has been an accepted fact, especially in Assam, that the leaders of the United Liberation Front of Asom (ULFA) have constantly been provided shelter in Dhaka, along with support towards training camps of Northeast insurgents along its borders with India. While Bangladesh has constantly refuted these charges, in April 2004, ten truck loads of arms worth more than $ 7.5 million intended for insurgent groups in the Northeast had been seized by Bangladeshi authorities in Chittagong.

India is keen on securing Bangladesh's firm cooperation in rooting out anti-Indian terror and insurgent outfits operating from its soil. With this objective in view, the armies from the two countries came together and held their first-ever counter-terrorism exercise in February 2009 in Jorhat, Assam, including heliborne and airborne operations. In the future, these exercises would prove instrumental towards joint patrolling of the Indo-Bangladesh border.

Given that the terrorists responsible for the Mumbai attacks came from the sea route, India and the Maldives have decided to scale up anti-piracy and marine counter-terrorism operations in the Indian Ocean. Underlining the importance of greater maritime surveillance in the Indian Ocean, Maldives President Mohamed Nasheed said, "We are a nation of sea-farers. We understand the topography of the Indian Ocean and there is a need for greater vigilance in the Indian Ocean."[30] With the Mumbai attacks as a backdrop, the two countries plan to intensify interaction between their coast guards. Joint exercises that are now held every two years would be held more frequently.

Conclusion

In order to use international cooperation as a tool against transnational terrorism, the efforts have to be focussed, and should go far beyond mere political rhetoric to demonstrate serious political will of the states involved. Transnational terrorism and transnational crime are being perpetrated largely by non-state actors across or beyond the political borders of a single state. Most governments respond to international terrorism at a tactical level and as a result, even after decades of combating the menace, the conventional response of either eliminating or apprehending terrorists has not deterred terrorism. This could be primarily attributed to the failure of the affected nations to obliterate the transnational support structures of terrorist groups.

Currently, India's international cooperation efforts are moderately placed and further need to be accelerated at both bilateral and regional levels. Therefore, the following steps need to be worked upon diligently in order to comprehend and counter transnational terror mechanisms:

- Intensify and accelerate the exchange of operational information.
- Emphasise counter-terrorism intelligence acquisition and coordination regarding actions or movements of terrorists in person or networks and organisations; hence, the need for multinational intelligence cooperation comes to the forefront.
- Create an international database to share intelligence/ information on terrorist movements, organisations, weapons, funding and international linkages.
- Build a new intelligence system to support transformed transnational security needs in order to counter unknown perpetrators, methods and targets.
- Put in place a coordinated crisis response system.
- Prevent the movement of terrorists or terrorist groups through effective border controls and measures for preventing counterfeiting, forgery or deceptive use of identity papers.
- Strengthen maritime counter-terrorism capabilities of the coast guard.
- Provide greatest measure of assistance in connection with criminal investigations or proceedings relating to the

financing or support of terrorist acts, including assistance in obtaining evidence in their possession necessary for the proceedings.

- Promote inter-agency coordination and the exchange of counter-terrorism information at the national, sub-regional, regional and international levels.
- Encourage states to establish dedicated and permanent counter-terrorism units, with the assistance of experts seconded from various specialised institutions, in areas such as criminal law, counter-financing of terrorism and border control.
- Upgrade the tactical abilities of security forces and train the forces to use technology competently.
- Hold joint military exercises at both bilateral and multilateral levels on a regular and frequent basis to practise counter-terror tactics.
- Encourage greater cooperation with INTERPOL and increased access towards utilisation of its resources and databases such as red corner notices and "watch lists".
- Implement strict measures towards the implementation of legal instruments to counter transnational terrorism.

Post-26/11, India needs to critically reflect upon the existing counter-terrorism mechanisms and accelerate deeper international cooperation, particularly through multilateral and bilateral arrangements/agreements. These initiatives at bolstering international cooperation to counter terror then need to be merged with a restructured system of national security intelligence and its stringent coordination with law enforcement mechanisms so as to break the nexus between international terrorism and transnational organised crime, money-laundering, illegal arms trafficking, illegal movement of nuclear and other potentially fatal materials that could prove instrumental in abetting more such strikes in the future.

Notes

1. United Nations General Assembly, Resolution 49/60, 09 December 1994, p. 4.
2. United Nations Security Council, Resolution 1373 (2001), adopted at the 4385th meeting of the Security Council, 28 September 2001.
3. For more details, see United Nations Security Council, Counter-Terrorism Committee Report No. 1, 03 December 2008.
4. See the draft statement, "ASEAN-India Joint Declaration for Cooperation to Combat International Terrorism," adopted 08 October 2003, Indonesia.
5. For more details, see Mahmoud Hmoud, "Negotiating the Draft Comprehensive Convention on International Terrorism: Major Bones of Contention," *Journal of International Criminal Justice*, Vol. 4, No. 5, 2006, pp. 1031-43.
6. Ashley J Tellis, "The US-India 'Global Partnership': How Significant for American Interests?" Testimony before the House Committee on International Relations, 16 November 2005.
7. Ian Storey, "Indo-US Strategic Ties on the Upswing," *Jane's Intelligence Review*, March 2003, pp. 40-43.
8. For more details, see Lisa Curtis, "After Mumbai: Time to Strengthen US-India Counterterrorism Cooperation," *Backgrounder*, No. 2217, 09 December 2008.
9. Bhabani Mishra, "India-US Relations: A Paradigm Shift," *Strategic Analysis*, Vol. 29, No. 1, 2005, p. 90.
10. US Department of State, *Country Reports on Terrorism 2007*, Office of the Coordinator for Counterterrorism, 30 April 2007.
11. "Sixth Meeting of the India-US Joint Working Group on Counter-Terrorism," Delhi, 31 August - 01 September 2004," US Consulate Press Release, Mumbai.
12. R S Vasan, "Terror from the Sea: Warning from the Indian Naval Chief," *South Asia Analysis Group*, Paper No. 3068, 24 February 2009.
13. "FBI Training Indian Sleuths in Fighting Terror," *Mail Today*, 17 June 2008.
14. Praveen Swami, "ISI Engineered Kabul Embassy Bombing: NYT," *The Hindu*, 02 August 2008.
15. US Department of State, n. 10.
16. Ibid.
17. For more details, see B Raman, "Evolution of India's Counter-Terrorism Capabilities," *International Terrorism Monitor*, Paper No. 55, 10 May 2006.
18. US Department of State, "Remarks with Indian Minister of External Affairs Pranab Mukherjee," New Delhi, 03 December 2008, http://www.state.gov/secretary/rm/2008/12/112622.htm, accessed on 11 January 2009.

19. John D McKinnon, "National Security Adviser Says Pakistan is Top US Challenge," *The Wall Street Journal*, 7 January 2009.
20. For more details see, Harry Ellis, *The Dilemma of Israel* (Washington: American Enterprise Institute for Public Policy Research, 1970).
21. "After Mumbai Attacks, Israel Ready to Share Anti-Terror Strategies," *The Indian Express*, 06 January 2009.
22. "Chinese forces arrive home after joint military training with India," 15 December 2008, http://news.xinhuanet.com/english/2008-12/15/content_10509034.htm, accessed on 11 January 2009.
23. B Raman, "Sino-Indian Cooperation in Counter-Terrorism," *International Terrorism Monitor*, Paper No. 311, 22 November 2007.
24. For more details, see "Joint Declaration on Security Cooperation Between Japan and India, Ministry of Foreign Affairs," Tokyo, 22 October 2008.
25. Russia Ready to Help India in Combating Terrorism," http://news.outlookindia.com/item.aspx?642260, accessed on 11 January 2009.
26. "India, Russia Vow to Jointly Counter Terror," *Press Trust of India*, 17 December 2008.
27. "Dawood's network involved in Mumbai attacks: Russia," http://economictimes.indiatimes.com/PoliticsNation/Dawoods_network_involved_in_2611_Russia/articleshow/3854964.cms, accessed on 11 January 2009.
28. Ashley J Tellis, "U.S. Strategy: Assisting Pakistan's Transformation," *The Washington Quarterly*, Vol 28, No. 1, Winter 2004-05.
29. Monika Chansoria, "Transnational Terror Mounting," *Central Chronicle*, 28 May 2008.
30. Sandeep Dikshit, "Maldives offers help to 'observe' Indian Ocean," *The Hindu*, 26 December 2008.

10

Terrorism and the Role of the Media

Shah Alam

The media provides information that communicates images, news, events, data, and analyses. It comprises both electronic (visual and audio) and print versions. The language with which the media reports and discusses terrorist acts and their organisations, is very important, since it often sets the parameters for public debate. The media today is omnipresent and contributes in setting agendas. In fact, in all contemporary conflicts, the media is not only a significant player but has also become a third party.[1] Moreover, the Internet offers another means by which terrorists and terrorist organisations can communicate their messages.

Terrorism gets publicity through the media. The reporting and coverage of the November 2008 terrorist incident in Mumbai generated debate about the role of the media in covering the government's rescue operation. The interrelationship among the media, terrorists, and government has many dimensions, is extremely complex and, hence, worthy of close examination.

The media influences public opinion. It affects not only the actions of the governments, but also of the terrorist groups. The Indian Airlines hijack episode of December 1999, the terrorist attack on India's Parliament on 13 December 2001, and the Mumbai incident of November 2008 are illustrative of the role and power of the media. However, there is a significant difference in the manner of reporting about terrorism between the television news programmes and the newspapers, as well as between the government-owned television and radio networks and other private news channels. The media in India is not always impartial and is often soft on some terrorist groups and organisations. Also, it has been seen in the past reporting and coverage of such events that the media brands even a mere 'suspect' as a terrorist, based on the police version. The media frequently uses the words 'militant' and 'terrorist' for those who belong to organisations like the Students Islamic Movement of India (SIMI) and Abhinav Bharat (Malegaon blast accused case).[2] It has been also seen that even terms like "Islamic terrorism" and "Hindu terrorism" are used commonly by the Indian media. The media in India widely used the term "Hindu terrorism" in the aftermath of the 29 September 2008 bomb blast in Malegaon town of Maharashtra.[3]

The media, particularly electronic, has become the leading news provider as a result of widespread networking. Terrorists and terrorist organisations are highly sensitive to the role of the media, especially the visual. The newspapers come second and serve to supplement television's instant, live, and highly emotional coverage. TV sets the agenda for all news media, compelling all others too to focus on the spectacular events on which TV itself flourishes. Events which produce strong pictures acquire maximum coverage. However, the role of the newspapers in disseminating information cannot be relegated or ignored because they can reach the remote areas where TV is not available. Even in towns and cities, despite the easy availability and wide reach of TV, the newspapers play an important role in disseminating information and starting debates on important issues. Both the newspapers and electronic media help in forming public opinion on important issues.

Media-Terrorism Relationship

There is no consensus on the definition of terrorism. Evidently, an incident of violence may be described differently by various groups and regions – some may see it as "a terrorist act" while another may portray the same as "fight for freedom". However, it is important to make a distinction between terrorism and criminal acts. In such a scenario, the role of the media becomes very complex.

Opinions vary on the relationship between the media and terrorism. Some scholars such as Paul Wilkinson say that the media and terrorism are in a "symbiotic relationship". He says that "if there is no aim to instil terror, then the violence is not of a terroristic nature."[4] The reporting and coverage of terrorist incidents advances the commercial interests of the media.

The media and terrorism have a "symbiotic relationship" because both require each other in advancing their interests.

> Just as the terrorists need to convey their often symbolic messages to various audiences, so too television networks and newspaper organisations have a general need to capture large numbers of viewers and readers in order to advance their own largely material self-interests. Concomitantly, journalists, print or electronic, have their careers to think about. These careers are often enhanced by higher salaries or more prestigious jobs when they gain exclusive access to a terrorist chieftain or on-the-spot coverage to a breaking terrorist event. Terrorism sells newspapers ..."[5]

The media is an intrinsic part of society. A particular TV channel or newspaper seeks to produce full coverage of an incident in order to enhance its business. As the media covers terrorism, it also, ironically enough, incites more terrorism, which, in turn, produces more media coverage. But if the media or the government censor the coverage, the controls tend to affect the credibility of the media or the government.

According to Yonah Alexander, the media provides terrorist groups useful tools that serve their propaganda and psychological war ends.[6] M Cherif Bassinouni says that the psychological effect of a particular violent act may be considerably more significant than the act itself and that the effect may be largely a creation of the media. J Bowyer Bell argues that the media-terrorist relationship is symbiotic, with the media coverage spreading the effect of a limited act to a wider public.[7] Ralph E Dowling says that for the terrorists, violence gives them access to the media that they would not be able to achieve through ordinary forms of discourse.[8]

On the other hand, the French sociologist Michel Wieviorka has denied that the media and terrorism are in a "symbiotic relationship". He argues that terrorists relate to the media in any of four different ways, from "pure indifference", "relative difference", a "media-oriented strategy", and finally to "coercion of the media".[9] Robert G Picard and Miquel Rodrigo have argued that the media forms an important part of society in which terrorists operate and there is no credible scientific evidence that establishes "a cause-effect relationship between media coverage and the spread of terrorism."[10]

It emerges from the arguments that while some terrorist acts are clearly carried out with the intention of seeking publicity, others are done without that intention, and some are even carried out in secret. It is generally agreed that the relationship between terrorism and the media is "symbiotic", in that terrorists and their organisations use the media as a conduit for their messages to be heard by the target audience while supplying "sensational news" for the media.[11] The experts disagree on the ways and degree to which the terrorists use and manipulate the media.

In both domestic and foreign cases, the media is a significant factor. The media reports the act and sets the agenda, and brings focus on the terrorists' aims and objectives. Each exploits the other. Apparently, terrorism has no meaning without media coverage. The media is attracted by terrorist acts not only because it is its duty to report any major event, but also because of the tragic nature or the human value of the incident. Terrorists exploit this and act in a way to attract maximum attention around the world. Terrorists use the media for both tactical and strategic purposes. It is a fact that terrorists direct their actions towards the public and utilise the media in order to have the strongest possible impact.

Terrorists seek publicity, usually free publicity, but also want secrecy. Terrorism gets publicity through the media – the terrorists act by itself is nothing, but publicity is all. The purpose of terrorism is to draw attention to a problem and the publicity surrounding a terrorist act is meant to convey this message to the world. Terrorists want a favourable understanding of their problems. Several people may not agree with their acts but may be sympathetic to their cause.

Terrorists and terrorist organisations build a cooperative relationship with the media personnel and organisations through various means to advance their interests. They seek sympathetic personnel in the media who could project their cause and wish to use the media to gain legitimacy to their cause. In hostage situations, terrorists use the media to put their demands before the authorities, as happened during the Indian Airlines hijack episode in December 1999.

Reporting, Images and Ethics

Strong, iconic and visual impressions determine and influence the public discourse more than detailed analyses and background information. Hence, the media struggles for the most powerful images. Sensationalism attracts audiences. Violence creates powerful images and in turn attracts far greater attention than peaceful negotiations can ever hope to achieve. This encourages the terrorists to indulge in violence. Terrorist acts are intended to create terror, fear, and chaos among the people. These depend largely on the images and messages being carried by media reports about the terrorist threats and acts. Terrorists also seek to create a situation where the people lose faith in their government's ability to protect them. The omnipresent media multiplies these effects out of proportion on the public psyche. The tragic incidents of November 2008 in Mumbai are a glaring example of this.

The media coverage of the November 2008 Mumbai incident was criticised at various levels. The media beamed the coverage live and projected the government rescue operation as inappropriate and lacking in coordination. It continued to beam the horrifying experiences for the entire 60 hours that it took to bring the situation under control. The media was widely criticised for having played an irresponsible role and for having become insensitive to others' grief, anxiety, and suffering.

Under pressure from the security agencies to keep the media at bay, the Union Information and Broadcasting Ministry is planning to amend the Cable Television Networks Rules (CTNR) 1994 to prohibit live coverage of such crises. The earlier attempts of the government to regulate the electronic media through the Broadcasting Services Regulating Bill were withdrawn because of stiff opposition from the media. The proposed CTNR amendment is also being resisted by the media.

It would be worthwhile to recall the role played by the media in another terrorist incident in December 1999 when an Indian Airlines flight had been hijacked. Initially, the Indian media played a responsible role during this crisis. When the hijackers demanded the release of terrorists, including Masood Azhar, from Indian jails in exchange for the passengers in the flight, or threatened to blow up the plane (along with all passengers), the Indian media played a significant role in forming public opinion in favour of securing the release of the passengers "at any cost". By playing up the demands of the relatives of the passengers, the media aroused the public sentiments. Consequently, the government came under pressure and released Masood Azhar and others in exchange for the release of the IC-814 passengers. The hijack drama dominated the headlines of newspapers and TV beamed non-stop the images of processions of wailing relatives of those on board 1C-814, demanding their rescue.

But as soon as the passengers were released, the same media that had been screaming for the rescue of the passengers, immediately changed its tune. The National Democratic Alliance (NDA) government came under severe criticism for the release of the militants. Even today, the media refers disparagingly to the incident where "Jaswant Singh escorted Masood Azhar to Kandahar." *The*

Times of India published a front page article entitled "Are We in the Media Playing into the Hands of the Hijackers?" after the episode of Kandahar. The article went on to say that publicity is the terrorist's oxygen and admitted that the turgid nature of Indian media coverage of the previous days might have greatly weakened the Indian government's negotiating powers.

However, there are no specific guidelines and standard codes in India for the use of images of violence in the media. It is expected to be aware of the professional, political and ethical implications of its information dissemination. A section of journalists are of the view that the suppression of any violent image would only increase the probability of an attack so extreme that coverage just could not be avoided any more. Telecasters, broadcasters, editors, journalists, and even publishers of online news have obligations in reporting terrorism-related news. And this is not only a matter of duty but also ethics, because what they report, or do not report, may make a difference between the life and death of thousands of people. The media coverage and reporting also vary from channel to channel and from newspaper to newspaper based on their commercial interests and targeted audience.

The media projection of a 'stereotype image' of a particular community is seen by many as inaccurate. For instance, the Indian media sometimes recklessly uses 'words' and 'language' to describe a particular community that might affect the cohesiveness of the diverse Indian society. Linking an individual attack to historical, societal or criminal contexts, even when none exists, may add further complexities. Linking of an incident to the whole region or community may complicate the situation instead of resolving it. An isolated use of a specific terror-image not only contributes to promoting violent political goals but also creates a wrong image of a whole region or a whole group and culture.

Irrespective of state control of the media, journalists should comprehend that they are responsible for the effects of using and distributing images. The media requires an honest approach in reporting events and maintaining its ethics and morality. By doing so, the media would be able to protect its central social role while also maintaining its credibility. The responsibility of the media is to tell the truth, and the whole truth. As BBC's John Wilson once said, "We have to be accepted as trustworthy reporters, especially in times of crisis."[12]

The media is a significant element in the considerations of the terrorists since it can act as an effective tool to convey their message to the large audience. But the media can play either a positive or a negative role, from the terrorists' perspective, arousing either support or rejection of their cause.[13] However, the media must be aware of its own power, responsibility, and limitations.

The media has to be responsible in its actions. After the bombings in Bangalore and Ahmadabad, the news came up about unconfirmed reports from sources in the Intelligence Bureau (IB) about SIMI, Laskhar-e-Tayyeba (LeT) and Harkat-ul-Jihad al Islami (HuJI) being responsible for the attacks. Covert operations by the Inter-Services Intelligence (ISI) were alleged to be responsible. According to the news reports, the intelligence agencies and the media had little or no proof. The media attempted to pacify the people by beaming such news and reports and there was no restraint in labelling a community as responsible for it.[14]

Meanwhile, it is also a fact that the media may be associated with the big corporate sector and business community. In such circumstances, it obviously takes sides, based on the predilections of its owners and, hence, may no longer be relied upon to be neutral.[15]

The media expects the following:

- The media want freedom to cover the issue without any restraint.
- It wants to be the first to disseminate the story accurately.
- It wants to project the incident in time, and attractively.
- The media personnel wish to be professional and not to disseminate false information.
- It wants to protect itself and operate freely and safely. It seeks to protect the legal right to publish and for it to remain relatively unrestrained.

- It seeks to uphold the society's right to know. The media wants to air the emotional reactions of the victims, family members, witnesses, and the people on the street, as well as information withheld by the government.
- It wants to play a constructive role in solving particular terrorist situations and terrorism-related problems.

The Internet is also a means by which terrorist organisations can communicate without relying on intermediaries (e.g. television and radio) to convey their messages in the way they want them to be presented. The terrorist organisations create their own websites and maintain them for this purpose. The websites are easily accessible and enable them to reach a wider audience. Some terrorist organisations, like Hizb-e Allah and Hamas have their own websites to convey the messages of the organisations in a number of different languages.

Media and the Government

The government wants loyalty, cooperation, understanding, and restraint from the media in its efforts to limit terrorist damage to society. It seeks to punish those who are responsible for terrorist acts and the media can play a constructive role in it.

- The government wants news coverage and reporting to advance its agenda and not that of the terrorists. It, therefore, expects that the media would support the government's courses of action when operations are under way and disseminate their information when requested.
- The government wants that the media should not be sympathetic to the terrorists. It should present terrorists as anti-national, anti-social, and evils of society. It wants to project that kidnapping, blowing up a building, or hijacking an airplane, is an unacceptable terrorist act regardless of the cause behind it.
- In a hostage-crisis situation, the government prefers to exclude the media from the surrounding area. But it wants both the print and electronic media to provide information to the authorities

when news reporters have access to the hostage sites.

- The government looks to publicity through the media to help in defusing tensions. Keeping the public calm is an important policy objective of the government.
- The government wants that the media, particularly television, avoids airing the emotional reactions of the victims, family members, witnesses, emotional stories about the relatives of the victims, and the people on the street. Apparently, such scenes may build public pressure upon the government to make concessions to the terrorists' demands.
- During terrorist incidents, the government wants the media not to reveal planned or ongoing counter-terrorism measures since that would forewarn the terrorists and affect counter-terrorism efforts.
- In the aftermath of incidents, the media should not reveal secrets or details of techniques of how the operations were performed. The media must avoid highlighting successful or unsuccessful operational methods.
- The government desires that the media must boost the image of government agencies. The media needs to be vigilant about disinformation from terrorists, their organisations, or others who gain from its coverage. The groups and organisations that indulge in such activities have many motives for disseminating inaccurate or false news.
- In cases where vital national security interests are at stake, the government seeks the cooperation of the media in disseminating information that could assist in neutralising the immediate threat posed by the terrorists and their organisations.

There is a fundamental conflict between the media and government. The Mumbai incident of November 2008 and its media coverage and report comprise a glaring example of the conflict of interests between the two institutions. The duty and responsibility of the media is to report the news as fully and accurately as possible, whereas the government seeks to protect sensitive information. The ways in which the security forces deal with the media, and how it reacts leads one to conclude that there are fundamental differences between the aims and interests of the government and the media.

The government wants to ensure that the media is not manipulated into promoting the causes of terrorism and its methods. In fact, neither the media nor the government want to see terrorism, or counter-terrorism, erode constitutional freedoms, including the right to access and freedom of expression—the pillars of democratic societies. But the government imposes restrictions on the freedom of media when it feels it is required.

Media's Impact on Government Policy and Counter-Terrorism

The effect of media reports and coverage on government policy may or may not be significant, depending on multiple factors. But fair and balanced reporting can help in shaping the government policy. The media may play an important role in the government's counter-terrorism policy by highlighting its achievements. Communication between the government and the media is one of the important ingredients in any strategy designed to prevent the cause of terrorism from prevailing. The media coverage and reporting of terrorist incidents like the Mumbai incident in November 2008, the Kandahar episode, and others significantly influenced government policy. For instance, Anita Joshua asked in *The Hindu* in December 2008: "Why is not the scene of crime – the Mumbai terror attack or any murder spot – ever cordoned off? Why should journalists – print and electronic are equally guilty – be walking all over the crime scene disturbing, and, in turn, destroying, evidence, and in this case, possibly impacting the operation?"[16] Indeed, media coverage and reporting may have an impact on government policy and could possibly hinder a counter-terrorism operation.

The media can be used as a counter-terrorism tool. The development of a detailed framework for media "cooperation" or "voluntary restraint" in reporting incidents of terrorism has become "of crucial importance in contemporary counter-terrorism techniques."[17] Openness, or at the least, appearance of openness with the media is recognised as a desirable policy in government counter-terrorism efforts. Miguel Rodrigo has linked the relationship of the media to terrorism. He opines that the media detects the presence of the problems of terrorism and underlying socio-political problems.[18] Social, economic, and political problems of a particular region or regions are highlighted by the media, thus, contributing to shaping government policy.

Many terrorists and terrorist organisations seek media hype and perpetrate their violent acts to gain publicity for their causes or to obtain concessions like the release of their fellow terrorists from prison. The Indian Airlines hijack incident in December 1999 was illustrative of this. The media is extremely vulnerable to manipulation by terrorists who are willing to use violence to publicise their cause. On the other hand, the media can be the enemy of the terrorists when carrying out counter-terrorist propaganda, and can strongly criticise and discredit the terrorists' motives and goals as well as their methods. The challenge for the government is to explore mechanisms that can increase government-media cooperation in such a manner that the interests of both are served. In fact, cooperation between the government and media would be an important element in any strategy to prevent the success of terrorist causes and strategies. The government can use the media as a tool in arousing world opinion against terrorism and terrorist organisations. The media can also be used to mobilise public opinion in other countries to bring pressure on governments to take or reject actions against terrorists and the organisations indulging in terrorism.

Need for Greater Interaction Between the Government and the Media

Greater interaction is required between the government and the media on the issue of terrorism. A number of options may improve government-media interaction when responding to, or covering, terrorist incidents. The government can adopt strategies to combat terrorist-driven initiatives, and the media can play a crucial role within the framework of such strategy.

The formation of the Terrorist Information Response Centre (TIRC) could provide one forum for coordination between the media and the government. The government should create a rapid reaction terrorism reporting pool, consisting of electronic and print media representatives. The coverage of incidents could be coordinated by the network representatives in the centre. The government should create a media pool of consensual news releases. But it is not an easy task.

The government should promote voluntary media coverage guidelines. The formulation of such guidelines by the media itself would not infringe on its right to access and reporting. The government should hold a special media summit to develop voluntary guidelines on coverage and reporting of terrorism. The creation of a Self-Regulation Press Council may help guide the media on what it should or should not report. Some broad guidelines could be: restricted information on hostages; limited information on force deployment during rescue operations; agreement not to air live unedited interviews with terrorists; checking and cross-checking information sources while reporting; avoidance of reporting that may cause widespread panic and fear among people, and help the terrorists to, in one way or another, exert undue pressure on the government.

Tackling Terrorism Against the Media

The media and media personnel are vulnerable to terrorist attacks and harassment. A trend toward terrorist attacks against media personnel and institutions has been emerging across the globe. Reporters in India, Pakistan, Afghanistan, and other parts of the world have been kidnapped and murdered. The American reporter, Daniel Pearl, was kidnapped by Islamic militants in Pakistan on 23 January 2002 and murdered. Daniel Pearl, the Wall Street

Journal's South Asia bureau chief, was based in Mumbai but had gone to Pakistan to cover a story connected to the the War on Terrorism.[19]

Journalists and reporters face insecurity while they cover such incidents. Musa Khan Khel, a journalist of Geo Television Network, was based in Mingora and had been covering the fighting in Swat Valley for many months. He was shot and killed after covering the rally that was organised by the hardliner Islamic clerics in Swat Valley.[20] Secretary General of the Pakistan Federal Union of Journalists, Mazhar Abbas said that four journalists were killed in Swat Valley in 2008. He further said that in the last several years, 45 journalists have been killed in various parts of Pakistan, including tribal areas under Taliban control.[21]

Journalists are highly vulnerable while they cover terrorist incidents. They are directly affected by terrorist activities. They become victims as hostages, are killed, and used for negotiations. They undergo physical security problems while they report, cover, interpret, and comment on the attacks. Journalists who are outspoken on issues of terrorists and terrorism are under attack. Such attacks on journalists appear to be rising. Journalists seek protection to operate as securely and freely as possible. Their concern goes beyond protecting their legal right to publish relatively unrestrained to include personal physical security. They seek protection from threats, harassment, or attacks during operations, and protection from subsequent murder by terrorists in retaliation aganist unfavourable coverage. There are numerous instances of murders of journalists who provided unfavourable coverage.

There is lack of comprehensive data on the media reporters being killed by terrorists. Governments have not yet evolved a mechanism to maintain records of the murders of media personnel. The database would include annual statistics that will show the number of journalists killed or injured in terrorist attacks, and the annual number of terrorist incidents against media personnel and organisations.

Conclusion

Terrorism should not be allowed to affect the importance of the freedom of the media because it is one of the essential foundations of a democratic society. Freedom of speech and expression and freedom of the media ensure the right of the people to be informed on matters of public concern, including terrorist threats and acts, as well as on the response of the government.

- The government should not restrict freedom of the media as an excuse in the fight against terrorism.
- The Indian media should highlight or present a balanced picture of the government's achievements and counter-terrorism policy.
- The government should keep the media informed about government strategies and action towards combating terrorism.
- The government must deny access to classified documents to the media. The media should refrain from leaking sensitive information.
- The media must be encouraged to pass information about terrorist activities and their plans to the government.
- Journalists/media in India should avoid playing into the hands of the terrorists. The media should avoid a race for sensational news and images which may help in strengthening the hands of terrorists.
- The Indian media should avoid promotion of terrorist objectives through images, reporting or any other means.
- The media should refrain from disseminating shocking pictures or images of terrorist acts because it may create panic in society.
- The media should fully inform the public about terrorist acts, including the suffering caused by these acts as well as the socio-cultural and political context of such acts.
- The media should not hurt the privacy and dignity of people, especially of the victims.
- The media should be professional in reporting terrorist acts and threats.

- The media should not help the objectives of the terrorists by creating fears among the people.
- The media should refrain from disseminating hate speeches.
- The government should provide adequate protection to mediapersons to help them to perform their tasks fearlessly.

Notes

1. Gurmeet Kanwal, "Learning from Lebanon," *The Indian Express*, 21 August 2006.
2. "Indian Media's softness on LTTE's terrorism", http://editindia.blogspot.com/2009/02/indian-medias-softness-of-lttes.html, accessed on 24 February 2009.
3. "Hindu Terrorism Debate Grips India," *BBC News*, 21 November 2008.
4. Paul Wilkinson, "The Media and Terrorism: A Reassessment," *Terrorism and Political Violence*, Vol. 57, No. 3, Summer 1997, pp. 51-55.
5. Leonard Weinberg, *Global Terrorism* (Oxford: Oneworld Publications, 2006), p. 97.
6. Yonah Alexander, "Terrorism, the Media and the Police," *Journal of International Affairs*, Vol. 32, No.1, 1978, pp. 101-02.
7. J Bowyer Bell, "Terrorist Scripts and Live-Action Spectaculars," *Columbian Journal Review*, No. 17, 1978, pp. 47-50.
8. Ralph E Dowling, "Terrorism and the Media: A Rhetorical Genre," *Journal of Communication*, Vol. 36, No.1, 1986, pp. 12-14.
9. Michel Wieviorka, *The Making of Terrorism* (Chicago: University of Chicago Press, 1988), pp. 43-45.
10. Robert G Picard, "News Coverage as the Contagion of Terrorism: Dangerous Charges Backed by Dubious Science," *Political Communication and Persuasion*, Vol. 3, Fall 1986, p. 51.
11. Brigitte Nacos, *Terrorism and the Media* (New York: Colombia University Press, 1994), pp. 48-54
12. William E Biernatzki, "Terrorism and Mass Media," *Communication Research Trends*, Vol. 21, No. 1, 2002, p. 21.
13. Ibid., p. 13
14. Pranay Rupani, "Responsibility of the Media and the Repercussions of Terror Strikes – Terrorism in India, Indian Mujahideen, Bangalore Blasts, Ahmadabad Blasts, Bombs," http://www.articlesbase.com/politics-articles/responsibility-of-the-media-and-the-repercussions-of-terror-strikes-terrorism-in-india-indian-

mujahideen-bangalore-blasts-ahmedabad-blasts-bombs-506717.html, accessed on 22 February 2009.

15. Kanwal, n. 1.
16. Anit Joshua, "Will the Proposed Emergency Protocol on Media Coverage Work?" *The Hindu*, 17 December 2008.
17. Jennifer Jane Hocking, "Governments' Perspectives," in David L Paletz and Alex P Schimd (eds.), *Terrorism and the Media* (New Bury Park: Sage Publication, 1992), pp. 86-104.
18. Miguel Rodrigo, *The Media of Communication Confront Terrorism* (Barcelona: Icariia, 1991), p. 30.
19. "Kidnapped American Reporter Murdered," *The Telegraph* (London), 22 February 2002.
20. Jane Perlez, "Pakistani Reporter is Killed After Celebration of Truce," *New York Times*, 19 February 2009.
21. Ibid.

11

The Role of Civil Society in Countering Terrorism

Avinash Godbole

The aftermath of the 26/11 terrorist attacks on Mumbai and the hostage situation that the terrorists created seem to have evoked a serious as well as unprecedented response from urban middle and upper middle class India. From the peace marches and human chains that were seen around the city of Mumbai to the anger apparent in the demands of carpet-bombing of Pakistan to using modern means of communication like the Internet and text messaging, the scale of collective action that emerged signified an awakening of activism among the hitherto politically dormant sections of the society.

Even media attention to the anger expressed on the streets of Mumbai and elsewhere seemed to have added to the enthusiasm of the 'soldiers' of change. Moreover, people from all walks of life openly expressed their views and rendered advice to the government on what needed to be done and why this was the right time to rectify the government's omissions of the past. The political class was targeted, particularly for their rash statements on various occasions. One could argue about whether this kind of public response was right or wrong and whether or not the government should have acted under the pressure of activism, but one cannot deny that it was heartening to see the emergence of a powerful voice in the public sphere in the form of an aware and concerned civil society. If the Home Minister had to resign on the issue of accountability, it is a good sign of activism. However, one must ask if the civil society activism emerged because of an exceptional act of terror and, hence, specific to that particular incident, or whether it would continue to act in a sustained manner in the future as well. Another question that must be answered is whether the anger of the upper middle class was biased in its response since its own constituents were affected, perhaps for the first time. Alternatively, was the event of 26/11 indeed exceptional in nature? Moreover, what will be the future nature and role of civil society in the fight against terrorism?

While India has been a long standing victim of terrorist activity, never had the country witnessed a hostage situation right in the heart of urban India until 26/11. In fact, never had the battle been so proximate and so prolonged. Therefore, the sense of vulnerability that 26/11 brought to the common citizen of the country was immense. This point needs to be kept in mind, as one feels optimistic over the role of the civil society in the aftermath of the Mumbai attacks. It may be the case that the hostage situation in the heart of the financial capital led to increased anxiety among urban Indians, and resulted in the heightened response. While this may well be true, one still needs to look at ways in which the civil society can play a meaningful role in the fight against terrorism. In the following sections, an attempt is made to discuss the role that a vibrant and vigilant civil society can play in the fight against terrorism.

Defining Civil Society

There are various definitions of the term 'civil society' based on different schools of political thought. Generally, civil society is described as liberal, radical or conservative, based on the three respective domains of economy, society and culture. This division is based on where one locates the centre of civil society.[1] The focus of this chapter is on the radical strand located in the domain of society.[2] Radical, in this context, means a domain of ideas, a critical, vigilant, united and broad-based endeavour aimed at ensuring qualitative and quantitative upgradation of efforts on the part of the governmental agencies. For the purpose of this chapter, the following definition is useful:

> Civil society refers to the arena of uncoerced collective action around shared interests, purposes and values. In theory, its institutional forms are distinct from those of the state, family and market, though in practice, the boundaries between state, civil society, family and market are often complex, blurred and negotiated. Civil society commonly embraces a diversity of spaces, actors and institutional forms, varying in their degree of formality, autonomy and power. Civil societies are often populated by organizations such as registered charities, development non-governmental organizations, community groups, women's organizations, faith-based organizations, professional associations, trade unions, self-help groups, social movements, business associations, coalitions and advocacy groups.[3]

This is the broadest possible definition of the term and it includes all the components of civil society as it is understood today. In theory, civil society is an indispensable component of democracy. Vigilant and participatory population is the critical element for the success of a democracy, and civil society is the means through which the process of participation and vigilance can take place.

Terrorism and Civil Society

Since the beginning of the 1990s, India has been witness to acts of terrorism in some form or the other. Particularly in the last six to seven years, the geographical reach, as well as the number of victims of terrorism, have increased manifold. The attack and hostage situation of 26/11 was only the latest in this series. Terrorism is not an end in itself but only a means of achieving larger ends. It is also defined as proxy war or war by other means when waged by a country that perceives itself to be inferior to its adversary in conventional warfare capability.

Many have argued that civil society is both an instrument and a victim of terrorism. The former means that terrorism finds its justification in civil society and the latter that terrorism challenges the fundamentals of civil society. While there is no dispute over the second idea, the former proposition is objectionable. By its very definition, civil society is supposed to give space for the expression of alternate voices and ideas. And if there are people in a healthy civil society who are interested in studying the factors and circumstances under which terrorism perpetuates, it should not be taken as amounting to the justification of terrorism. On the contrary, the presence of debate in civil society can be used, in a constructive manner, to root out the causes that lead to dissent that eventually turns into terrorism. However, for this to happen, state organs urgently need to get over the sense of unease with the critical role of civil society. The state must begin to accept the criticism that emanates from civil society in a positive, constructive manner.

In fact, there are many ways in which civil society can play a role in the fight against terrorism. These are discussed in the forthcoming paragraphs.

Public Sphere: Protest and the State-Society Relationship

The public sphere is the central tenet of the concept of civil society. It is the democratic space where the ideal definition of democracy as "a system of the people, by the people and for the people" can be seen in action. It is this sphere that civil society can protect through vibrant activism. This was the basic aspect of public action as seen on the streets of urban India. It signified that the citizens wanted the government to act fast and in a decisive manner. In this sense, civil society was not anti-government but rather in support of strong state action. The United Progressive Alliance (UPA) government's urgency to upgrade the country's anti-terror laws is an example of this. And, the power of civil society is evident in the fact that the UPA brought in essentially the same laws that it had been against as the opposition party.[4] The sense of urgency shown by the UPA in the wake of the public outcry for a strong anti-terror law proves the classic dictum that a government must not only act but must also be seen to act.

The public protest led to the change of guard in the political arena as the Union Home Minister and the Chief Minister of Maharashtra had to resign, taking moral responsibility for the failure of the state to prevent the attacks. Every statement made by the state leadership was scrutinised to the core and the ministers were made accountable for their remarks. In particular, the Chief Minister of Maharashtra faced public ire for letting his actor son and a filmmaker accompany him on the inspection tour of the Taj Hotel, which later came to be termed as "terror tourism". In a similar fashion, the central government witnessed the exit of the Union Home Minister who was increasingly being perceived as inefficient.

Another area where civil society must act is in saving the democratic nature of the Indian police and judicial system. But it is in this field that one saw a conspicuous absence of collective action. One is referring here to the debate that surrounded the provision of legal aid to the lone captured terrorist in Mumbai, Mohammad Ajmal Kasab. When members belonging to certain political groups were pelting stones on the houses of lawyers willing to take up the case of Kasab, the collective action of Mumbai was absent. There was no group that stood up for it and it is here that one must ask if collective action is equivalent to civil society, and ponder over the steps that can turn the collective into civil. Even earlier, there have been instances of this kind when blasts took place in Jaipur, Faizabad and Varanasi.

Check on State Excesses

Even as public protests and citizens' collective action can force the government to act in the case of terrorism, it can also ensure that state mechanisms do not cross the line in their efforts. India is a democratic country and even as the country develops mechanisms to fight terrorism, it must be ensured that democratic principles of justice are not violated and the state action does not violate human rights. In this sense, civil society can act as a check on state excesses. However, there was no protest when the UPA government legislated 180 days of detention in the case of terrorism suspects as against 90 days that the National Democratic Alliance (NDA) government had proposed in the Prevention of Terrorism Act (POTA). One can only wait and see if in the future, a mature civil society raises its voice to check state excesses.

Similarly, civil activism can ensure that the fight against terrorism does not curtail civil liberties that are characteristic of a democratic society. There will be certain restrictions on movement and assembly, depending on the nature of the threats faced, but it should not mean restrictions on the constitutional rights of the citizens. Instances of fake encounters where innocent civilians tend to be victims is another area that needs to be checked and it must be accepted that India's record in this field is not completely unblemished. Recent history has instances to show that this kind of atrocity has taken place in India. This problem is true especially in the terror-affected regions of India like the state of Jammu and Kashmir (J&K). Provisions like the promulgation of the Armed Forces Powers Special Act (AFPSA) have led to antagonism against the armed forces in these regions. If the local populace does not support the Indian state's initiatives then the success achieved will also be limited. Civil society can play a role in providing legal help and justice to the kin of the victims, whether in terms of bringing the perpetrators to book or ensuring that they also get adequate compensation. In a preventive capacity, this would mean sensitising the state agencies to the issues at hand to ensure no civilian casualties, or at least, minimum collateral damage.

Another way in which non-governmental organisations (NGOs) and other groups can check state action is by ensuring that the state response to terror is not disproportionate and that terrorism does not become a political weapon. In other words, if there is a terror attack in the country and if the government is willing to fight an all out war without ensuring domestic security, then it might be the case that by generating jingoistic fervour the government might be diverting attention from other urgent issues. Therefore, a vibrant civil society can ensure that a generally inefficient government does not hide its failures in the name of the response to terrorism.

Spreading Information and Checking Corruption

Free flow of accurate information is critical for the proper functioning of civil society and every effort must be made to ensure this because the enlightened individual alone can be the backbone of a vibrant civil society. By getting to know what the government is doing and how it is functioning in its anti-terror efforts, civil society can bring in checks and balances into the whole process. This will bring not just more ideas but also alternate perspectives into the picture.

What then is the method to ensure the free flow of information? In theory, it can happen in two ways: one, through transparency on the part of the law-making and law-enforcing agencies; and, two, through the willingness of civil society to take the trouble of seeking information. In reaching this objective, tools like the Right to Information Act (RTI) can help civil society organisations and citizens' groups. This can also help in keeping a check on corruption of all forms, be it in the acquisition of weapons and other equipment, use of time, and strategic efficiency in deployment, or in ensuring the quality and frequency of police patrols. Vigilant activism can be extremely useful in not letting the state machinery off guard. The role of the mass media will also be crucial in this respect. One only needs to recall here the public scrutiny of the state response in the immediate aftermath of the attacks of 26/11.

Avoiding Polarisation of Communities

Civil society can play an important role in this respect as well. In the United States, there were several attacks and hate crimes against the Sikh community of Indian origin in the aftermath of 9/11, confusing them with Osama bin Laden and his accomplices because of their headgear. Examples like this show that terrorism inevitably leads to polarisation of communities. In fact, one of the purposes of terrorism is to divide and polarise the society based on the particular identities, thereby going well beyond the number of immediate victims of a terror attack. It would be a failure of civil society if any terror attack by people belonging to a particular religion or community was to lead to a polarised society. It would amount to directly playing into the hands of the terrorists.

A vibrant civil society can be crucial in ensuring that terrorism is not confused with identity and, thus, avoid stereotyping of religious identities. There have been similar instances of this kind where people belonging to particular groups were ordered to exit planes and arrested for alleged suspicious activity when in reality they were harmless business persons.[5] Similarly, in another recent instance of this kind, a Muslim family of Indian origin was barred from flying when they discussed safe exit plans on board an aircraft.[6] That these instances happened in a democratic state like the US is a matter of serious concern. It also underlines the need for an active civil society.

India is no exception to this trend. In the wake of the recent terror attacks in India, the name of Azamgarh has been tarnished as a nurturing ground of terrorist activity and agenda. In addition, many youths from this region have either lost their jobs, or have been denied employment opportunities and have become targets of suspicion and ridicule. Such damaging tendencies must be avoided at all costs. India surely does not want terrorism to be nurtured because of polarisation of this kind. Here the preventive role of civil society can be critical in eliminating polarisation.

Sometimes, even the state machinery plays a role in the polarisation of communities when it portrays the captured terrorists in a certain manner. The mass media becomes a tool in this process. For example, in the case of the alleged terrorists captured in connection with the Delhi blasts of September 2008, almost all national dailies published their pictures, showing the achievement of the Delhi Police. The alleged terrorists' faces were seen covered by identical Palestinian *rumaals*, a vestment that was used as headgear, and made popular, by the late Yasser Arafat. This sort of racial profiling of the alleged perpetrators of terror does not help. More shameful is the revelation that the Delhi Police had stocked up these *rumaals* to use in a similar manner in cases relating to terrorism.[7] It is in areas like this that one would like to see greater civil society activism by way of petitions and public interest litigations to avoid stereotyping of terror.

Avoiding Communalisation of Terrorism

This issue is of particular significance as far as India is concerned. Given the country's diversity of communities and religions, terrorism has been communalised ever since it has emerged in India. It has even been used for political purposes to increase societal tensions to disrupt the fragile democratic secular ethos of the Indian Union. However, if a terrorist attack leads to communal violence resulting in death and destruction on a mass scale, then it aids the terrorists' agenda, which is to divide the country on the lines of religious identity. It also puts a question mark on the unity and strength of the country and on the ability of the state to manage its internal affairs.

Stereotyping of communities and religions can lead to exploitation. Multi-faith dialogues and interaction can be of great help in solving this issue as lack of communication and interaction between different communities leads to misunderstandings and lack of trust. Civil society organisations can play a role by designing mechanisms to introduce religious practices of different religions to other communities in ways that eliminate misinformation about each other.

The role of religious preachers will be critically important in this respect. An attempt must be made to ensure that religious preaching remains secular in character and that there are no attempts to prove the superiority of any faith by pointing to the apparent or imagined shortfalls of another. Thus, it must be ensured that religious education is not contradictory to the values of secularism and tolerance, which are enshrined in the Indian Constitution.

Role of Discrimination and Poverty

Discrimination, poverty and alienation are fertile grounds for the growth of terrorism. Social harmony can be achieved through civil society, and NGOs and social organisations can play an important role in this direction. The argument here is that when any sort of disadvantage is present, it is easy for the perpetrators of terror to instill a sense of alienation or discrimination. Young, uneducated, poor youths tend to be easy prey of the hate doctrine and are willing to take up the 'cause of justice,' even if it means embracing terrorism. One only needs to recall here that Ajmal Kasab, the only terrorist captured alive in the Mumbai attack, came from a poor background and joined radical outfits probably because his father could not afford a set of new clothes. The point of this argument is not to justify his actions, but to highlight the fact that if the society does not channelise the abilities and energies of the youth in a constructive manner, these will be exploited by destructive forces like those of terrorism, crimes against women, and hate crimes. Civil society organisations can play a role in assimilation of the members from the disadvantaged sections of the society by activities that increase social trust and faith in common welfare. Therefore, if the well-off sections of the society take the first steps, however small, a lot could be achieved. This can take various forms like educational and vocational facilities for the disadvantaged groups and equal employment opportunities to avoid discrimination. Civil society organisations and private industry can lead the way in this respect and set an example for the government.

At a more general level, a fragmented country will be more vulnerable to a divisive agenda, whether home-grown or coming from across the borders, than one that is known for its strength and unity. Strengthening the country from within before taking the battle to the enemy across the border is the need of the hour.

Channel for State-Society Interaction

At the most basic level, by ensuring a sustained dialogue, the state and the society can keep each other informed. It will also ensure that the political elite are not scared of social activism and do not consider it a threat but an effective tool of state functioning in a democracy. A serious role of civil society will also ensure that the political elite does not ignore it, as was seen in the instances of Mumbai protests when politicians attracted public ire for ridiculing the demonstrations that targeted the political class. In order for this to happen, however, both sides need to establish a mode of sustained dialogue and take it to a certain level of maturity and trust. Civil society can also ensure that there is no sense of antagonism between the state and the people and that there is trust between the two. Civil society can become the space for the peaceful expression of opinion and, thus, act as a safety valve to defuse pressure situations that threaten to lead to a state-society clash.

Ensuring Preparedness and Post-event Response and Role of the Individual

State machinery can develop plans on how it expects the citizens to react in case of terrorist attacks of the scale of Mumbai and perhaps even for larger attacks. Unfortunately, there are no such plans as of now. NGOs and citizens groups can play a significant role in educating the people on tasks such as informing the police in the case of suspicious movements in the area or in the case of finding any suspicious object or clearing an area to minimise the casualties. Equally important is the verification of the accuracy of the information and controlling the spread of misinformation because the latter could lead to spread of panic and cause unprecedented havoc. Civil society organisations can play a greater role in this respect. Verification of information for accuracy and channelising of the accurate information to the people is one way. Civil society can use the mass media for this purpose. Having the contact details of nodal agencies dealing with terrorism can be useful to get accurate information. Civic organisations can play an important role in educating the citizens on response and preparedness to situations where terrorists may use unconventional means and methods like chemical or biological weapons for attacks. This can be done through workshops, demonstrations of rescue efforts, stocking and distribution of first aid, and so on. The role of the alert and active individual will be crucial for all of this to take place.

Conclusion

While civil society can play a crucial role in helping counter terrorism, a word of caution is, nevertheless, needed before one can begin to reap the benefits of the possible positive influence of civil society in the case of terrorism. At the outset, one must ensure that civil society must amount to more than the sum of its parts. One must also have an inherent faith in the constructive role played by collective activism. It must also be ensured that the citizens united for sloganeering are really concerned about the menace of terrorism and that national interest is above everything else. It is also necessary that, at all times, civil society does not lose its 'civil' and democratic character and start promoting hardline views instead. Civil society organisations must also ensure that nationalism does not mask national interests. These are the pitfalls that one sees many public groups falling into. Civil society organisations must be aware of these, particularly when the fight is against terrorism because of the extremely complex nature of the threat of terrorism that India faces today.

It can be stated that Indian civil society is rich with exciting possibilities as far as its role in dealing with terrorism is concerned. It can become the space where the society and state interact over the issues of mutual interest and concern. However, for this, the 'civil' in civil society must mature to a certain level. And, indeed, for this to take place, the state must warm up to the idea of increased scrutiny and questioning of its performance, which unfortunately is not the case as of now. The state and civil society must be ready to play complementary roles. Civil society has tools like RTI that it can use to great benefit in its efforts to deal with terrorism. It can also play a crucial role in ensuring social harmony and avoiding communalisation of terror. Social activism can lead the fight against discrimination of all forms and can channelise energies towards positive outcomes.

Terrorism is a challenge to the authority of the state in a non-conventional manner and to deal with it effectively, the state has to take several initiatives. However, this cannot be done in isolation. All organs of the state and society must design a comprehensive response by which the vulnerability of the country to the menace of terrorism can be minimised. Often, state-led mechanisms fail because excessive secrecy keeps other important elements out of it and is, therefore, unable to exploit their possibilities of playing a constructive role. Individuals and civil society can unite to play their roles in assisting the state initiatives and by asking the state critical questions by which it can improve its mechanisms and methods. Often, there is a danger that in a rather overcautious response to terrorism, the state might curtail the democratic space. Civil society can safeguard it and ensure its usage in aiding the fight against terrorism.

Civil society in a democratic state is the ultimate manifestation of the success of the democratic space. If developed and used in the right manner, it can play a significant role in reducing the instances and intensity of terrorism.

Notes

1. For more discussion on this, see Sunil Khilnani, "The Development of Civil Society" in Sudipta Kaviraj and Sunil Khilnani (eds.), *Civil Society: History and Possibilities* (Cambridge: Cambridge University Press, 2001), pp. 11-32.
2. The liberal strand locates the centre of civil society in the economy, property rights and market mechanisms and for the conservative, it is in cultural norms and values, historical patterns of societal relations in any civility. Ibid., pp. 13-14.
3. Centre for Civil Society, London School of Economics, "What is Civil Society?" 01 March 2004, http://www.lse.ac.uk/collections/CCS/what_is_civil_society.htm, accessed on 15 January 2008.
4. The UPA had opposed POTA by calling it draconian and a political tool. It was also quick to remove POTA after it came to power in May 2004.

5. "No Racial Consideration Behind Plane Incident: Dutch Govt," http://www.outlookindia.com/pti_news.asp?id=410237, accessed on 30 January 2008.
6. "Safest Seat Remarks get Muslim Family Kicked off Plane," http://edition.cnn.com/2009/US/01/01/family.grounded/, accessed on 03 February 2008.
7. For more on this, see Sadanand Menon, "Burnt to the Grain," *Better Photography*, November 2008, p. 37.

12

Counter-Terrorism Policies of the US, Japan and Israel: Lessons for India

Rajesh Kapoor

This chapter analyses the counter-terrorism approaches of the US, Japan and Israel and suggests lessons that India can learn from their experiences. There is no exaggeration in the statement that the US and Japanese approaches to counter-terrorism have emerged as exemplary since they have been considerably successful in preventing the recurrence of terrorist attacks on their soil and, therefore, have a lot to offer to other terrorism afflicted countries.

This does not mean that their policies are flawless. In fact, the US policies are criticised the world over and several theorists have suggested that waging a war against countries on flimsy grounds is unjustifiable and unacceptable. Japanese policies too are criticised within and outside Japan. Moreover, Japan works in conjunction with the US. Like the US, Israel follows the military model of counter-terrorism. It is interesting to note that the US, Japan and Israel are long-term allies, whereas India has only recently enhanced its cooperation with the US.

The counter-terrorism approach of each individual country is shaped by both domestic and international determinants. The three countries mentioned above are located in militarily vulnerable or strategically significant regions. Japan has China and North Korea in its vicinity, Israel has several hostile nations surrounding it, while the US has many enemies all over the world due to its interventionist policies. Similarly, India also has hostile countries in its neighbourhood covertly sponsoring and supporting several terrorist outfits. While India and the US are pluralistic and multi-cultural societies, Israel and Japan are largely homogeneous. They are also smaller in size, but densely populated. The US is bigger in terms of geographical size with few densely populated cities. The US, Japan, Israel and India all figure on the hit list of Islamic fundamentalists. Even Japan has received threats from Osama bin Laden in a few of his interviews.

Of all these countries, India is the most vulnerable. Despite the long history of terrorism, the country has not come out with an effective and long-term strategy to counter terrorism. Given the size and population of India, it will not be feasible for the country to blindly follow the approaches of other countries.

Time and again, the US, Japan, Israel and India have been subjected to terrorism. Japan faced the terrorism propagated and perpetuated by the left wing Japanese Red Army (JRA) and also by religious sects like Aum Shinrikyo. Left wing terrorism lost its momentum with the rapid urbanisation and industrialisation of the country. Acts of terrorism were dealt with the utmost care and state policies not only addressed the security needs of the citizens but also the grudges of disgruntled youths, workers and farmers. The US, ever since its inception, remained an important target for terrorists. As a country, the US has created an effective shield against terrorism around its citizens across the world though US citizens have been targeted abroad. Other than securing the homeland, the US has also waged a global war against the so-called states sponsoring terrorism. Israel has responded to terrorism through retaliation and also through preemptive measures. India is a soft state and instead of preventing the terrorist attacks through a well defined strategy, reacts only after a terrorist attack, and that too usually rather mildly.

India's counter-terrorism capabilities are inadequate and require much more than has been done so far. In the last few years, the occurrence of terrorist strikes has considerably increased. Few countries have effectively prevented, if not tackled, this problem. It is argued here that as India borrowed the best democratic practices from across the world, it should also borrow the best concepts and practices to counter terrorism, and adapt them sufficiently to evolve its own strategy of safeguarding its citizens and national assets from terrorists. Before analysing the effectiveness of the counter-terrorism policies of these countries, a few facts must be recounted.

According to American sources, between February 2004 and June 2008, a total of 21 incidents of terrorist attacks took place in the US. Only nine people were wounded and none died. During the same period, in Japan, 10 terrorist attacks took place which were perpetuated by unknown people or groups. In all, there were no injuries or death. Such is the preparedness of these states against terrorist attacks that instead of targeting them on their soil, terrorists prefer to hit their citizens outside their boundaries. In Israel, around 2,417 incidents took place, killing 218, while 3,142 were injured. Six people were taken hostage and the total number of people directly affected in Israel was 3,366. In the same period, more than 4,300 terrorist attacks took place in India, killing more than 5,000 people, injuring more than 11,316 and more than 2,500 were taken hostage. All these add up to 19,000 direct victims of terrorism in India.[1]

These figures show that countries like the US, Japan and Israel have remained comparatively successful in securing their land and citizens from terrorist threats. These countries have left no stone unturned to reach higher levels of immunity from the continuously evolving terrorism, which also includes the potential threats of chemical, biological and nuclear weapons. In addition, terrorists are constantly changing their tactics. According to several reports, due to the possibilities of weapons of mass destruction (WMDs) falling into the hands of non-state actors, each country, while designing its policies, has remained committed in staying ahead of the terrorists. There are unconfirmed reports to the effect that easy availability of WMD experts in some Eastern European countries has made the situation more alarming.

Counter-Terrorism Policies: Identifying Challenges and Evaluating Effectiveness

Security at the cost of individual liberties and privacy does not go well with the democratic ethos. As a result, counter-terrorist operations in the democratic set-ups remain a challenging and complex task. Anti-terrorism laws are often criticised for their draconian characteristics. In addition, surveillance beyond a point is detrimental to the overall well-being of an individual as there exists the possibility of the state becoming a highly guarded garrison state. Such fears also exist among the civil societies in India. Effectiveness and overall acceptability are two parameters of good governance and counter-terrorism policies. Several domestic and international compulsions also have a detrimental effect on such policies. There are political parties and their representatives who covertly or overtly support criminalisation of politics and subsequently encourage terrorism. International agencies like Amnesty International also criticise the high-handedness of state agencies.

The US, Japan and Israel have adopted a comprehensive approach of dealing with terrorism at different levels, domestic as well as international. In this regard, a series of laws have been passed in each country to prevent terrorist strikes in the last few years. These laws are passed in accordance with Resolution 1373 of the Security Council under which each member state is mandated to frame anti-terrorism laws and enhance international cooperation to support anti-terrorism efforts. These laws are not free from criticism, especially when individual liberty is infringed upon. The PATRIOT Act of the

US provides extraordinary powers to the agencies handling terrorism related issues, including prospective terrorist strikes. Nevertheless, these laws and other measures are instrumental in securing these countries.

In these countries, the entire security apparatus has been beefed up by integrating several existing agencies, creating new counter-terrorism agencies and improving inter-agency as well as intra-agency interoperability and coordination. The issue of command and control has been resolved. Duties and authorities are appropriately defined. Surveillance systems have been strengthened. Intelligence gathering and sharing systems have also been consolidated and made to react promptly in the case of any contingency.

In the US, Japan and Israel, the feeling of nationalism is different than in India. In these countries, it has been observed that a majority of the people are ready to sacrifice their freedom and privacy for the sake of security. These countries can go to any extent to protect the interests of their citizens at home and abroad. This is clearly manifested in their policy documents. India lacks both – the feeling of nationalism of that sort as well as visionary and upright policies.[2]

These countries have achieved a greater degree of immunity because of their ability to muster the necessary resources, political will and public support. They have also taken stringent measures, including punitive and preventive laws, to ensure the safety and security of their citizens anywhere in the world. In the absence of the above factors, and the peculiarity of its geo-political and geo-strategic environment, India has to develop its own counter-terrorism methods and apparatuses. India lacks political will, public support and effective policies to counter terrorism. Therefore, it is imperative that the government learns how to manage public perceptions and evolve equilibrium amongst the advocates of security and liberty.

Counter-Terrorism Approaches of Israel, Japan and the US

Israel

Ever since its creation in 1948, Israel has suffered from terrorism because of the prevalent religious sentiments and the Israeli policy in the Occupied Territories. Since then, Israel has been under siege by its neighbours in the Middle East. Not surprisingly, therefore, counter-terrorist policies have been a critical aspect of Israel's security structure. Israel realised, quite early, the need to have well defined laws and a consistent counter-terrorism approach. Israeli anti-terrorist policies are predominantly retaliatory, repressive, at times proactive and preemptive, and often entail military measures. With the promulgation of the Prevention of Terrorism Ordinance (POTO) in 1948, and the following amendments, most notably in 1980, 1986 and 1993, Israel showed its far-sightedness and efficiently countered its adversaries. After the 9/11 attacks, Israeli policy was viewed by many as a useful model for emulation, though certainly not the best one.

The Israeli approach to counter-terrorism is considered controversial because of the pervasive domestic use of the military in policing actions, imposition of curfew in certain areas, and prolonged detention or deportation of suspected terrorists out of the country even in the absence of incontrovertible evidence. Israel has also augmented the powers of the state in dealing with terrorism to include some very aggressive and controversial measures that have invited international criticism.

Post-9/11, Israel declared the Palestinian attacks as a terrorist threat, though these were earlier considered civil disturbances. James Beckman observes, "Israel views the terrorist threats as armed conflict short of war, and has implemented some very aggressive counter-terrorism measures which reflect this mindset of being at war – or close to it."[3] The Israeli government has now resorted to targeted killings which involve preemptive or anticipatory self-defence against the individual terrorists.

Israel's counter-terrorism stance is three-fold: extra-territorial judicial powers to prosecute elements perpetuating terror, retaliation if provoked, and fighting terrorists even beyond its sovereign territory.[4] It is clearly mentioned in the policy document of the Israel government that "Israel will continue to act determinedly in order to guarantee the security of its citizens and residents in and outside of Israel, against terror organisations threatening to harm them. Israel will continue to act, any where and any time, in order to foil, disrupt and prevent terror attacks against its citizens or residents."[5]

Japan

War-ravaged Japan, in the process of rebuilding its lost glory, economic and military might, suffered several instances of popular uprising and acts of terrorism during the Occupation era (1945-52). However, one considerable achievement of Japan has been that it could secure its citizens and territories from all kind of potential threats. Japan has also put in place a mechanism to deal with chemical and biological weapons. No major incident has been reported since 1995, when members of the Aum Shinrikyo attacked the subway in Tokyo.

The basic policy of Japan's international counter-terrorism measures is three-fold; first, to strengthen national counter-terrorism measures; second, to counter terrorism through international cooperation; and third, through capacity building measures which include assistance to other countries in need.[6]

USA

Right from its inception in 1776, the US has suffered from terrorism. However, it became a primary concern of the US government in the 1970s when terrorists began engaging in hijackings, assassinations, bombings, and hostage taking aimed at undermining US interests, not only inside the country but across the world. The government policies are as much responsible as the other socio-economic, racial or religious factors for the emergence of the anti-US terrorism. The biggest blow to the US military and economic pride came on 11 September 2001, when terrorists attacked and destroyed the World Trade Centre and part of the Pentagon, symbols of US economic and military might. This was followed by a retaliatory military response from the US when President Bush declared the "War on Terror".

With regard to the preparedness of the US, an official document of its Justice Department says that in more than the last seven years, "the Justice Department has significantly improved its ability to identify, penetrate, and dismantle terrorist plots as a result of a series of structural reforms, the development of new intelligence and law enforcement tools, and a new mindset that values information sharing, communication and prevention. Working with its federal, state, and local partners as well as international counterparts, the Justice Department has not rested in its efforts to safeguard America."[7] The US has shown the rest of the world the effectiveness and comprehensiveness of its counter-terrorism policies. Even now, agencies dealing with counter-terrorism are constantly at work.

The US counter-terrorism policy is primarily focussed on preventing terrorist attacks before they occur, using a broad range of tools, denying terrorist organisations as well as state-sponsors of terrorism access to WMD, denying terrorist groups the support and sanctuary of rogue states, and also denying the terrorists control of any nation that they could use as a base and launching pad for terror.[8]

Legal Measures

Israel

Israeli legal measures include the POTO which has already been discussed.[9] The POTO does not create a separate criminal offence for terrorism and leaves the term undefined in the ordinance. Interestingly, those convicted under acts of terrorism, to the extent they survive, are tried under the normal penal laws of Israel. In Section 1 of POTO, "terrorist organisation" is defined as "a body of persons resorting in its activities to acts of violence calculated to cause death or injury to a person or to threats of such acts of violence." The law also prohibits participation in its activities, publication of propaganda and collection of money or articles for the benefit of a terrorist organisation or activities. There is a provision of severe punishment ranging from 5 to 20 years for the members of different ranks, and depending on the degree of involvement in the terrorist activities. Israeli law prohibits terrorists from propagating their messages and intentions through speeches or otherwise, and has been functional for the longest period. A person can be criminalised on the basis of the words of praise or sympathy, delivered in the public places, for terrorist organisations. Israel's law on explosives prohibits the manufacture, transport, or trade of explosive devices or materials without a government issued permit to handle the substances.

Israel's penal law permits the death penalty in cases of terrorism and also allows for the prosecution of those who do not directly participate in terrorist acts. Some special provisions of the penal law also provide Israeli courts with extra-territorial jurisdiction in the cases of crimes against humanity, against the state of Israel, or against Israeli residents or nationals. The military has been given special powers to detain and try suspected terrorists and also to demolish homes or dwellings of terrorists caught or killed, and persons offering assistance or shelter to terrorists, particularly in the Occupied Territories.

Basically, in the Occupied Territories, there is a dual justice system based on the nationality of the accused: Jewish underground terrorists are tried in Israeli courts, and others are tried in military tribunals. Israeli laws are periodically subject to revision and several existing controversial provisions are repealed in the subsequent amendments to POTO like the trial of civilians by a military court which was similar to the US practice of trying combatants.

Israel treats all terrorists as unlawful combatants, and to deal with them, the country has evolved its own practice of eliminating them only on the basis of proven evidence. They are not entitled to rights and liberties enjoyed by rest of the citizens or, for that matter, human beings. In this way, Israel has thwarted several terrorist attacks but the likelihood of loss of innocent lives has also been very high. Israel has even destroyed terrorist camps beyond its territories. Israel takes refuge in international laws, such as various UN Resolutions to justify its acts of targeted killing.

Japan

Unlike the US and Israel, Japan does not have a separate statute regulating and defining terrorism. After the 1995 Sarin gas attack, Japan amended its laws for dealing with religious groups and also improved the government's capability to gain more information about crimes by enhancing its surveillance capabilities. Japan amended its Religious Corporation Law of 1951. Under Article 81 of this law, Japanese courts are empowered to dissolve any group that violates the law. According to James Beckman, "This law has clear implications to Islamic-based groups which might also be engaged in militant activities."[10] Under the 1996 amendment to the Act, all registered religious groups are required to submit annual details of properties owned by them and also details of their leaders, executive members and financial accounts. Any member of the group can be questioned if the authority feels that there is enough ground to do so. The government can suspend the profit-making activities of any group and can review the certification paper on the request of any citizen who has been negatively impacted by the activities of that group.[11]

More surveillance powers were given to the police by amending the Anti-Subversion Act (refer to surveillance section later in the chapter) under which terrorism related crimes also fall. In 1999, through an amendment, the powers of law enforcing agencies were further augmented. In the wake of the 9/11 attacks, Japan reviewed its position on terrorism and worked to strengthen its crisis management and information gathering systems.[12] The anti-terrorism special measures law was implemented to provide the Self-Defence Forces (SDF) with powers to support non-combat and humanitarian operations, including the transport of weapons and ammunition, to the US-led Coalition in the Indian Ocean, and to carry, and if necessary, use weapons. The Japanese Coast Guard was also authorised to fire at suspicious vessels in Japanese territorial waters by a separate legislation.

In 2002, the Diet passed the "Emergency Legislation to Deal with Military Attacks from Abroad", "Self-Defence Revision Law", and "Security Council Revision Law", which taken together constitute the War Contingency Bills.[13] These laws are meant to transform Japan into a country that participates in war. Since the Constitution lays down the three basic laws mandating Japan's renunciation of war, its refusal to take part in combat, and to bear arms, the three Bills were necessary to revise the country's position. However, some Japanese scholars consider them unconstitutional.

The Japanese government has amended its Immigration Control and Refugee Recognition Act, which was enacted in May 2006, and made it mandatory for foreign nationals to submit personal identification information (fingerprints and a facial photograph) on landing.[14] Steps have also been taken to deport foreign terrorists, and it has been made compulsory to submit a report about crew members and passengers prior to landing at any air or sea port.

USA

The US Congress had enacted several Acts to enhance the capabilities of federal agencies. A wide range of activities are clearly covered under the definition of the act of terrorism. Taking notice of the inadequacies and lacunae of the existing Acts, the US government introduced the PATRIOT Act immediately after the 9/11 attacks. Now the Department of Justice has the authority to investigate all terrorism related offences. This puts an end to the confusion which existed earlier because of the concurrent authority of various other departments to investigate such cases.

PATRIOT Act: There existed several domestic and international mechanisms before 9/11 to combat terrorism, including the use of military and intelligence apparatuses.[15] However, 9/11 forced several drastic legal changes. The US Congress enacted several pieces of legislation in the months following the attacks. These included: the Aviation and Transportation Security Act; Bioterrorism Response Act of 2001; Enhanced Border Security and Visa Entry Reform Act of 2002; Terrorist Bombings Convention Implementation Act of 2001; and Victims of Terrorism Relief Act of 2001. The most important piece of legislation, however, was the Uniting and Strengthening America by Providing Appropriate Tools Required to Intercept and Obstruct Terrorism Act of 2001 (USA PATRIOT). A few of the provisions in the Act were supposed to expire with time, but these provisions, including the critical information sharing provisions, were reauthorised by the US PATRIOT Act Improvement and Reauthorisation Act of 2005, which allowed investigators to continue to exercise more powers in countering terrorism. The 2005 version of the PATRIOT Act contains all the expiring provisions of the USA PATRIOT Act, and several additional safeguards to protect privacy interests and civil liberties; and strengthened port security has also been added to it.

The US government was successful in taking advantage of the post-9/11 panicked public and introduced a 342-page Bill to acquire expansive powers in combating terrorism for its different agencies. It took 45 days in getting the final approval of the Congress and little debate took place over the deliberations of the Bill.[16]

The PATRIOT Act had several components that were intended to improve the ability of the domestic security apparatus to prevent further attacks. Through the Act, the historical barriers among different agencies, particularly intelligence and law enforcement, were blurred, and interoperability among the agencies was enhanced to an unprecedented level. Centralised information sharing and creation of provisions to allow disclosure of historically secret grand jury testimony to federal officials without a court order were other significant steps. The Act has allowed federal agents to better track sophisticated terrorists trained to evade detection and has given national security investigators tools comparable to those used in criminal cases. It has also increased penalties for those who commit certain terrorist crimes and those who support them. It has also, more generally, allowed information sharing among law enforcement, intelligence, immigration, and national security officials.

More powers were given to the agencies engaged in countering terrorism through amending the Foreign Intelligence Surveillance Act of 1978. The FISA Amendments Act of 2008 allows intelligence professionals to quickly and effectively monitor terrorist communications, while protecting the civil liberties of Americans. The Act ensures all the essential powers to the intelligence agencies, to keep a watch on terrorists' communications, and decisive power to acquire foreign intelligence information about persons even outside US territories. The Act also makes it mandatory to seek court orders to target Americans for foreign intelligence surveillance.

President George W Bush signed the Military Commissions Act (MCA) on 17 October 2006, which provided statutory authority to try alien unlawful enemy combatants for violations of the law of war. Prior to this, the Bush Administration gave unprecedented powers to the military, especially in matters pertaining to detention and torture of people who were believed to be involved in international terrorism. Guantanamo Bay prison is one of the examples in this regard where human rights were also violated.[17] The United States has employed military commissions to try its enemies for violations of the law of war since the Revolutionary War. Through a commission system under the MCA, an unprecedented set of protections for war-time prosecutions has been provided.[18] Besides, equal attention is being paid to protect the rights, liberties and interests of US citizens through timely review of existing policies.

Military in Counter-terrorism

As discussed in the legal measures, the Israeli military enjoys special powers in the Occupied Territories and a type of martial law is still in effect there. The emergency regulations give the military great leeway in imposing restrictions, detentions and expulsions as a means of controlling the region. It is under this special authority that Israel has conducted such operations as demolishing homes and targeted killings. In the Occupied Territories, the total number of troops has been considerably increased and nearly three divisions are operating there.

Israel utilises its military to arrest militants, secure certain borders in the occupied areas, and try terrorists in military courts. The utilisation of the military is permissible under the emergency orders which govern the contested regions of the West Bank and the Gaza Strip.

The Israeli Defence Forces (IDF) have envisioned and implemented the counter-terrorism policy in the Occupied Territories. The policy is based on the principle of the use of force against terrorists and even civilian targets who are suspected of sheltering terrorists residing in the territories beyond its sovereignty. Israel's three intelligence services – the General Security Service (GSS, or SHABAK), the Israeli Defence Forces Intelligence Branch, and the Mossad (Israeli intelligence service) – are primarily responsible for Israeli counter-terrorism policy. Israel's domestic security apparatus has been fortified over a period of time and the country has given a lot of freedom to its intelligence agencies. Israeli investigators have broader investigative capabilities than are available in regular criminal investigations such as investigative arrests and prolonged interrogations of terrorists. Following complaints of atrocities and mishandling of people under detention, Israeli courts have instructed the investigative agencies to mellow down their torture tactics and stop taking forced confessions from the arrested.

The Israeli security apparatus is thoroughly backed by the government in power. There have been reports that GSS officers were pardoned and their actions over looked. The prolonged planning and counter-terrorism measures have certainly strengthened various agencies but turned the entire state into a "garrison police state". This implies that the state is highly guarded and even public places are subject to security screening. Where the agencies are unable to get a clear picture, especially in places occupied by the Palestinians, "lock-down mechanisms" to prevent unwanted incidents are followed.[19]

In the post-War period, the Japanese SDF did not have a very good reputation among the masses. However, owing to the sustained efforts of the government to popularise its defence forces, the SDF has created some space for itself and is usually used in disaster relief and humanitarian aid activities within and outside Japan. The SDF carries out drills with the NPA (National Police Agency) and other agencies on a regular basis. Japan has also utilised the SDF to play a significant role in Afghanistan and Iraq where they have provided rear echelon and constructive support to the US and other allies.

In the US, the military is not used for maintaining internal law and order. This has been ensured by the Posse Comitatus Act.[20] There are certainly more views than the strict restriction about the use of the military domestically. A few scholars are of the opinion that there is erosion in the Act and, if required, the military can be used domestically as well. The last domestic deployment took place during the 1996 Atlanta Olympics where troops were engaged more in menial tasks than actual security purposes. In fact, the US Congress has reaffirmed under the Homeland Security legislation that the Posse Comitatus Act has served the nation well and there is no need to deploy the military for internal security maintenance.[21] The US Army is continuously engaged in fighting insurgents in Afghanistan and Iraq. In addition, the US has strategic military bases around the globe which provide it with the leverage and the ability to respond quickly on issues of international concern.

Policing and Intelligence

Israel has a single, centralised police structure with a very aggressive approach to homeland security, which is significantly augmented by its military forces. The country also has an effective warning system, an aggressive intelligence network, the capability to anticipate potential attacks and their prevention. Military forces remain instrumental in maintaining the security of the country, from both inside and outside. To address the threat of terrorism,

Israel has overhauled its security apparatus and created a new ministry of Home Security, with control over the police, border guards and other units.[22] All the Israeli police stations in Israel have Community Policing Centres. This experiment has shown mixed results on crime as these centres have helped in building up friendly ties between the police and public, but not all the people are aware of these centres. Prof David Weisburd observes, "The idea of including local authorities in decision-making has become an established part of the Israeli policing philosophy."[23]

Israel has also enhanced its intelligence capabilities, including human intelligence. The number of security personnel has seen an unprecedented increase and according to a study in 2003, police and security personnel outnumbered total employees in Israel's top three corporations. Almost everything is under the tight scrutiny of the state and its law and order maintenance agencies. The biggest criticism of this system is that the security personnel are not well educated and are ill-trained because of the high cost of specialised training. Consequently, they often end up harassing and killing innocent people. The strongest point of Israeli counter-terrorism is its intelligence. Martin Ven Creveld observes that "the Israeli success in gathering intelligence has been extraordinary."[24]

Japan has also strengthened its National Police Organisation (NPO) which is constituted of the National Public Safety Commission (NPSC) and NPA. At the fundamental level, NPA is a very effective agency in the prevention of terrorist acts. NPA operates through small kiosks built on the sides of roads. It is said about the Japanese policeman that he knows virtually everybody by name and face in the area under his jurisdiction. He is more like a postman than a policeman and has mastered the art of covertly checking anybody's residence without hurting their sentiments. The NPA conducts biannual surveys through the policeman, and the data, thus collected and updated is kept in the *Kobans* (police kiosks) for the use of the police. This is a very effective method of policing. Unlike other developed countries, the Japanese public is overwhelmingly cooperative and forthcoming in sharing personal information with the police.[25] Another interesting detail about the NPO is that the NPSC exercises administrative supervision over the NPA. While the Commission is under the jurisdiction of the prime minister, he is not empowered to exercise direct command or control. This ensures the Commission's independence and its political neutrality.[26]

The US has several decentralised law enforcement agencies at city, state and federal levels. Taking lessons from the failure of state machinery to anticipate and prevent another 9/11, and on the basis of suggestions of the 9/11 Commission, various law agencies were brought under the jurisdiction of the Department of Homeland Security by the passing of the Homeland Security Bill in 2002.[27] It is clearly stated in the policies of the Department of Homeland Security that in order to prevent and protect US citizens and their freedom, critical infrastructure, property and the economy from acts of terrorism, natural disasters and other emergencies, the department works to anticipate, preempt, detect and deter threats to the homeland security. The department is also responsible for preparation required in case there is a terrorist attack, natural disaster or other large-scale emergency. In such cases, the department will provide a coordinated, comprehensive federal response and mount a swift and effective recovery effort.[28] The department assumes primary responsibility for ensuring that emergency response professionals are prepared for any situation. Yet, the policing is quite decentralised and unlike in Israel, the military is not used to maintain internal law and order. For this reason, the law and order situation varies from state to state in the US. Terrorism related cases are mostly dealt with by the federal agencies whose powers have been augmented to unprecedented levels, with no financial constraints.[29]

Surveillance

Israel has made frequent usage of electronic surveillance and wiretap intercepts to prevent acts of terrorism. An elaborate database on terrorist activity and the movements of terrorist operatives and their chiefs has been maintained and is continuously updated. Each Israeli citizen is required to carry a national identification card on his/her person, having the person's picture, name and date of birth. Most Israeli citizens prefer their security over privacy.

Through an Act passed by the Japanese Diet in 1999, the law enforcement agencies acquired wiretapping surveillance powers. In Japan, anybody can be put under electronic surveillance by seeking a judicial warrant from a district court judge.

In the US, the domestic surveillance capabilities of law enforcement and intelligence officials are incredible. Surveillance blended with speedy trials and the strictest punitive measures has produced noteworthy results. Nothing has been left outside the purview of the monitoring agencies, and e-mails, Internet usage, all sorts of communication and even financial transactions can be put under the scanner if there is a reasonable suspicion to validate the action. Prior to 11 September, international financing and money laundering for terrorist networks was widely regarded as a significant problem. To correct this, the Patriot Act requires banks to monitor and report suspicious transactions. Such reports are to be shared by the Treasury Department with the intelligence and law enforcement communities. The Act also provides for government access to credit records without notification. The surveillance capabilities of the government were also substantially increased through an expansion of the ability of investigators to obtain FISA warrants. FISA authorised wiretaps where the purpose of the tap was to obtain intelligence about a foreign power (including a terrorist organisation). The PATRIOT Act changed the word "purpose" to "significant purpose" in the FISA warrant requirement.

International Cooperation

Israel has shown willingness to cooperate in international attempts at countering terrorism. The US is its major ally in this activity. Both countries have a good intelligence sharing network.

Japan has shown keenness on promoting international cooperation to overcome its vulnerability against terrorism, and deny terrorists safe havens and means for their activities. Japan has played a constructive role at various international platforms such as the United Nations (UN), G-8, Association of Southeast Asian Nations (ASEAN) and ASEAN Regional Forum (ARF). It has also ratified and implemented all 13 international counter-terrorism conventions and protocols, and the government has shown active interest in combating all forms of terrorism. Japan has made a vital contribution to the fight against terrorism in the Indian Ocean with the Coalition forces engaged in activities such as Operation Enduring Freedom (OEF), International Security Assistance Force (ISAF), Provincial Reconstruction Teams (PRT) in Afghanistan and OEF-Maritime Interdiction Operations (OEF-MIO) in the Indian Ocean. Japan has been contributing to peace and stability by conducting refuelling of vessels participating in the OEF-MIO from 2001 to 2007 under the Anti-Terrorism Special Measures Law, and from February 2008 under the Replenishment Support Special Measures Law.

Other than domestic security arrangements, in order to address the problem at the basic level, Japan is providing assistance to developing countries like Pakistan through official development assistance (ODA) so that socio-economic factors conducive for the growth of the terrorism can be tackled. Japan is advocating peaceful solution of the conflicts and consolidation of peace, sustainable development and poverty reduction and assistance to moderation and promotion of dialogue between civilisations. Japan is also providing technical knowhow and counter-terrorism capacity building assistance to several countries, particularly in Southeast Asia.[30]

The US has signed several international treaties and also assists various countries in evolving new counter-terrorism policies and strengthening existing ones. Being a multi-cultural country, the US has recognised the need for reconciliation of interests and has taken effective measures to prevent the radicalisation of the society.

Regional Instruments to Counter Terrorism

African Union (AU)

- Convention on the Prevention and Combating of terrorism, 1999
- Protocol to the OUA Convention on the Prevention and Combating of terrorism, 2004

Association Of South East Asian Nations (ASEAN)

- ASEAN Convention on Counter Terrorism, 2007

Black Sea Economic Cooperation

- Additional Protocol on combating terrorism to the Agreement among the Governments of the Black Sea Economic Cooperation participating States on cooperation in combating crime, in particular its organised forms, 2004

Commonwealth Of Independant States (CIS)

- Treaty on cooperation among States Members of the Commonwealth of Independant States in combating terrorism, 1999

Communauté Economique Et Monétaire De L'Afrique Centrale (CEMAC)

- Règlement N. 08/05-UEAC-057-CM-13 portant adoption de la Convention relative à la lutte contre le terrorisme en Afrique Centrale, 2005
- Règlement N.01/03 CEMAC-UMAC portant prévention et répression du blanchiment des capitaux et du financement du terrorisme en Afrique Centrale, 2003

Cooperation Council For The Arab States Of The Gulf (GCC)

- Convention against terrorism, 2004

European Union

- European Convention on the suppression of terrorism, 1977
- Protocol amending the European Convention on the suppression of terrorism, 2003
- Convention on the prevention of terrorism, 2005
- Convention on laundering, search, seizure and confiscation of the proceeds from crime and on the financing of terrorism, 2005
- ECHR Case Law Related to Terrorism
- EU Instruments and Case Law relating to Terrorism

Financial Action Task Force (FATF)
- Special recommendations on Terrorist Financing, 2004

League Of Arab States
- Arab Convention on the suppression of terrorism, 1998
- Arab Convention on Extradition, 1952

Organization Of American States (OAS) / Inter-American Committee Against Terrorism (CICTE)
- Convention to prevent and punish acts of terrorism taking the form of crimes against persons and related extortion that are of international significance, 1971
- Inter-American Convention against terrorism, 2002

Organization Of The Islamic Conference (OIC)
- Convention of the Organization of the Islamic Conference on combating international terrorism, 1999

Shangai Cooperation Organization (SCO)
- Shangai Convention on Combating Terrorism, Separatism and Extremism, 2001

South Asian Association For Regional Cooperation (SAARC)
- Regional Convention on suppression of terrorism, 1987
- Additional Protocol to the Regional Convention on suppression of terrorism, 2004. Entered into force on 12 January 2006.

Union Economique Et Monétaire Ouest Africaine (UEMOA)
- Règlement N.14/2002/CM/UEMOA relatif au gel des fonds et autres ressources financières dans le cadre de la lutte contre le financement du terrorisme, 2002
- Décision N.09/2008/CM/UEMOA relative à la liste des personnes, entités ou organismes visés par le gel des fonds et autres ressources financières dans le cadre de la lutte contre le financement du terrorisme, 2008
- Directive N.04/2007/CM/UEMOA relative à la lutte contre le financement du terrorisme dans les Etats membres de l'UEMOA, 2007

Source: United Nations Office on Drugs and Crime: Terrorism Prevention Branch - https://www.unodc.org/tldb/en/regional_instruments.html

Post 9/11, the US has leveraged international law enforcement and other counter-terrorism cooperation to target and dismantle terrorist enterprises both at home and abroad. The US has shared thousands of pieces of threat-related information with its international allies and provided critical evidence to other countries for use in terrorism-related prosecutions and received critical evidence from others for its own use. Several US agencies, including the Federal Bureau of Investigation (FBI) and Drug Enforcement Administration continue to play important roles in Afghanistan, particularly to assist the Afghan state agencies to nab and spoil the plans of the terrorist organisations that benefit from illegal drug trade.

More generally, the US has declared a policy of preemptive military strikes in order to deter future attacks. The Administration first employed a broad-based military operation as part of the war on terrorism in Afghanistan under the "Bush Doctrine" of preemptive military strikes on states that pose an imminent threat to the United States. Subsequently, continuing the same war, the US launched an invasion on Iraq to depose the ruling government under Saddam Hussein based on the assumption that Iraq had WMD. India is unlikely to follow such a hawkish policy but can learn some lessons, and should strategise to use such methods in a controlled and covert manner.

Conclusion

To strengthen any counter-terrorism apparatus, well defined laws and a focussed approach are the basic prerequisites. India needs to carry out structural as well as functional reforms of all its agencies by drawing lessons from other countries. There is an urgent need to identify the areas of contention among the various agencies responsible for countering terrorism. On the lines of the US Department of Justice, one single ministry should be given the responsibility to investigate terrorism related offences so as to minimise confusion. It will help law enforcement and intelligence agencies to identify, dismantle, and disrupt terrorist plots by eliminating the differences and miscommunication among various agencies. India can also minimise the time loss during procedural enquiries by updating investigative tools and allowing authorities to obtain a search warrant from a single court regardless of where the terrorist-related activity occurred. India also needs a separate set of rules and prosecutorial system for the perpetrators of extreme violence. Military courts can be assigned with some powers under duly laid down rules and also in consultation with the Indian judiciary.

India needs to seriously consider the powers that security agencies in the US, Israel and Japan have derived owing to the PATRIOT Act, POTO (of Israel) and Anti-Terrorism Special Measures Law, respectively. A post-mortem strategy will not work for India. Instead, prevention is better than cure, and preemption is the best of all. India should keep all options open, including use of the military whenever required, be it against domestic terrorism or a threat abroad. It should also be ensured that such manoeuvres are carried out in a controlled manner.

Being a pacifist country, Japanese counter-terrorism policy, especially its legal measures, have several inherent limitations. However, the Japanese strategy of maximisation of national interests by taking advantage of the situation should be studied and replicated. Japanese nationalists are trying to create a favourable environment for revising their pacifist Constitution so that the country may regain normalcy.[31] An amended version of the Japanese Religious Corporation Law can be useful for streamlining religious organisations in India.

Israeli intelligence agencies are the best in gathering information, be it inside Israel or elsewhere. They exercise unlimited powers and enjoy state protection. Indian intelligence agencies can enhance their capabilities through joint training programmes and intelligence sharing.

The Posse Comitatus Act of the US should be studied in detail to draw some lessons so that over-burdened armed forces fighting insurgents can be utilised exclusively for national defence.

Indian parliamentarians can take some lessons from the political will and unanimity shown by all the lawmakers of the US Congress and the Japanese Diet while enacting the strictest anti-terrorism laws. Like the US, Japan and Israel, India should be proactive in keeping a tight vigil on suspicious financial transactions through advanced business monitoring and be prompt in freezing the assets of the individuals and organisations involved in terrorist acts. India should start issuing e-passports. A national level database and tracking system for every foreigner entering India from any of its borders should be put in place with immediate effect. This can subsequently graduate to issuing identification cards with unique numbers so that vital information about an individual can be accessed from anywhere at the click of a mouse. A national level database for all the terrorists and terrorist organisations is also urgently required.

No single country or its counter-terrorism approach can offer the best solution to India. Besides, while framing any counter-terrorist policy, it should not be forgotten that liberty and privacy of the citizens are as important as their security. Therefore, a combination of the best practices which are feasible under Indian conditions, can and must be emulated.

Notes

1. See Worldwide Incidents Tracking System, National Counterterrorism Center, http://wits.nctc.gov/
2. The US has waged a Global War on Terror (GWOT) against its adversaries since 2001. Japan has shifted its stance from non-combat and post-combat humanitarian and reconstruction assistance to actively participate in GWOT. Israel's policy manifests non-tolerance of any act of terrorism on its soil as well as against its citizens.
3. James Beckman, *Comparative Legal Approaches to Homeland Security and Anti-Terrorism* (Hampshire: Ashgate, 2007), p. 149.
4. Arunabha Bhoumik, "Democratic Responses to Terrorism: A Comparative Study of the United States, Israel and India," Bepress Legal Series, Working Paper 287, 17 June 2004, http://law.bepress.com/expresso/eps/287, accessed on 20 March 2009.
5. Prime Minister's Office, Government of Israel, "Government Policy," http://www.pmo.gov.il/PMOEng/Government/Policy/, accessed on 20 March 2009.

6. Ministry of Foreign Affairs, Japan, "Japan's International Counter-Terrorism Cooperation," http://www.mofa.go.jp/policy/terrorism/coop0208.pdf, accessed on 20 March 2009.
7. "What We Do: Combat Terrorism," United States Department of Justice, http://www.usdoj.gov/whatwedo/whatwedo_ct.html, accessed on 20 March 2009.
8. Office of the President of the United States, *The National Security Strategy of the United States of America* (Washington: The White House, March 2006).
9. POTO applies only in Israel's permanent territory, including Jerusalem and the Golan Heights and not in the West Bank and Gaza Strip, locations subject to Palestinian Authority control.
10. Beckman, n. 3, p. 141.
11. For more details about religious corporations, see http://www.mext.go.jp/b_menu/hakusho/html/hpae199401/hpae199401_2_189.html, accessed on 20 March 2009.
12. Prior to that, in order to counter cult like organisations, several laws had already been amended.
13. Hisao Maeda, tr. by Adam Lebowitz, "The 2002 Defense Ministry White Paper: Full Speed Ahead to the National Warfare State," 13 February 2003, http://iticwebarchives.ssrc.org/ZMag/www.zmag.org/content/print_article8d6d.html?itemID=3036&sectionID=44, accessed on 20 March 2009.
14. Most notably, the legislation requires that all foreign individuals who are 16 years of age or older must be fingerprinted and photographed upon the individual's entry into Japan.
15. In 1974, Congress passed the Anti-hijacking Act and the Air Transportation Security Act; in 1984, the Act to Combat International Terrorism; and in 1986, the Omnibus Anti-terrorism Act, all of which consequently strengthened the investigating and prosecuting agencies like the FBI and the Department of Justice and have made terrorist acts against Americans abroad a federal crime and allowed the arrest of perpetrators even overseas for trial in US courts. In 1979, through an amendment to the Export Administration Act, the Secretary of State was made to designate states that consistently support terrorism. These laws have allowed the US to impose sanctions against "state sponsors" of terrorism and arms exports to states designated as state sponsors of terrorism through Arms Export Amendments Act of 1989. With the introduction of the Foreign Intelligence Surveillance Act (FISA), provisions such as seeking secret warrants from the FISA court to investigate matters on foreign soil, were created. After the Oklahoma City bombing, Congress

passed the Anti-Terrorism and Effective Death Penalty Act of 1996 (AEDPA). The Act prohibits the US to give any military or economic aid to the terror sponsoring countries and power to the Secretary of State to designate some organisations as Foreign Terrorist Organisations (FTOs). Under the Act, provisions like asset freezing of FTOs, denial of asylum to alien terrorists and criminal sanctions related to developing biological weapons and plastic explosives were also created.

16. Such was the unanimity over the necessity of the stringent and comprehensive law that in the House of Representatives, only 66 of the 435 representatives voted no, and only one of the 100 Senators voted against the legislation.

17. After Bush signed an executive order that stipulated that the US military could indefinitely detain any non-citizen involved in international terrorism and the Justice Department's advice that the Guantanamo Bay Detention Camp could be considered outside US legal jurisdiction, prisoners captured in Afghanistan were moved there beginning in early 2002. It was also asserted that detainees were not entitled to any of the protections of the Geneva Conventions or very minimal protections listed under Common Article 3 of the Geneva Conventions. The Department of Defence issued an internal memo stating that prisoners would in the future be entitled to protection under Common Article 3. The detainees currently held as of June 2008 have been classified by the United States as "enemy combatants." There is nothing that India needs to learn from Guantanamo Bay and even President Obama is trying hard to shut down this detention camp. However, the US Congress is opposing such moves.

18. United States Department of Justice, "Fact Sheet: Justice Department Counter-Terrorism Efforts Since 9/11," http://www.usdoj.gov/opa/pr/2008/September/08-nsd-807.html, accessed on 20 March 2009.

19. "Lock-down mechanism," involves security screenings in public places, and the limiting of the freedom of movement, especially the movement of Palestinians to and from the Occupied Territories. Bhoumik, n. 4.

20. The Act was passed on 18 June 1878 and states, "From and after the passage of this Act it shall not be lawful to employ any part of the Army of the United States, as a posse comitatus, or otherwise, for the purpose of executing the laws, except in such cases and under such circumstances as such employment of said force may be expressly authorized by the Constitution or by Act of Congress; and no money appropriated by this Act shall be used to pay any of the expenses incurred in the employment of any troops in violation of this section and any person willfully violating the provisions of this section

shall be deemed guilty of a misdemeanor and on conviction thereof shall be punished by fine not exceeding ten thousand dollars or imprisonment not exceeding two years or by both such fine and imprisonment."

21. Beckman, n. 3, pp. 35-37.
22. Martin Van Creveld, "Israel's Counterterrorism," in Doron Zimmermann and Andreas Wenger (eds.), *How States Fight Terrorism: Policy Dynamics in the West* (New Delhi: Viva Books, 2008), p. 166.
23. David Weisburd et. al., "Community Policing In Israel: A National Evaluation" http://www.mops.gov.il/NR/rdonlyres/46710B03, accessed on 20 March 2009.
24. Creveld, n. 22, p. 169.
25. Beckman, n. 3, pp. 140-41.
26. "National Police Agency," http://www.npa.go.jp/english/index.htm, accessed on 20 March 2009.
27. Twenty-four separate federal agencies were combined into the Department of Homeland Security and put into one of four subdivisions: Border and Transportation Security, Science and Technology, Emergency Preparedness and Response and Information Analysis and Infrastructure Protection.
28. "Department of Homeland Security," http://www.dhs.gov, accessed on 20 March 2009.
29. The US government has roughly doubled the FBI's budget between Fiscal Year 2001 and Fiscal Year 2008. $7.1 billion has been requested for the FBI in Fiscal Year 2009.
30. Ministry of Foreign Affairs, n. 6.
31. Owing to the restrictions put by Article 9 of the post-Occupation Constitution imposed by the US authorities, Japan cannot maintain offensive capabilities. This provision raises serious doubts about the sovereignty and hence 'normal' status of the country. It has been stressed that revision of the Constitution, particularly Article 9, will ensure normalcy.

13

Conclusion: Beginning of an End

Gurmeet Kanwal and N Manoharan

The 'new terrorism' that India presently confronts is more lethal, more audacious, more innovative and more diabolical than the hit-and-run attacks that had characterised militancy in Jammu and Kashmir and the Northeastern states during the early decades of independence. Consequently, the Indian government and the security forces are taken by surprise every time. Religion and revenge constitute the major ingredients of motivation for the new cohort of terrorists. They are high-tech, thoroughly professional and trained to leave fewer footprints. The present day terror groups are difficult to penetrate. Their sources of funds have become diverse and, at the same time, more opaque. Therefore, it is becoming increasingly more difficult to identify and eliminate these sources. Since the urban population is being targeted more frequently, the terrorists enjoy an advantage as indiscriminate counter-terrorist operations by the state would result in high collateral damage. For the same reason, the use of heavy weapons and aerial bombardment against the terrorists can be ruled out.

Countering this complex nature of terrorism effectively requires a new set of counter-terrorism policies and mechanisms, including pragmatic laws. India's counter-terrorism approach needs a thorough overhaul based on a clear understanding of the threat potential of 'new terrorism'. A comprehensive approach that relies on lateral thinking and goes beyond conventional methods is urgently required. The basic premise for any counter-terrorism policy for India, at the least, should be "zero tolerance". Terrorism, as a means of redressing grievances, should be deemed unacceptable under any circumstances. A fundamental flaw in India's approach to fighting terrorism is the lack of a comprehensive national security strategy for external and internal security, including counter-terrorism. Such a strategy should have a multi-disciplinary, inter-ministerial, inter-departmental, inter-agency and inter-Service approach, to meet the ongoing and emerging threats and challenges to national security. Without a comprehensive national security strategy, policy formulation and implementation will remain incoherent as the threats are amorphous and complex in nature. The National Security Council (NSC) Secretariat must initiate a nation-wide debate on formulating a national security strategy so that all stakeholders can give their inputs and the NSC can arrive at holistic deductions.

The next logical step would be to formulate a viable national counter-terrorism strategy that addresses the 'root causes' underlying terrorism. Some of the important 'root causes' that require immediate attention are socio-economic deprivation, political inequity, religious intolerance, and discrimination on various grounds. By neutralising the causes, most, if not all, militants can be dissuaded from resorting to violence as a means of achieving their ends. Understanding the true nature and causal factors of present day terrorism is a vital first step to provide the right antidote. Over and above this fundamental step, appropriate methods should be used to prevent as well as to deter terrorists. Accordingly, two broad categories of counter-terrorism strategies are proposed: "Prevention Strategies" and "Deterrence and Operational Strategies".

Prevention Strategies

Building a Database

The first step must be to identify the enemy. A comprehensive database of the terror groups inimical to India must be drawn up detailing their ideology, organisational set-up, leadership, goals, *modus operandi*, training systems, support network, weapon systems at their disposal and sources of funding. The Indian linkages of the foreign terrorist organisations need to be clearly identified. Most importantly, this data should be updated constantly and maintained in such a format that it can be exchanged with friendly foreign powers and international organisations like INTERPOL.

Of late, terrorism in India has been driven mainly by religious fundamentalists operating from across India's borders, often with the support of sections of the foreign government machinery. The most active foreign terrorist organisations are the Pakistan-based Lashkar-e-Tayyeba (LeT), Jaish-e-Mohammed (JeM) and Harkat-ul-Mujahideen and the Bangladesh-based Harkat-ul-Jihad-al-Islami (HuJI), which also has a Pakistan chapter. All four organisations are loosely affiliated with Osama bin Laden's International Islamic Front, whose ultimate aim is to establish an Islamic Caliphate (one nation under Allah with 1.5 billion Muslims) with India as an integral part of it. Of late, these terrorist organisations have been known to receive local support from the banned Students Islamic Movement of India (SIMI) and Indian Mujahideen, which wish to liberate India from the materialistic cultural influence of the West and to create an Islamic society.

The aim of the terrorist organisations planning and executing strikes in India is to create an environment of panic leading to a majority community backlash against the minority so that India's secular credentials are undermined. They also seek to force the government machinery to react with repression and violence. The tools of terror are car and scooter bombs, improvised explosive devices (IEDs) placed in trains and buses and, occasionally, suicide bombings. Assassination attempts and kidnappings are bound to follow. The tactics, techniques and procedures adopted by the Pakistan-based 26/11 attackers clearly indicate that they had been given commando training either by the Special Services Group (SSG), the elite Special Forces of the Pakistan Army, or by retired Pakistani mercenary commandos who have joined ranks of the LeT.

This apart, a national database can be created by integrating existing databases of the Crime Records Bureau, Railways, Customs, Intelligence Services, Regional Passport/Registration Offices, immigration/emigration, state police records, census, electoral offices, etc. This can then be networked to link all 14,000-odd police stations of India through a cyber highway "for investigation of crime and detection of criminals in real time." It must be appreciated that the central government has finally moved to implement the long-pending "Multi-purpose National Identity Card Project". The project, however, should be foolproof and be completed in the earliest possible time period. Once implemented, a biometric national identity card will go a long way in easily identifying infiltrators and illegal migrants.

Securing India's Borders

Border security is critical for preventing terrorist attacks from across India's porous borders. India's land borders have long been used for infiltration by inimical forces. Vigilance along the borders needs to be substantially enhanced, including through the use of hi-tech surveillance devices. Border management also needs to be more efficiently coordinated between the various central agencies that operate along the country's borders. In this respect, the report of the Border Management Task Force, established by the Group of Ministers that studied the recommendations of the Kargil Review Committee, must be implemented in full at an early date. The idea of Integrated Check Posts that has been lying mute for long should be revived.

India's 7,600-km-long coastline along nine states and four union territories (UTs) and 1,197 islands is especially vulnerable. The Coast Guard and the state-level police forces, the primary agencies responsible for guarding the coastline, do not have adequate trained personnel or infrastructure to discharge their responsibilities. For instance, speed boats for effective patrolling of the coasts are not available in sufficient numbers with the states concerned. The concept of 'marine policing' is still on paper. This should be revived. To meet the shortage of trained manpower, the coastal states can consider recruiting retired naval personnel.

The "Coastal Security Scheme" launched in March 2006 by the Union Home Ministry, in which 73 coastal police stations, 97 check posts, 58 outposts and 30 barracks were planned, requires to be revisited in terms of quantity and quality of the proposed infrastructure. Indian 'maritime domain awareness' on the lines of the US should be set up to carefully monitor incoming ships and aircraft on the coastline. There is a need to induct satellites, unmanned aerial vehicles (UAVs) and long-range spy planes to improve surveillance over land and sea. The recent decision to install coastal radars all along India's coast is to be commended. In addition, police personnel of coastal states and UTs should be given specialised training in mounting maritime vigilance. Needless to say, better coordination among the Indian Navy, Coast Guard, Customs and state police is required. The idea of Coastal Commands, which was floated soon after the Mumbai terror attacks, has not been found to be practical; command and control for coastal security needs to be reviewed and the Indian Navy given a greater say in the management of coastal security. There is also an urgent need to register and regulate around 300,000 fishing boats operating in the seas off the Indian coasts. High security number plates and beacons (to make distress call in times of danger and indicate its exact location) for all fishing vessels should be made compulsory.

Strengthening Intelligence

The key to success in fighting terrorism effectively lies in obtaining accurate intelligence about impending attacks and neutralisation of terrorists before they can launch their planned attacks. In the age of 'new terrorism', conventional methods of intelligence gathering are less relevant; they are increasingly yielding diminishing returns. Innovative measures should, therefore, be evolved for the collection of intelligence on terrorist groups. Accurate, timely and focussed intelligence is an important tool for preventing terror attacks. Intelligence gathering in India, especially preventive aspects of intelligence, needs substantial improvement. Terrorist attacks have occurred either due to the absence of precise actionable intelligence or lack of follow-up action when such intelligence was available.

In order to improve intelligence acquisition, it is necessary to penetrate the networks and sleeper cells of key terrorist organisations for the collection of actionable human intelligence (HUMINT) and monitor their communications set-up for the collection of technical intelligence (TECHINT). There is a need to synergise the advantages of human intelligence with the technological expediency of technical intelligence. The beat constable has been neglected for long as an important source of grassroots intelligence. This lacuna must be rectified early. In this regard, the network of informers has to be expanded. There is a severe shortage of staff, especially in central intelligence agencies like the Intelligence Bureau (IB), Research and Analysis Wing (RAW) and National Technical Research Organisation (NTRO). The IB is reported to have as many as 3,000 vacancies. Filling up of vacancies, therefore, is an urgent need. In addition, improvement of the analytical skills of intelligence agents is vital.

For better coordination among intelligence agencies and other law enforcement bodies that rely on intelligence, a separate intelligence assessment and coordination cell should be instituted at the national level. This should be the apex body for intelligence assessment for both conventional threats and challenges, internal and external, and terrorism. It could be established on the lines of the US National Intelligence Council (NIC). Through this, a central command structure for intelligence collation, analyses and dissemination can be established. Most importantly, the central and state intelligence agencies should share information methodically and it must trickle down in real-time to the user who is required to take action. To achieve this, a central database or a national intelligence grid should be set up so that all intelligence agencies can pool their inputs for use by any state or central bodies. This way, the existing problem of slack inter-agency intelligence sharing could be avoided. Since the threat of terrorism is transnational in nature, there is an urgent need for regional and international networking of friendly intelligence agencies for mutually beneficial intelligence sharing. The existing Multi-Agency Centre (MAC) can provide the building blocks for an apex-level body for intelligence assessments.

Stifling Resources

So far, Indian efforts at combating terror financing have proved to be inadequate. Unfortunately, in general, India is yet to formulate clear-cut procedures to check the flow of funds into the country, leave alone funds transfers by terrorists. The Prevention of Money Laundering Act (PMLA), the nodal Indian legislation meant for monitoring financial flows, requires radical amendments. The Financial Investigative Unit (FIU) has to work in coordination with other intelligence and investigative agencies to effectively identify suspicious financial activities, especially in real estate and stock markets. At the same time, India should make conscious efforts to become a member of the United Nations Financial Action Task Force (FATF), a 34-member inter-governmental body for devising and promoting measures aimed at combating money laundering and terrorist financing. Recognising the vital importance of taking action to combat the financing of terrorism, the FATF has agreed to implement nine Special Recommendations which set out the basic framework to detect, prevent and suppress the financing of terrorism and terrorist acts.

India should also seriously take measures to regulate the movement and sale of explosive substances. In this regard, the Explosive Substances Act requires amendment to include ammonium nitrate, a commonly used fertiliser, which has explosive properties.

Nine Special Recommendations of the United Nations Financial Action Task Force

I. Ratification and implementation of UN instruments

Each country should take immediate steps to ratify and to implement fully the 1999 United Nations International Convention for the Suppression of the Financing of Terrorism.

Countries should also immediately implement the United Nations resolutions relating to the prevention and suppression of the financing of terrorist acts, particularly United Nations Security Council Resolution 1373.

II. Criminalising the financing of terrorism and associated money laundering

Each country should criminalise the financing of terrorism, terrorist acts and terrorist organisations. Countries should ensure that such offences are designated as money laundering predicate offences.

III. Freezing and confiscating terrorist assets

Each country should implement measures to freeze without delay funds or other assets of terrorists, those who finance terrorism and terrorist organisations in accordance with the United Nations resolutions relating to the prevention and suppression of the financing of terrorist acts.

Each country should also adopt and implement measures, including legislative ones, which would enable the competent authorities to seize and confiscate property that is the proceeds of, or used in, or intended or allocated for use in, the financing of terrorism, terrorist acts or terrorist organisations.

IV. Reporting suspicious transactions related to terrorism

If financial institutions, or other businesses or entities subject to anti-money laundering obligations, suspect or have reasonable grounds to suspect that funds are linked or related to, or are to be used for terrorism, terrorist acts or by terrorist organisations, they should be required to report promptly their suspicions to the competent authorities.

V. International cooperation

Each country should afford another country, on the basis of a treaty, arrangement or other mechanism for mutual legal assistance or information exchange, the greatest possible measure of assistance in connection with criminal, civil enforcement, and administrative investigations, inquiries and proceedings relating to the financing of terrorism, terrorist acts and terrorist organisations.

Countries should also take all possible measures to ensure that they do not provide safe havens for individuals charged with the financing of terrorism, terrorist acts or terrorist organisations, and should have procedures in place to extradite, where possible, such individuals.

VI. Alternative remittance

Each country should take measures to ensure that persons or legal entities, including agents, that provide a service for the transmission of money or value, including transmission through an informal money or value transfer system or network, should be licensed or registered and subject to all the FATF Recommendations that apply to banks and non-bank financial institutions. Each country should ensure that persons or legal entities that carry out this service illegally are subject to administrative, civil or criminal sanctions.

VII. Wire transfers

Countries should take measures to require financial institutions, including money remitters, to include accurate and meaningful originator information (name, address and account number) on funds transfers and related messages that are sent, and the information should remain with the transfer or related message through the payment chain.

Countries should take measures to ensure that financial institutions, including money remitters, conduct enhanced scrutiny of and monitor for suspicious activity funds transfers which do not contain complete originator information (name, address and account number).

VIII. Non-profit organisations

Countries should review the adequacy of laws and regulations that relate to entities that can be abused for the financing of terrorism. Non-profit organisations are particularly vulnerable, and countries should ensure that they cannot be misused: by terrorist organisations posing as legitimate entities; to exploit legitimate entities as conduits for terrorist financing, including for the purpose of escaping asset freezing measures; and to conceal or obscure the clandestine diversion of funds intended for legitimate purposes to terrorist organisations.

IX. Cash couriers

Countries should have measures in place to detect the physical cross-border transportation of currency and bearer negotiable instruments, including a declaration system or other disclosure obligation.

Countries should ensure that their competent authorities have the legal authority to stop or restrain currency or bearer negotiable instruments that are suspected to be related to terrorist financing or money laundering, or that are falsely declared or disclosed.

Countries should ensure that effective, proportionate and dissuasive sanctions are available to deal with persons who make false declaration(s) or disclosure(s). In cases where the currency or bearer negotiable instruments are related to terrorist financing or money laundering, countries should also adopt measures, including legislative ones consistent with Recommendation 3 and Special Recommendation III, which would enable the confiscation of such currency or instruments.

(Source: http://www.fatf-gafi.org/document/9/0,3343,en_32250379_32236920_34032073_1_1_1_1,00.html)

'Target Hardening'

Terrorists usually choose high-profile soft targets like markets, railway stations, airports, bus stands, hotels, places of worship, national monuments, heritage buildings, and government infrastructure to attract maximum attention. Such targets should be put under maximum surveillance and protection and a broad security advisory should be issued in this regard. The staff manning these places should be trained in rendering first aid, evacuation techniques, and relief and rescue operations. Surveillance cameras, metal and explosive vapour detectors and X-ray scanning machines should be installed at key access points. Technology to detect and alert against suspicious activity such as loitering by an individual or vehicle should be made use of. Use of appropriate technology will immensely reduce manpower intensive monitoring. Security personnel should be sensitised to spotting and segregating suspicious objects that are left behind. Protection of critical infrastructure should be made shared responsibility of the government, private sector and the people.

Community Policing

Without the eyes, ears and intuition of the general public, it is difficult to identify a terrorist who is anonymous and blends seamlessly into the environment in which he lives and operates. An effective battle against terrorism can be waged only by involving members of the public. This includes creating societal awareness to keep a steady eye on tentative or errant behaviour in the neighbourhood and sharing of information of suspicious movements with point persons in the police and intelligence agencies. For instance, on every New York City subway train, the message to passengers since the terrorist attacks of 9/11 has been clear: "If you see something, say something." For this purpose, Indian citizens must organise themselves into neighbourhood watch committees through community consensus mechanisms based on genuine concern to prevent future terrorist attacks. All communities should be co-opted in counter-terror measures instead of perceiving some as the "other". The community of Indian fishermen should keep a constant tab on coastal waters. Awareness creation among people should also include 'golden rules' to be followed by the people in case of a terrorist attack. Every citizen should know the basic tenets of first aid. Such familiarisation will not only minimise the lethality of terrorist attacks, but also reduce the consequent panic.

Cooperation with Other Countries

Since terrorism has become a global menace, cooperation with friendly countries that are also victims of terror is crucial in countering it. The United Nations Security Council (UNSC) Resolution 1373 mandates all member countries to initiate steps in this regard. International cooperation should be based on a global strategy against terrorism that "would be free from double standards and self-serving interests, and would unite the world rather than divide it." The strategy should be to identify breeding grounds of terrorism all over the world and gradually neutralise them through socio-economic measures and military action where necessary. One of the major such breeding grounds is Pakistan. India should launch an intense diplomatic campaign to link international aid to Pakistan with the dismantling of the terror mechanism on its soil. Any peace process and normalisation between India and Pakistan should be conditional on credible action of the latter on the terror infrastructure based on its territory.

The Indian government must enter into extensive cooperative arrangements with friendly countries to maximise the advantages of intelligence sharing, seek training assistance and acquire expertise available with countries like Israel and the United States that have had a head start in this field. Joint military and police exercises aimed at enhancing counter-terrorism skills should be made routine. Each country can benefit immensely from the other's experience, technology, intelligence and threat evaluation. For instance, Latin American countries like Columbia and Peru have immense experience in countering urban terrorism; the US possesses the requisite technology; Israel has compiled an enormous data base on pan-Islamist terrorist organisations. India should tap these resources on priority basis. Also, in the absence of bilateral extradition treaties, a clear legal basis for international cooperation in investigating terrorist attacks is missing. The UN, at the global level, and the South Asian Association for Regional Cooperation (SAARC), at the regional level, can contribute meaningfully to bridge this gap.

Deterrence and Operational Strategies

National Counter-Terrorism Centre (NCTC)

Preventing and countering terrorism needs a coordinated response at the national level. For this, a vital prerequisite is a clear-cut command and control structure. Presently, there is no single central agency responsible for coordination of operations during a terror strike. The government's plan to set-up a National Counter-Terrorism Centre "to take proactive anti-terrorism measures" is a good move. But, this should gradually become a nodal agency to counter terrorism.

The NCTC should be a combination operations room-cum-command and control centre with access to the intelligence data base and hot lines to similar centres in the states as well as the new National Security Guard (NSG) hubs in the four metros other than New Delhi. Nominated counter-terrorism forces such as the NSG and the special forces of the armed forces, with dedicated air, rail and road transport resources should be available to the NCTC for emergency deployment. This centre can be the nodal point for other crises as well and it is here that the Crisis Management Group should hold its meetings during emergencies. Empowered representatives of the armed forces and central paramilitary forces (CPMFs) should also be co-located in the NCTC. In fact, it will be more appropriate to call it a National Crisis Management Centre.

Specialised Counter-Terrorism Forces

The success of counter-terrorism operations depends to a considerable extent on a speedy response, with operations being executed by the right force that is trained, armed and equipped suitably for the job at hand. As the NSG is India's primary strike force for counter-terrorist operations, it must be given the wherewithal to respond swiftly to terrorist attacks to minimise casualties and deny the perpetrators the ability to consolidate. The central government's recent decision to locate NSG echelons in the four metros (Chennai, Hyderabad, Kolkata and Mumbai) that have been targeted most frequently will enable the force to respond in a timelier manner.

At the same time, the NSG must also be equipped with state-of-the-art technology and equipment to enable the commandos to enhance their operational performance and minimise their own casualties. They should have periodic interaction and joint exercises with similar special forces of important countries. Most importantly, the NSG should be divested of VIP security duties. A separate force can be created for that purpose. Where necessary, the Indian Army's elite special forces should be employed to counter terrorist attacks. Every state should have a NSG-type commando force to counter lethal terror strikes. They can be called State Security Guards (SSG). Local availability of such forces will ensure that precious time is not lost.

Enhancing Police Equipment and Training Standards

Although special forces will help, the local police should be made the first responders in the event of a terrorist strike. Policing at the grassroots level should be strengthened. As the Padmanabhaiah Committee had advocated, what India requires is a "highly motivated, professionally-skilled, infrastructurally self-sufficient and sophisticatedly trained police force." Ironically, however, India has ill-trained and ill-equipped police forces to counter hi-tech terrorism. Without any exception, police forces of all states of India are understaffed. There are just 146 police personnel per 100,000 population – one of the lowest policemen per population ratios in the world. Vacancies should be filled immediately to overcome this anomaly. In this regard, the state governments have to revamp their recruitment procedures and make them quick, time-bound and transparent. Most importantly, postings and transfers should be handled with care, devoid of any political considerations. The National Police Commission has already stipulated (also endorsed by the Supreme Court) a minimum of at least two years for senior police officers. This should be implemented by all the states.

Lack of proper equipment like weapons, gadgets, protection gear and communication devices for police personnel is yet another issue that came to the fore during the recent Mumbai terror attacks. Police constables are poorly armed and the firemen lack protection. There must be speedy upgradation of equipment as per world standards as the lives of citizens are involved. Use of the state-of-the-art technology is important to have an edge over well-armed terrorists. The Centre has already been assisting the states by providing separate funds for police modernisation. But not all states have taken the modernisation drive seriously and have often failed to utilise the funds allotted to them. Apart from insisting on a national standard, monitoring of modernisation of state police forces should be periodically undertaken by the central government. A case can also be made out for a centralised approach to weapons and equipment acquisition so as to benefit from the buyers' clout and have some commonality among the states and the central forces. Every city should have a modern police control room with digitised maps and each police station should possess the requisite resources like anti-riot gear, better weapons, the nucleus of a mobile forensic unit and be connected to a networked criminal data base management system.

Proper training is a prerequisite for effective counter-terrorism operations. Unfortunately, a policeman is trained only once every 20 years on an average; this should be rectified. The available training resources in the country must be optimally utilised to train selected police and paramilitary officers and non-commissioned officers (NCOs) as trainers for training personnel of their own battalions. The army's training facilities should also be utilised for this purpose and army instructors should be sent on deputations or short-term attachments to police training academies and schools. New training facilities should be established at the national level to impart training on dealing with new tools of terror and methodologies and for acquiring the right skills for counter-terrorism operations. Rehearsals should be periodically undertaken for search-and-rescue operations after large-scale terrorist strikes. Different contingencies should be simulated and practised. Periodic training and counter-terrorism drills should be made compulsory. Future training should also cater for terrorist attacks in the form of weapons of mass destruction (WMDs). In short, what is required is a "new-age policeman" who is more professional, better-motivated, suitably empowered, well-trained, and one who places greater emphasis on technology for investigation and other tasks.

Police-Population Ratio in Important Countries

Sl. No.	Country	Total Police Personnel			
		Count		Rate per 100,000 inhabitants	
1	2	3	4	5	6
		2001	2002	2001	2002
1	Italy	320,657	322,483	555.7	559.0
2	Mexico	448,210	495,821	451.0	491.8
3	USA	927,759	941,139	325.2	326.4
4	Australia	57,239	59,812	294.8	304.2
5	Hungary	28,845	29,113	283.2	286.6
6	Poland	100,772	99,014	260.8	259.0
7	United Kingdom	148,932	152,576	252.2	257.6
8	South Africa	99,520	101,582	222.1	224.0
9	Switzerland	14,884	14,847	205.8	203.7
10	Romania	44,670	46,345	199.4	207.8
11	Nepal	46,444	46,481	196.9	192.7
12	Chile	29,706	30,090	192.9	193.0
13	Canada	57,076	58,422	183.6	186.3
14	Japan	228,000	231,700	179.5	182.2
15	Myanmar	68,924	68,959	143.1	141.4
16	India	1,428,267	1,433,555	139.1	136.4
	2003		1,496,276		139.5
	2004		1,530,389		140.1
	2005		1,579,697		142.7
	2006		1,632,651		145.2

Source: United Nations Division for Policy Analysis and Public Affairs, released on 31 March 2005, and for India, from 2003-2006, "Data on Police Organisations in India," Bureau of Police Research and Development (BPR&D)

Covert Operations

In order to achieve a lasting impact and ensure that the actual perpetrators of terrorism are targeted, while simultaneously avoiding collateral damage, it is necessary to employ covert capabilities to neutralise the leadership of terrorist organisations. Clandestine operations can be methodically planned and stealthily executed at opportune times. These must not only be time-critical responses but also must have an element of 'plausible deniability' built into them. Other advantages include relatively low political, economic and military cost and low risk of casualties to own operatives as local personnel – who harbour grudges against the targeted organisations – can often be used.

Young operatives must be selected and trained – first in the rudiments of intelligence gathering and after being given some in-country experience, in the complexities of high-risk special operations in a hostile foreign environment. They will also need to be imparted specialised instructions in selecting, training and motivating local agents to carry out pre-planned and opportunity strikes against nominated targets. It will take at least three to five years to put in place basic capabilities for covert operations as both terrorist organisations and their handlers will have to be penetrated. Targets should include the leaders of fundamentalist terrorist organisations who are known to sponsor terrorist strikes in India, their handlers and fugitives from Indian justice like Dawood Ibrahim and Hafiz Saeed.

Anti-Terror Laws

Counter-terror laws in India are a perfect reflection of the Indian style of handling terrorism: adhocism. No single law has prevailed over a secular time-frame. From time to time, depending on the regime at the Centre, legislation came into being and faded. India still lacks a comprehensive legal framework to prosecute terrorists. There has been no political consensus on the nature and use of laws as an effective antidote to terrorism in India. While the right wing parties advocate a pro-legal framework against terrorism, the centrist parties follow a more liberal approach. The opposition parties oppose anti-terror laws on the grounds of "repressive character", and when they come to power, they invariably resort to lesser laws. There is, thus, a cyclical pattern of enactment and repeal without addressing the underlying structural issues. Counter-terror laws in most cases have been enacted in response to a particular crisis and often been repealed when faced with strong political opposition or a perception that the crisis has passed. 'Urgency' of a situation cannot be an excuse for hasty enactment of special laws. What is required is careful drafting with an understanding of 'effects' and 'side effects' of such laws. The draft should be widely circulated and given sufficient time for parliamentary and public scrutiny. In that case, the government can expect wider acceptance by the people than in a situation where laws are suddenly introduced. Simultaneously, the laws should be placed for intense judicial examination before being enacted.

The main deficiency in Indian terror laws is the lack of sufficient tools to prevent a terrorist attack. Monitoring of e-mails, telephones and illegal financial transactions can be incorporated in the existing legislation. Yet another issue is implementation of existing laws. India has a very low conviction rate of less than 10 percent in terrorism-related cases. This was so even under laws like the Prevention of Terrorism Act (POTA) and Terrorism and Disruptive Activities Act (TADA) – which are now considered draconian – as against 80 percent plus in Western countries. The provisions of terror laws should be clear and unambiguous enough so as not to give room for discretion to law enforcement agencies. What constitutes a 'terrorist act' should be clearly defined without any ambiguity. Or else, counter-terror laws may be misused for political advantage. Proper safeguards should be built-in to prevent any kind of misuse by law enforcement agencies. Overall, the success of counter-terrorism legislation depends on how the provisions relating to all three levels – 'prevention', 'deterrence' and 'correction' – are incorporated and implemented in a balanced manner.

In the wake of the Mumbai attacks on 26 November 2008, the central government, apart from amending the existing Unlawful Activities Prevention Act, set up the National Investigation Agency (NIA) to investigate terror-related cases throughout the country. It is a good first step, but it has generally been felt that the powers entrusted to the NIA are not adequate to tackle terrorism in an effective way. The major lacuna is that the NIA comes into the picture only after a terror attack and not before it, making it just another body of post-incident investigation. The NIA also does not possess powers of monitoring fund flows, immigration, telephones, e-mails etc. At the same time, the move has been criticised for violating the principles of federalism. Some states felt that the NIA was "an attempt to sidetrack" the states in the fight against terrorism. These concerns should be kept in mind when the NIA takes up cases for investigation.

India is one of the countries worst affected by terrorism. In the recent period, India has witnessed more terrorist incidents than any other country in the world. Yet, an analysis of how India has responded to all terrorist attacks reveals a broad pattern: immediately after every attack, the system goes into hyper active mode and gets back to business as usual in a short while. The underlying reason for this is 'systemic lethargy'. It is important, therefore, to get over this and increase the level of preparedness. Fixing accountability helps in this regard. It was partly due to extra alertness that there has been no major terrorist attack in India since 26/11. Our success in preventing terrorist attacks can be sustained only at the price of unrelenting vigilance. During 2008-09, about 25 terrorist modules have been busted. But this is not enough. What is urgently required is a nuanced counter-terrorism strategy that approaches the problem of militancy in a holistic manner. Good governance, improved and credible intelligence, better coordination, use of innovative technology, and a net-centric information command structure will go a long way in enhancing the counter-terrorism capabilities of India.

Appendix

MAJOR TERRORIST ATTACKS IN INDIA: 1993-2009

Rohit Singh

---

12 March 1993: Mumbai [serial bomb blasts]

A series of 13 explosions rocked the city of Bombay at different commercial locations, in a span of three hours, leaving close to 260 people dead and more than 700 injured. This was the first and the most destructive incident of mass-casualty terrorism in India orchestrated by underworld don Dawood Ibrahim's crime syndicate, the 'D-Company', in collusion with Pakistan's intelligence agency, Inter-Services Intelligence (ISI). The blasts were purportedly carried out in retaliation to the demolition of the Babri Masjid mosque in December 1992 and the subsequent riots that broke out all over the country, including in Mumbai.

In 2006, a special Terrorist and Disruptive Activities (Prevention) Act (TADA) court convicted nearly 100 accused in the conspiracy cases. However, the prime accused, including Dawood Ibrahim and Tiger Memon took refuge in Pakistan and Dubai, and are still absconding.

30 December 1996: Kokrajhar [train bombings]

Thirty-three passengers were killed in an improvised explosive device (IED) blast carried out by Bodo insurgents on the Brahmaputra Mail between Kokrajhar and Fakiragram stations in Lower Assam.

26 January 1997: Ganderbal [firing]

Twenty-five Kashmiri Pandits were killed by Lashkar-e-Tayyeba (LeT) terrorists in Wundhama village of Ganderbal district, near Srinagar. The massacre was another in a series of killings aimed at driving out minority communities, mainly Hindus, out of the Kashmir Valley.

14 February 1998: Coimbatore [serial bomb blasts]

Forty-six people were killed and around 200 injured when 13 bombs ripped through 11 locations in Coimbatore city in Tamil Nadu. Bharatiya Janata Party (BJP) leader LK Advani was scheduled to address a rally in the city on the same day. Local Islamic fundamentalist groups like the Al-Umma and All India Al-Jihad Committee, which had come up following incidents of rioting in Coimbatore, were held responsible for the blasts. In 2007, 13 accused mainly belonging to Al-Umma were convicted by a sessions court, while the prime accused – the chairman of the Kerala-based People's Democratic Party (PDP) – was acquitted.

03 August 1998: Chamba [firing]

In the early hours of the day, militants belonging to Hizbul Mujahideen (HM), gunned down 35 Hindus, mostly labourers in Kalaban and Satrundi villages in Chamba district of Himachal Pradesh, bordering Doda in Jammu and Kashmir.

24-31 December 1999: IC 814 [hijacking]

Indian Airlines flight IC 814 from Kathmandu to New Delhi was hijacked shortly after it entered Indian airspace over Varanasi, on 24 December, with 189 passengers and crew on board. After a landing at Amritsar, a refuelling stop at Lahore and a night halt at Dubai, the aircraft was taken to Kandahar, where the week-long hijack situation finally came to an end following the release of three Pakistani terrorists lodged in Indian jails by the Government of India, as demanded by the hijackers – Maulana Masood Azhar, Ahmed Omar Saeed Sheikh and Mushtaq Ahmed Zargar. Masood Azhar, the ideologue of the proscribed militant group Harkat-ul-Ansar (HuA), formed the terrorist outfit, Jaish-e-Mohammed (JeM), in Pakistan upon his release. Omar Sheikh, a British national of Pakistani origin, later killed the American journalist Daniel Pearl in Karachi.

The hijacking was a result of meticulous planning done by members of the Harkat-ul-Mujahideen (HuM), and is believed to have received active collaboration from the Pakistani intelligence agency, the ISI, and the Taliban. In Mumbai, four persons with ISI links were arrested and charged with providing logistics support to the hijackers. Three of them were sentenced to life imprisonment by a Patiala court in February 2008.

20 March 2000: Chitisinghpora [firing]

Thirty-six members of the Sikh community were killed in village Chitisinghpora in Anantnag district of Jammu and Kashmir on the eve of the then-US President Bill Clinton's visit to the subcontinent. The massacre was believed to have been carried out by the Pakistan-based militant groups the LeT and HM.

01-02 August 2000: Anantnag [firing]

In a continuing spate of violence, 87 people were killed in different attacks, in the Doda, Anantnag and Kupwara districts of strife-torn Jammu and Kashmir. In Pahalgam, 30 pilgrims were gunned down at a base camp for the holy Amarnath Yatra. The attacks were carried out by the LeT, on the eve of talks between the central government and the indigenous group, HM, which had recently declared a ceasefire.

22 December 2000: Delhi [firing]

On the night of 22 December, six LeT terrorists stormed the Red Fort in Delhi, killing two army men and one civilian. The attack on the historic fort, guarded by an army battalion, was aimed at derailing peace efforts by the central government following a unilateral declaration of ceasefire during the holy month of Ramzan in Jammu and Kashmir, which was extended just two days before the attack. A few days later, the Delhi Police claimed to have killed one suspect and arrested a Pakistani national, Mohammed Ashfaq and his Indian wife from a South Delhi locality. In September 2007, the Delhi High Court upheld the death sentence of Mohammed Ashfaq while the remaining six accused were acquitted. Ashfaq's death sentence was stayed by the Supreme Court in December 2007.

25 December 2000: Srinagar [bomb blast]

In continuing attacks during the ceasefire, a car bomb explosion outside Badami Bagh Cantonment in Srinagar killed eight people. Further, an abortive suicide attack on Srinagar airport by six LeT members on 16 January 2001, killed four security force personnel and two civilians, apart from the six terrorists.

01 October 2001: Srinagar [bomb blast]

A JeM suicide bomber blew up his car outside the entrance of the Jammu and Kashmir Legislative Assembly building in Srinagar. Shortly afterwards, three more JeM terrorists carried out an armed assault on the building. Thirty-eight people were killed and several others injured in this major *fidayeen* attack in Jammu and Kashmir, while several legislators had a narrow escape.

13 December 2001: Delhi [attack]

Five heavily armed Pakistani terrorists belonging to the LeT and JeM rammed their car at the then Vice-President's cavalcade and entered the compound of the Parliament house in New Delhi, killing nine people and injuring 16 others before they were eliminated. They could not enter the main building where several top Parliamentarians were present.

The attack led to the deterioration of relations between India and Pakistan and what followed was a 10-month-long mobilisation of Indian troops on the border with Pakistan ('Operation Parakram'). The United States banned the LeT and JeM, and Pakistan, under international pressure, took some steps to rein in terrorists operating from its soil.

In India, four suspects accused of providing logistical support to the five terrorists were arrested, of whom one, Mohammed Afzal, has been sentenced to death by the Supreme Court, but his mercy petition is pending with the President of India. One more suspect, Shaukat Guru, Afzal's cousin, has been sentenced to 10 years in prison. Two others, Shaukat's wife Afsan Guru and Delhi University lecturer SAR Geelani were acquitted.

The JeM commander in Kashmir, Ghazi Baba, said to be one of the masterminds behind the Parliament attack, was gunned down by security forces in Srinagar in August 2003. The Jaish commander, Maulana

Masood Azhar, another mastermind named in the case, is on India's list of wanted terrorists handed over to Pakistan.

22 January 2002: Kolkata [attack]

Gunmen on a motorcycle opened fire on policemen stationed outside the American Information Resource Centre in Kolkata, killing seven of them.

One suspect was killed a week later in an encounter with the police in Hazaribagh in Jharkhand. In 2005, seven accused in the case, including a Dubai-based underworld don, Aftab Ansari, were sentenced to death.

The attack was believed to have been carried out by members of a group called Amir Reza Khan Commando Force. Its leader Amir Reza Khan, a native of Kolkata, wanted for masterminding the attack, is known to be living in Pakistan. The case took a new turn when Sadiq Sheikh, an Indian Mujahideen (IM) operative arrested by the Mumbai Police on 24 September 2008, in connection with the Delhi and Ahmedabad blasts, is reportedly claimed to be one of the persons who fired on the policemen outside the American Centre.

30 March 2002: Jammu [attack]

On 30 March, two *fidayeen* terrorists belonging to the LeT stormed the Raghunath and Panjbakhtar Temples in Jammu city. In the indiscriminate firing and lobbing of grenades, 11 persons were killed and 20 injured. One of the terrorists blew himself up, while the other was killed by security forces. In 2006, all six people arrested on charges of providing explosives and transporting the two terrorists from Surankote to Jammu, were acquitted due to lack of evidence.

14 May 2002: Jammu [attack]

In the early hours of 14 May, three terrorists boarded a Himachal Tourism bus at Vijaypur, south of Jammu on National Highway 1. They alighted outside the Kaluchak army camp, on the outskirts of Jammu, and entered the residential quarters of family members of soldiers deployed on the border. Thirty-one people, including women and children, were killed in this attack, inviting worldwide outrage and condemnation. A little-known group, Al-Mansoorian, believed to be an LeT front organisation, along with Jamiat-ul-Mujahideen, claimed responsibility for the attack.

This incident brought India and Pakistan almost to the brink of war, coming as it did in the wake of 'Operation Parakram', where the troops were already mobilised on the borders.

13 July 2002: Jammu [attack]

Two terrorists opened fire and lobbed grenades at a labour camp on the outskirts of Jammu, namely Rajiv Nagar and Kasimpura, killing 31 people. Police claimed to have killed one of the two LeT terrorists in an encounter on 02 August 2002, while later, seven LeT men were arrested on charges of operational and logistics planning.

24 September 2002: Gandhinagar [attack]

Two terrorists suspected to be from the LeT entered the famous Akshardam Temple in Gandhinagar, killing 33 people, mainly devotees, and injuring 79 others. The two terrorists were later killed by National Security Guard (NSG) commandos who were flown in from Delhi. The attacks were executed purportedly to avenge the riots in Gujarat, earlier that year, following the Godhra train burning. Three out of six arrested for their involvement in the conspiracy and planning, were sentenced to death.

13 March 2003: Mumbai [train bombing]

A bomb ripped through a local train compartment as it entered Mulund railway station. Eleven people were killed and 65 injured in the explosion. Sixteen accused, including Saquib Nachan, said to be the mastermind and a former general secretary of the banned Students Islamic Movement of India (SIMI) are serving sentences in jail for their complicity in the blast.

25 August 2003: Mumbai [serial bomb blasts]

In the afternoon of 25 August, bombs placed in two taxis went off near the Gateway of India and the busy Zaveri Bazaar locality in South Mumbai killing 52 people and injuring around 184. The prime accused, Mohammed Hanif, his wife Fahmida Hanif, and Arshad Ansari were arrested for placing the bombs in the hired taxis before alighting. They are believed to have links with the LeT. Sentencing in the case is pending, while two others accused were acquitted. One more accused was arrested in Dubai, where the conspiracy was allegedly hatched. One accused, Nasir Ahmed, was killed in a police encounter in Mumbai in September 2003.

02 January 2004: Jammu [firing]

Two terrorists belonging to the JeM opened fire at the busy Jammu railway station in the evening, killing four security personnel and injuring 15 others. The two terrorists were eliminated by the army and evacuated more than 700 passengers to safety.

15 August 2004: Dhemaji [bomb blast]

Thirteen women and children were killed in an IED explosion at a school during Independence Day celebrations. The blast was triggered by the United Liberation Front of Asom (ULFA), an insurgent outfit demanding separation of the state of Assam from the Indian union.

05 July 2005: Ayodhya [attack]

Five terrorists believed to be from the JeM attempted to storm the Ram Janam Bhoomi Temple complex in Ayodhya. Posing as devotees, they came in an explosive laden Ambassador car and later hijacked a jeep. All five were killed by the Central Reserve Police Force (CRPF) personnel guarding the complex. One civilian got killed in a grenade blast by the terrorists and two CRPF personnel sustained injuries. Four persons from Jammu and Kashmir and one from Uttar Pradesh have been arrested for providing logistics support to the Pakistani terrorists in the case, where a chargesheet is yet to be filed.

28 July 2005: Jaunpur [train bombing]

Seventeen passengers were killed and more than 50 injured when a bomb went off in a coach of the Shramjeevi express near Harpalganj railway station in Jaunpur district of Uttar Pradesh. A chargesheet has been filed against seven accused including two former SIMI members and the trial is currently underway.

29 October 2005: Delhi [serial bomb blasts]

On the eve of Diwali, near simultaneous explosions rocked two market places teeming with people at Sarojini Nagar and Paharganj in the national capital. Sixty-two people were killed and 210 injured. Further casualties were averted as alert passengers and the driver of a city bus removed a bomb placed beneath a seat in Govindpuri locality.

A group calling itself the Inquilab Mahaz of Pakistan, involved in earlier terror activities in Karachi, claimed responsibility for the serial blasts. But investigators believe the blasts were carried out by the LeT. The trial is on against Tariq Ahmed Dar, arrested by the Delhi Police in Anantnag district of Jammu and Kashmir for allegedly selecting the blast sites and making satellite phone calls to LeT commanders in J&K and two others for assisting with finances, as also one Rafiq, whom the police claim is one of the four bomb planters. Zarar Shah and Abu Huzefa, top Lashkar commanders in the Valley, were believed to be the masterminds behind the bombings. Abu Huzefa was killed in an encounter in Kashmir in January 2006, while Zarar Shah remains at large.

28 December 2005: Bangalore [firing]

A retired Indian Institute of Technology (IIT) Delhi professor was killed and four others were injured when an armed gunman opened fire on delegates coming out of an international seminar at the Indian Institute of Science (IISc) in Bangalore. A Type 56 rifle and ammunition were recovered from outside the IISc auditorium.

Police claimed that the six LeT terrorists arrested after the Rampur CRPF camp attack in January 2008, were involved in the attack while Ajmal Amir Kasab, the lone terrorist to be arrested in the Mumbai attacks of 26/11, revealed that Abu Hamza, an LeT terrorist, had carried out the shooting and managed to escape to Pakistan. He is reported to have motivated the 26/11 terrorists to carry out the attacks citing his own example.

07 March 2006: Varanasi [bomb blast]

Three blasts took place in the evening at the revered Sankat Mochan Temple and Varanasi Cantonment railway station in the holy city. Twenty people were killed and more than 100 injured. A little known outfit, calling itself the Lashkar-e-Kahar, claimed responsibility. The police later arrested six Harkat-ul-Jihad-al-Islami (HuJI) terrorists, who they claimed, were trained by the JeM for carrying out the blasts. Explosives were smuggled in through Nepal. A HuJI commander, Waliullah, and another accused have been awarded jail sentences in cases related to the Arms Act, while the trial is yet to begin in the case.

11 July 2006: Mumbai [train bombings]

Seven blasts ripped through compartments of suburban trains on the western line in a span of eleven minutes. About 209 commuters were killed and more than 700 injured in the carnage. All the trains had departed from Mumbai's busy Churchgate station, where the bombs were believed to have been placed by 11 Pakistani nationals, who subsequently fled the country later. The blasts were masterminded by the ISI and executed by the LeT in collusion with local operatives of SIMI. A mixture of ammonium nitrate and RDX was used in the blasts. The trial against the 13 accused in the case has been stayed by the Supreme Court following appeal by the accused, questioning the framing of charges under the Maharashtra Control of Organised Crime Act (MCOCA).

06 September 2006: Malegaon [bomb blasts]

Two bombs attached to bicycles exploded near a Muslim graveyard in the cotton town of Malegaon on the occasion of a Shia religious procession, killing 40 people and injuring more than 25. The blasts were believed to have been carried out by SIMI operatives with LeT support aimed at disturbing communal harmony in the sensitive town in Nashik district. RDX was used in the blasts. The trial has been stayed against the nine arrested accused, some of whom are also believed to have a role in the 7/11 Mumbai train blasts following their appeal against being tried under MCOCA.

19 February 2007: Panipat [train bombings]

IEDs packed with inflammable objects exploded in two train compartments on the India-Pakistan train link, the Samjhauta Express, near Dewana station in Panipat, Haryana. Sixty-eight passengers travelling to Lahore were killed and around 50 injured. Three unexploded IEDs were later recovered from the train. The bombing on the eve of the then-Pakistan Foreign Minister Mehmood Kureshi's visit to India was believed to have been carried out by the LeT and JeM. Safdar Nagori, the founder of the banned outfit SIMI, was arrested in the case. He was allegedly aware of the conspiracy and providing logistical aid to the bomb planters.

18 May 2007: Hyderabad [bomb blast]

Nine people were killed and many injured when a bomb placed under a concrete pipe was set off using a cell phone in the Mecca Masjid near Charminar in Hyderabad during Friday prayers. Five people were killed in subsequent police firing on protesters and rioters. Mohammed Shaheed alias Bilal, an operative of the HuJI, was believed to be behind the blasts. The trail in the case went cold after Bilal and another suspect were killed in shooting incidents in Pakistan, a few days after the blast.

25 August 2007: Hyderabad [serial bomb blasts]

Forty-two people were killed and more than 50 injured after three blasts rocked crowded areas, including Gokul Chat and Lumbini Park in Hyderabad in the evening. Police say HuJI militants based in Bangladesh and Pakistan were involved. Several local youths arrested in the case were later acquitted by the court. A chargesheet is expected to be filed soon in one of the blast cases.

23 November 2007: Uttar Pradesh [serial bomb blasts]

A series of near-simultaneous explosions ripped through court complexes in Lucknow, Faizabad and Varanasi, killing about 14 and injuring 50 people. An outfit calling itself the Al-Hind Mujahideen claimed responsibility in an e-mail to media houses. The blasts were purportedly carried out in retaliation to the assault by lawyers on three JeM militants in a Lucknow court. It is now established that the blasts were carried out by a module of Indian Mujahideen operatives led by Mohammed Saif, arrested from Batla House in South Delhi in September 2008.

01 January 2008: Rampur [attack]

In the early hours of the day, LeT militants attacked a CRPF recruitment centre in Rampur. They fired with AK-47s and lobbed grenades at a sentry post and an administrative building inside the centre, killing seven CRPF personnel and one civilian. On 10 February 2008, Sabauddin and two Pakistani nationals were arrested with arms and ammunition from the Lucknow railway station while they were boarding a train to Mumbai. Forensic reports have established that the two Pakistani nationals, Imran Shahzad and Mohammed Farooq, had fired in Rampur from the same AK-47s recovered from their possession. The trial is on against them and four others arrested from Uttar Pradesh for harbouring the terrorists.

13 May 2008: Jaipur [serial bomb blasts]

A series of nine explosions within a span of 15 minutes rocked the Pink City, killing 70 people and injuring nearly 200. The IEDs, packed with ball bearings and ammonium nitrate, were attached to bicycles in areas frequented by tourists in the Old City. The Indian Mujahideen (IM), an offshoot of the banned SIMI supported by the LeT, claimed responsibility. The trial is poised to commence against three arrested in the case, while two IM members were killed in the Batla House encounter in September 2008. Six accused are absconding in the case.

25 July 2008: Bangalore [serial bomb blasts]

One person was killed and 11 injured when a series of seven low-intensity crude bombs were detonated at several road junctions in the IT city of Bangalore. In February 2009, the Bangalore Police claimed to have solved the case with the arrest of an eight-member LeT module based in Kerala and one member from Karanataka (who had planted the bombs) disguising themselves as labourers. In March 2009, one Sarfaraz Nawaz, a native of Kerala and resident of Muscat, was arrested for allegedly providing Rs 350,000 to Abdul Sattar who had led the IM module that carried out the blasts on the instructions of LeT.

26 July 2008: Ahmadabad [serial bomb blasts]

A series of 21 explosions shook Ahmadabad a day after the blasts in Bangalore, killing 59 people and injuring more than 150. The pattern of the blasts was similar to that of Jaipur and Bangalore where low grade explosives mixed with shrapnel were used. The bombs in Ahmadabad were placed at busy intersections and commuter buses, going off in the evening. Later, as casualties were being evacuated to hospitals, car bombs went off, killing the injured patients. At least three bombs were defused in the city. The IM claimed responsibility for the blasts, terming it as "revenge" for the Gujarat riots of 2002. Around 26 SIMI and IM members have been arrested from different parts of the country and chargesheets have been filed in the case. In August 2008, Gujarat Police arrested Mufti Ahmed Basheer, a SIMI operative from Azamgarh in Uttar Pradesh, for allegedly masterminding the blasts.

13 September 2008: Delhi [serial bomb blasts]

Five near-simultaneous explosions took place in market places in Karol Bagh, Connaught Place and Greater Kailash during the busy evening hours, killing 26 people and injuring nearly 100 others. At least three bombs were defused in India Gate and Connaught Place in the heart of the National Capital. The IEDs bore the hallmark of earlier blasts in the year – a mixture of crude explosives and shrapnel, triggered by timer devices. A week later, two IM operatives were killed, including the team leader Atif Ameen, in a shootout at Batla House locality of South Delhi. Two other suspects were arrested in the raid. More than a dozen suspects linked with IM and SIMI were arrested from across the country. The chargesheet filed in the case refers to the involvement of this module in the Jaipur, Ahmedabad and Hyderabad (2007) serial blasts as well. Abu al-Qama, a top LeT operative, based in Pakistan, was named the mastermind of the Delhi blasts.

29 September 2008: Delhi [bomb blast]

Two motorcycle-borne men dropped a bomb placed in a tiffin box in a narrow market lane in Mehrauli locality of South Delhi. The explosion killed six people and injured nearly 20 others. No headway has been made in the case which came a fortnight after the earlier blasts on 13 September 2008. A separate IM module is suspected to be responsible for the blast.

21 October 2008: Imphal [bomb blast]

At least 17 persons, many of them police personnel, were killed and 30 injured as an IED placed in a two-wheeler vehicle was detonated near the Assam Rifles and Police Commando complex in Imphal West district. The blast was targeted at security forces personnel indulging in pre-Diwali revelry at a hotel outside their camp. Metei underground organisations such as the Kangelipak Communist Party (KCP-MC) and People's Revolutionary Party of Kangleipak (PREPAK) were held responsible for the blast.

30 October 2008: Lower Assam [serial bomb blasts]

Nine blasts across Lower/Western Assam killed 89 people and injured more than 450 others. Most of the IEDs were placed in cars and motorcycles and contained explosives such as RDX. The blasts took place in markets in Guwahati, Barpeta, Bongaigaon and Kokrajhar towns. A little-known outfit calling itself the Islamic Security Force claimed responsibility but the police termed it as a hoax. Several people associated with the outlawed National Democratic Front of Bodoland (NDFB), currently under a ceasefire agreement with the Centre, were arrested for purchasing the cars in which the bombs were placed, and contributing other logistical support. However, it is not yet established whether NDFB had masterminded the blasts on its own or had supported the Bangladesh based Islamic terror group, HuJI, in carrying out the explosions. The investigations have been handed over to the Central Bureau of Investigation (CBI).

26 November 2008: Mumbai [attack]

The series of bombings throughout the country in the year 2008 reached a climax on 26 November 2008, when 10 armed terrorists, now established to be members of a highly trained LeT squad, carried out a simultaneous armed assault at various prominent locations in South Mumbai, killing 189 people and injuring more than 300. They kept the city under siege for nearly 60 hours, taking several people hostage in the Taj and Oberoi hotels and a Jewish family at Nariman House. They were finally neutralised by NSG commandos. One terrorist, Mohammed Amir Ajmal Kasab, a native of Punjab province in Pakistan, was captured alive on the first night after he and his partner had killed commuters at the busy Chattrapati Shivaji Terminus railway station and ambushed three senior Mumbai Police officers. The carnage at Mumbai outraged the entire country and India went on a diplomatic offensive, demanding action by Pakistan on dismantling terror infrastructure on its soil and bringing the perpetrators to justice. A mammoth chargesheet has been filed in the case, with the plethora of technical and material evidence pointing towards some "state" and "non-state" actors in Pakistan. The United Nations proscribed the LeT front Jamaat-ud-Dawa and froze its financial assets. But Pakistan is yet to take any verifiable or substantive action against the main conspirators of the attacks based on its soil. In India, the trial has begun against the captured terrorist and two others arrested in the Rampur CRPF camp attack case.

01 January 2009: Guwahati [serial bomb blasts]

A series of three explosions rocked the city, killing at least five, and injuring 67 others, hours before Home Minister P Chidambaram was due to visit. All the blasts were reported to be the result of low intensity IEDs. ULFA is suspected to have carried out the bombings, though suspicions of the involvement of Bangladesh-based fundamentalist groups were also voiced. Chief Minister Gogoi admitted to security lapses and called for a full enquiry into the incident.

06 April 2009: Assam [bomb blasts]

Two blasts in locations approximately 210 km apart went off hours after each other, killing two and injuring 60 others, a day before Prime Minister Manmohan Singh was due to visit the region as a part of election campaigning. ULFA was suspected to be behind the blasts, given the *modus operandi*, as also since it occurred on the eve of the 30th anniversary of ULFA. Later in the day, a grenade attack on a police station in Northern Assam took place, in which two policemen were injured.

22 November 2009: Nalbari [bomb blasts]

At least seven people were killed and 53 injured in two bomb blasts, which took place within 15 minutes and 50 metres of each other, in Nalbari district, 70 km from Guwahati. The bombs were mounted on bicycles and left near a police station. ULFA was suspected to be behind the blasts.